THE PERSONAL NARRATIVE OF JAMES O. PATTIE

KEYSTONE WESTERN AMERICANA SERIES

Archibald Hanna and William H. Goetzmann,
General Editors

THE PERSONAL NARRATIVE OF

# James O. Pattie

---

*The 1831 Edition, Unabridged*

*Introduction by William H. Goetzmann*

---

J. B. LIPPINCOTT COMPANY

*Philadelphia and New York*

# INTRODUCTION

ONE DAY IN THE FALL OF 1830 an authentic American hero appeared at the office of the *Western Monthly Review* in Cincinnati and offered to sell the story of his life for a new start in the Old Northwest. His name was James Ohio Pattie. He was only twenty-six years old but he looked at least forty, and he had recently come upriver from New Orleans where he had been down on his luck and forced to depend upon charity for his steamboat passage. Before that he had been in Mexico where, according to his story, he had gone to protest his ill-treatment at the hands of authorities in California, and instead had been robbed and left penniless in a foreign land, his "dreams of success . . . vanished forever." What had he been doing in California that led to such a tragic fate? He had gone there to hunt furs with his father and six other men—walked all the way from Santa Fé, as he put it, "over rugged and pathless mountains, subject to every species of danger, want, and misery. . . ."

Timothy Flint, the editor of the *Western Monthly Review,* was interested. Flint was a Harvard man and a clergyman besides, but he was a good editor, and most of his literary career had been devoted to heroes of one kind or another. When he lived in St. Louis he had known James Mackay, the Scotsman in the employ of the Spaniards who had gone up the Missouri River before Lewis and Clark. In Louisiana his good friend was Henry Bullard who had been to Mexico and Santa Fé. Out of their stories and those of

v

others Flint had written two important novels, *Francis Berrian, or the Mexican Patriot,* and *Shoshone Valley.* The former was the first American novel to portray the Santa Fé trader, and the southern Rockies. The latter, which he had just published that very year (1830), was the first novel to celebrate the exploits of the fur hunters of the Far West, the famous free-booting mountain men. In addition to these works Flint had written widely about the commerce of the West with its picturesque characters and frightful dangers. But out of the whole range of western characters the one that interested him most was Daniel Boone, the archetype of all western adventurers, the original hunter from Kentucky. Now with the arrival of James Ohio Pattie from the Far West, Flint had just what he wanted, a man who had been a mountain man, who had hunted the romantic Rockies and known Indians, and who had moreover been a captive of the Spaniards in far-off, exotic California. Perhaps best of all, he had in Pattie an authentic Kentucky hunter. And for Flint just being a Kentuckian was enough. Yes, the Reverend Editor was interested in Mr. Pattie's story.

As might be expected, what Pattie had to say bordered always on the incredible. He had come from a long line of Kentucky hunters going back to 1782, when his grandfather had saved Bryant's Station from massacre. His father, Sylvester Pattie, had moved west to Missouri where, during the War of 1812 as a young lieutenant of the militia, he became the hero of the siege of Fort Cap au Gris, saving his entire command by means of a daring dash for help through British lines. After the war he opened a sawmill on the Gasconade River, and with his wife and nine children settled down to the prosperous life of a yeoman-mechanic. Evil times befell the family, however, and Mrs. Pattie died of the fever, leaving nine children behind, the eldest of whom was James Ohio, barely twenty years old. So stunned was Sylvester Pattie by the loss of his wife that in a fit of despair he determined to abandon his children to friends and relatives and seek solace among the outcast mountain men out West. He was not the first or the last American to go west seeking peace and rejuvenation. By the summer of 1824 he had settled on his plan. Taking his eldest son, James Ohio, with him, he would go to the upper Missouri and trap for beaver. And so in that year, in a scene reminiscent of a Charles Dickens story, he set off with his son for the wilderness, leaving behind eight destitute children. He never saw them again.

Taking on three men as partners, the Patties started out up the Missouri to seek their fortune. They got only as far as the Council Bluffs when they were stopped by the Indian agent and turned back for failing to secure a trapper's license. So instead they turned toward the Southwest, joining young Sylvester Pratte's party of would-be Santa Fé traders. Almost immediately the elder Pattie was elected captain of the train.

Eventually, on November 5 of 1824, they reached Santa Fé, one of many such trading caravans to reach the brick-kiln capital on the Rio Grande that year. Since 1821, when the Mexicans achieved their independence and William Becknell had taken his first trainload of goods into the capital, Santa Fé had been a wide-open city, the focal point of dozens of caravans moving south by southwest from St. Louis, Westport, Franklin, and other frontier outposts. As such it soon became notorious for its gambling hells, its stabbings and shootings, its faro and monte, all-night fandangoes, and comely, compliant, and irresistible señoritas, who were a far cry from the homespun farm girls of frontier Missouri.

It was one of these señoritas in fact who gave the Patties their start. No sooner had they arrived in the Valley of the Rio Grande than young James Ohio rescued the beautiful Jacova, daughter of a Mexican grandee, from the Indians, and deposited her, clad only in his buckskin hunting shirt and blushing demurely, upon her father's doorstep. Ever afterwards the Patties could do no wrong in New Mexico.

It will not do in an introduction to chronicle in detail all of the Patties' adventures as James Ohio recounted them to Timothy Flint. Suffice to say that after a short career as a fur trapper along the Gila River in New Mexico, the elder Pattie retired to become proprietor of the Santa Rita Copper Mines—an operation made hazardous by the fact that the mines stood dead in the center of the hostile Apache country. Young James Ohio continued the life of the trapper and in so doing explored all of the Southwest from the Rio Grande to the Colorado, made the trip across north Mexico to

Guaymas on its Pacific shores and, if his account be true, made an incredible journey northward along the Colorado River, the Grand, and then via the parks of Colorado to the Big Horn, the Yellowstone, and finally the Upper Missouri. In so doing he was the first American to see the Grand Canyon.

When ultimately he came back to his father at Santa Rita, James Ohio Pattie had seen more of the West than any other man excepting perhaps Jedediah Smith and Peter Skene Ogden.

In September of 1827 (Pattie's dates are for the most part inaccurate), due to the press of finance, the Patties made one last hunt into the West to seek their fortunes. The hunt took them from the mouth of the Colorado River across the desert to California, where they were imprisoned by Governor Echeandia, and where Sylvester Pattie died in a Spanish jail. From California, after a further series of adventures, James Ohio Pattie had made his way to Cincinnati, where he arrived broken and penniless, old beyond his years, and ready to sell his story to whomever would pay. He was a character out of a romance, come back from the ends of the earth to find his brothers and sisters all gone and everything changed. This was the story that under the editorship of the Reverend Flint was published in Cincinnati in 1831 under the title *The Personal Narrative of James O. Pattie of Kentucky*. . . . It was the best book Flint ever did, and one of the classics of western Americana.

For students of the American West Pattie's book has always been one of the greatest puzzles. With all its color and detail, its panoramic scope and strong narrative, it is difficult to assess its true historical value because no one knows for certain just how much of Pattie's adventure was true, and how much was the characteristic elaboration of the teller of tall tales. If, indeed, the *Personal Narrative* is true for the most part, then it serves as the prime source on the fur trade of the Old Southwest. Intrigued with the problem, scholars have chipped away little by little in checking its authenticity. As mentioned previously, most of Pattie's dates can be shown to be in error by as much as two years. However, the historian H. H. Bancroft, working in the Mexican Archives, established the fact of Pattie's entrance into and captivity in California. He declared the Patties' treatment to have been much milder than that chronicled in the *Personal Narrative,* and he toned down the exploits of James Ohio to a considerable degree. In the end Bancroft characterized Pattie as "a self-conceited and quick-tempered boy with a freedom of speech often amounting to insolence, and unlimited ability to make himself disagreeable."

In 1923, in a brilliant article in the *Southwestern Historical Quarterly,* Joseph J. Hill of the Bancroft Library succeeded in unraveling the complicated chronology of the southwestern fur trade to the extent of establishing Pattie's participation in the massacre of the Michel Robideau party by the Papagos in 1826 along the Gila River, and his subsequent association with a party led by Ewing Young that reached the Grand Canyon and the Upper Colorado. Beyond that scholarship has been unable to penetrate. But Hill's picture of Pattie agrees substantially with that of Bancroft and he demonstrated rather forcefully that if he had done nothing else young Pattie had, to use Mark Twain's term, told a few "stretchers" that made him seem the *leader* of parties where he had in fact been only a rather minor participant. Hill calls him "an egotistical boy who happened to be picked up along the way." But then perhaps Hill failed to realize that after all Pattie was from Kentucky, a land of tall-tale tellers whose place has only recently been usurped by Texas.

Perhaps historians will never know the precise factor of truth in Pattie's *Personal Narrative,* though they seem to go on using it as source material year after year anyway. But once having read the *Narrative* the dispute over its factual authenticity seems merely limiting, for above all else it is one of the documents of American mythology. It belongs with John Filson's work on Daniel Boone, Henry T. Bonner's *The Life and Adventures of Jim Beckwourth,* and Davy Crockett's autobiography. Somehow it does not seem to matter much that its author was an "egotistical boy," penniless and boasting of his own importance, for what Pattie's book presents us with is an authentic culture hero. He is Odysseus or Beowulf as the "Hunter of Kentucky," on the move and acting out the vivid story of the American conquest of the Far West on a scale so grand that every detail seems larger than life and even the irony of his eventual failure seems unimportant.

Suffice to say then that the Reverend Timothy Flint knew a hero when he saw one, and this is a fortunate thing because in the case of Pattie's *Personal Narrative,* heroes did indeed make for good stories and good reading.

WILLIAM H. GOETZMANN

*Yale University*
*November 1, 1961*

# THE

# PERSONAL NARRATIVE

OF

# JAMES O. PATTIE,

OF

# KENTUCKY,

DURING AN EXPEDITION FROM ST. LOUIS, THROUGH THE VAST REGIONS
BETWEEN THAT PLACE AND THE PACIFIC OCEAN, AND THENCE BACK
THROUGH THE CITY OF MEXICO TO VERA CRUZ, DURING JOURNEY-
INGS OF SIX YEARS; IN WHICH HE AND HIS FATHER, WHO
ACCOMPANIED HIM, SUFFERED UNHEARD OF HARDSHIPS
AND DANGERS, HAD VARIOUS CONFLICTS WITH THE IN-
DIANS, AND WERE MADE CAPTIVES, IN WHICH
CAPTIVITY HIS FATHER DIED; TOGETHER
WITH A DESCRIPTION OF THE COUNTRY,
AND THE VARIOUS NATIONS THROUGH
WHICH THEY PASSED.

---

## EDITED BY TIMOTHY FLINT.

---

CINCINNATI:
PRINTED AND PUBLISHED BY JOHN H. WOOD.
1831.

# CONTENTS

Editor's Preface (by Timothy Flint)     1
Introduction to the Narrative     5

THE NARRATIVE OF JAMES O. PATTIE     11

Appendices     231
  *Inland Trade with New Mexico*     233
  *Downfall of the Fredonian Republic*     260
  *Mexico*     263

MAP
The Southwest and Far West, showing the travels of
James O. Pattie     xiv-xv

PATTIE'S ROUTE ———
CONJECTURAL ROUTE -------
*

# EDITOR'S PREFACE

## by Timothy Flint

IT HAS BEEN MY FORTUNE to be known as a writer of works of the imagination. I am solicitous that this Journal should lose none of its intrinsic interest, from its being supposed that in preparing it for the press, I have drawn from the imagination, either in regard to the incidents or their coloring. For, in the literal truth of the facts, incredible as some of them may appear, my grounds of conviction are my acquaintance with the Author the impossibility of inventing a narrative like the following, the respectability of his relations, the standing which his father sustained, the confidence reposed in him by the Hon. J. S. Johnston, the very respectable senator in congress from Louisiana, who introduced him to me, the concurrent testimony of persons now in this city, who saw him at different points in New Mexico, and the reports, which reached the United States, during the expedition of many of the incidents here recorded.

When my family first arrived at St. Charles' in 1816, the fame of the exploits of his father, as an officer of the rangers, was fresh in the narratives of his associates and fellow soldiers. I have been on the ground, at Cap au Gris, where he was besieged by the Indians. I am not unacquainted with the scenery through which he passed on the Missouri, and I, too, for many years was a sojourner in the prairies.

1

These circumstances, along with a conviction of the truth of the narrative, tended to give me an interest in it, and to qualify me in some degree to judge of the internal evidences contained in the journal itself, of its entire authenticity. It will be perceived at once, that Mr. Pattie, with Mr. McDuffie, thinks more of action than literature, and is more competent to perform exploits, than blazon them in eloquent periods. My influence upon the narrative regards orthography, and punctuation and the occasional interposition of a topographical illustration, which my acquaintance with the accounts of travellers in New Mexico, and published views of the country have enabled me to furnish. The reader will award me the confidence of acting in good faith, in regard to drawing nothing from my own thoughts. I have found more call to suppress, than to add, to soften, than to show in stronger relief many of the incidents. Circumstances of suffering, which in many similar narratives have been given in downright plainness of detail, I have been impelled to leave to the reader's imagination, as too revolting to be recorded.

The very texture of the narrative precludes ornament and amplification. The simple record of events as they transpired, painted by the hungry, toil-worn hunter, in the midst of the desert, surrounded by sterility, espying the foot print of the savage, or discerning him couched behind the tree or hillock, or hearing the distant howl of wild beasts, will naturally bear characteristics of stern disregard of embellishment. To alter it, to attempt to embellish it, to divest it of the peculiar impress of the narrator and his circumstances, would be to take from it its keeping, the charm of its simplicity, and its internal marks of truth. In these respects I have been anxious to leave the narrative as I found it.

The journalist seems in these pages a legitimate descendant of those western pioneers, the hunters of Kentucky, a race passing unrecorded from history. The pencil of biography could seize upon no subjects of higher interest. With hearts keenly alive to the impulses of honor and patriotism, and the charities of kindred and friends; they possessed spirits impassible to fear, that no form of suffering or death could daunt; and frames for strength and endurance, as if ribbed with brass and sinewed with steel. For them to traverse wide deserts, climb mountains, swim rivers, grapple with the grizzly bear, and encounter the savage, in a sojourn in the wilderness of years, far from the abodes of civilized men, was but a spirit-stirring and holiday mode of life.

To me, there is a kind of moral sublimity in the contemplation of the adventures and daring of such men. They read a lesson to shrinking and effeminate spirits, the men of soft hands and fashionable life, whose frames the winds of heaven are not allowed to visit too roughly. They tend to re-inspire something of that simplicity of manners, manly hardihood, and Spartan energy and force of character, which formed so conspicuous a part of the nature of the settlers of the western wilderness.

Every one knows with what intense interest the community perused the adventures of Captain Riley, and other intrepid mariners shipwrecked and enslaved upon distant and barbarous shores. It is far from my thoughts to detract from the intrepidity of American mariners, which is known, wherever the winds blow, or the waves roll; or to depreciate the interest of the recorded narratives of their sufferings. A picture more calculated to arouse American sympathies cannot be presented, than that of a ship's crew, driven by the fierce winds and the mountain waves upon a rock bound shore, and escaping death in the sea, only to encounter captivity from the barbarians on the land. Yet much of the courage, required to encounter these emergencies is passive, counselling only the necessity of submission to events, from which there is no escape, and to which all resistance would be unavailing.

The courage requisite to be put forth in an expedition such as that in which Mr. Pattie and his associates were cast, must be both active and passive, energetic and ever vigilant, and never permitted to shrink, or intermit a moment for years. At one time it is assailed by hordes of yelling savages, and at another, menaced with the horrible death of hunger and thirst in interminable forests, or arid sands. Either position offers perils and sufferings sufficiently appalling. But fewer spirits, I apprehend, are formed to brave those of the field,

> 'Where wilds immeasurably spread,
> Seem lengthening as they go.'

than of the ocean, where the mariner either soon finds rest beneath its tumultuous bosom, or joyfully spreads his sails again to the breeze.

# INTRODUCTION TO THE NARRATIVE

THE GRANDFATHER OF THE AUTHOR of this Journal, was born in Caroline county, Virginia, in 1750. Soon after he was turned of twenty-one, he moved to Kentucky, and became an associate with those fearless spirits who first settled in the western forests. To qualify him to meet the dangers and encounter the toils of his new position, he had served in the revolutionary war, and had been brought in hostile contact with the British in their attempt to ascend the river Potomac.

He arrived in Kentucky, in company with twenty emigrant families, in 1781, and settled on the south side of the Kentucky river. The new settlers were beginning to build houses with internal finishing. His pursuit, which was that of a house carpenter, procured him constant employment, but he sometimes diversified it by teaching school. Soon after his arrival, the commencing settlement experienced the severest and most destructive assaults from the Indians. In August, 1782, he was one of the party who marched to the assistance of Bryant's station, and shared in the glory of relieving that place by the memorable defeat of the savages.

Not long afterwards he was called upon by Col. Logan to join a party led by him against the Indians, who had gained a bloody victory over the Kentuckians at the Blue Licks. He was present on the spot, where the bodies of the slain lay unburied, and assisted

5

in their interment. During his absence on this expedition, Sylvester Pattie, father of the author, was born, August 25, 1782.

In November of the same year, his grand-father was summoned to join a party commanded by Col. Logan, in an expedition against the Indians at the Shawnee towns, in the limits of the present state of Ohio. They crossed the Ohio just below the mouth of the Licking, opposite the site of what is now Cincinnati, which was at that time an unbroken forest, without the appearance of a human habitation. They were here joined by Gen. Clark with his troops from the falls of the Ohio, or what is now Louisville. The united force marched to the Indian towns, which they burnt and destroyed.

Returning from this expedition, he resumed his former occupations, witnessing the rapid advance of the country from immigration. When the district, in which he resided, was constituted Bracken county, he was appointed one of the judges of the court of quarter sessions, which office he filled sixteen years, until his place was vacated by an act of the legislature reducing the court to a single judge.

Sylvester Pattie, the father of the author, as was common at that period in Kentucky, married early, having only reached nineteen. He settled near his fathers house, and there remained until there began to be a prevalent disposition among the people to move to Missouri. March 14, 1812, he removed to that country, the author, being then eight years old. Born and reared amidst the horrors of Indian assaults and incursions, and having lived to see Kentucky entirely free from these dangers, it may seem strange, that he should have chosen to remove a young family to that remote country, then enduring the same horrors of Indian warfare, as Kentucky had experienced twenty-five years before. It was in the midst of the late war with England, which, it is well known, operated to bring the fiercest assaults of savage incursion upon the remote frontiers of Illinois and Missouri.

To repel these incursions, these then territories, called out some companies of rangers, who marched against the Sac and Fox Indians, between the Mississippi and the lakes, who were at that time active in murdering women and children, and burning their habitations during the absence of the male heads of families. When Pattie was appointed lieutenant in one of these companies, he left his family at St. Charles' where he was then residing. It may be imagined, that the condition of his wife was sufficiently lonely, as this village contained but one American family besides her own, and she was unable to converse with its French inhabitants. His company had several skirmishes with the Indians, in each of which it came off successful.

The rangers left him in command of a detachment, in possession of the fort at Cap au Gris. Soon after the main body of the rangers had marched away, the fort was besieged by a body of English and Indians. The besiegers made several attempts to storm the fort, but were repelled by the garrison.—The foe continued the siege for a week, continually firing upon the garrison, who sometimes, though not often, for want of ammunition, returned the fire. Lieutenant Pattie, perceiving no disposition in the enemy to withdraw, and discovering that his ammunition was almost entirely exhausted, deemed it necessary to send a despatch to Bellefontaine, near the point of the junction of the Missouri and Mississippi, where was stationed a considerable American force. He proposed to his command, that a couple of men should make their way through the enemy, cross the Mississippi, and apprize the commander of Bellefontaine of their condition. No one was found willing to risk the attempt, as the besiegers were encamped entirely around them. Leaving Thomas McNair in command in his place, and putting on the uniform of one of the English soldiers, whom they had killed during one of the attempts to storm the fort; he passed by night safely through the camp of the enemy, and arrived at the point of his destination, a distance of over forty miles: 500 soldiers were immediately dispatched from Bellefontaine to the relief of the besieged at Cap au Gris. As soon as this force reached the fort, the British and Indians decamped, not, however, without leaving many of their lifeless companions behind them.

Lieutenant Pattie remained in command of Cap au Gris, being essentially instrumental in repressing the incursions of the Sacs and Foxes, and disposing them to a treaty of peace, until the close of the war. In 1813 he received his discharge, and returned to his family, with whom he enjoyed domestic happiness in privacy and repose for some years. St. Louis and St. Charles were beginning rapidly to improve; American families were constantly immigrating to these towns. The timber in their vicinity is not of the best kind for building. Pine could no where be obtained in abundance, nearer than on the Gasconade, a stream that enters on the south side of the Missouri, about one hundred and fifty miles up that river. Mr. Pattie, possessing a wandering and adventurous spirit, meditated the idea of removing to this frontier and unpeopled river, to erect Mills upon it, and send down pine lumber in rafts to St. Louis, and the adjoining country. He carried his plan into operation, and erected a Saw and Grist Mill upon the Gasconade. It proved a very fortunate speculation, as there was an immediate demand at St. Louis and St. Charles for all the plank the mill could supply.

In this remote wilderness, Mr. Pattie lived in happiness and prosperity, until the mother of the author was attacked by consumption. Although her husband was, as has been said, strongly endowed with the wandering propensity, he was no less profoundly attached to his family; and in this wild region, the loss of a beloved wife was irreparable. She soon sunk under the disorder, leaving nine young children. Not long after, the youngest died, and was deposited by her side in this far land.

The house, which had been the scene of domestic quiet, cheerfulness and joy, and the hospitable home of the stranger, sojourning in these forests, became dreary and desolate. Mr. Pattie, who had been noted for the buoyancy of his gay spirit, was now silent, dejected, and even inattentive to his business; which, requiring great activity and constant attention, soon ran into disorder.

About this time, remote trapping and trading expeditions up the Missouri, and in the interior of New Mexico began to be much talked of. Mr. Pattie seemed to be interested in these expeditions, which offered much to stir the spirit and excite enterprize. To arouse him from his indolent melancholy, his friends advised him to sell his property, convert it into merchandize and equipments for trapping and hunting, and to join in such an undertaking. To a man born and reared under the circumstances of his early life— one to whom forests, and long rivers, adventures, and distant mountains, presented pictures of familiar and birth day scenes—

one, who confided in his rifle, as a sure friend, and who withal, connected dejection and bereavement with his present desolate residence; little was necessary to tempt him to such an enterprise.

In a word, he adopted the project with that undoubting and unshrinking purpose, with which to will is to accomplish. Arrangements were soon made. The Children were provided for among his relations. The Author was at school; but inheriting the love of a rifle through so many generations, and nursed amid such scenes, he begged so earnestly of his father that he might be allowed to accompany the expedition, that he prevailed. The sad task remained for him to record the incidents of the expedition, and the sufferings and death of his father.

# THE NARRATIVE OF JAMES O. PATTIE

I PASS BY, as unimportant in this Journal, all the circumstances of our arrangements for setting out on our expedition; together with my father's sorrow and mine, at leaving the spot where his wife and my mother was buried, the place, which had once been so cheerful, and was now so gloomy to us. We made our purchases at St. Louis. Our company consisted of five persons. We had ten horses packed with traps, trapping utensils, guns, ammunition, knives, tomahawks, provisions, blankets, and some surplus arms, as we anticipated that we should be able to gain some additions to our number by way of recruits, as we proceeded onward. But when the trial came, so formidable seemed the danger, fatigue distance, and uncertainty of the expedition, that not an individual could be persuaded to share our enterprize.

June 20, 1824, we crossed the Missouri at a small town called Newport, and meandered the river as far as Pilcher's fort, without any incident worthy of record, except that one of our associates, who had become too unwell to travel, was left at Charaton, the remotest village on this frontier of any size. We arrived at Pilcher's fort, on the 13th day of July. There we remained, until the 28th, waiting the arrival of a keel boat from below, that was partly freighted with merchandize for us, with which we intended to trade with the Indians.

On the 28th, our number diminished to four, we set off for a trading establishment eight miles above us on the Missouri, be-

longing to Pratte, Choteau and Company. In this place centres
most of the trade with the Indians on the upper Missouri. Here
we met with Sylvester, son of Gen. Pratte, who was on his way
to New Mexico, with purposes similar to ours. His company had
preceded him, and was on the river Platte waiting for him.

We left this trading establishment for the Council Bluffs, six
miles above. When we arrived there, the commanding officer demanded to see our license for trading with the Indians. We informed him, that we neither had any, nor were aware that any was
necessary. We were informed, that we could be allowed to ascend
the river no higher without one. This dilemma brought our onward progress to a dead stand. We were prompt, however, in
making new arrangements. We concluded to sell our surplus arms
in exchange for merchandize, and change our direction from the
upper Missouri, to New Mexico. One of our number was so much
discouraged with our apparent ill success, and so little satisfied
with this new project, that he came to the determination to leave
our ranks. The remainder, though dispirited by the reduction of
our number, determined not to abandon the undertaking. Our
invalid having rejoined us, we still numbered four. We remained
some time at this beautiful position, the Council Bluffs. I have
seen much that is beautiful, interesting and commanding in the
wild scenery of nature, but no prospect above, around, and below
more so than from this spot. Our object and destination being the
same as Mr. Pratte's, we concluded to join his company on the
Platte.

We left the Bluffs, July 30th, and encamped the night after our
departure on a small stream, called the Elkhorn. We reached it at
a point thirty miles S. W. from the Bluffs. The Pawnee Indians
sometimes resort upon the banks of this stream. The country is
so open and bare of timber, that it was with difficulty we could
find sufficient wood to cook with, even on the banks of the river,
where wood is found, if at all, in the prairie country.

Early the next morning we commenced our march up the bottoms of the stream, which we continued to ascend, until almost
night fall, when we concluded to cross it to a small grove of timber that we descried on the opposite shore, where we encamped

for the night, securing our horses with great care, through fear
that they would be stolen by the Indians.

In the morning, as we were making arrangements to commence
our march, we discovered a large body of Indians, running full
speed towards us. When they had arrived within a hundred yards
of us, we made signs, that they must halt, or that we should fire
upon them. They halted, and we inquired of them, as one of our
number spoke their language, to what nation they belonged?
They answered the Pawnee. Considering them friendly, we permitted them to approach us. It was on our way, to pass through
their town, and we followed them thither. As soon as we arrived
at their town, they conducted us to the lodge of their chief, who
posted a number of his warriors at the door, and called the rest of
his chiefs, accompanied by an interpreter. They formed a circle in
the centre of the lodge. The elder chief then lighting a pipe, commenced smoking; the next chief holding the bowl of his pipe. This
mode of smoking differed from that of any Indians we had yet
seen. He filled his mouth with the smoke, then puffed it in our
bosoms, then on his own, and then upward, as he said, toward the
Great Spirit, that he would bestow upon us plenty of fat buffaloes,
and all necessary aid on our way. He informed us, that he had two
war parties abroad. He gave us a stick curiously painted with characters, I suppose something like hieroglyphics, bidding us, should
we see any of his warriors, to give them that stick; in which case
they would treat us kindly. The pipe was then passed round, and
we each of us gave it two or three light whiffs. We were then
treated with fat buffaloe meat, and after we had eaten, he gave us
counsel in regard to our future course, particularly not to let our
horses loose at night. His treatment was altogether paternal.

Next morning we left the village of this hospitable old chief, accompanied by a pilot, dispatched to conduct us to Mr. Pratte's
company on the Platte. This is one of the three villages of the Republican Pawnees. It is situated on the little Platte River, in the centre of an extensive prairie plain; having near it a small strip of
wood extending from the village to the river. The houses are cone-
shaped, like a sugar loaf. The number of lodges may amount to
six hundred.

The night after we left this village, we encamped on the banks of a small creek called the Mad Buffaloe. Here we could find no wood for cooking, and made our first experiment of the common resort in these wide prairies; that is, we were obliged to collect the dung of the buffaloe for that purpose. Having taken our supper, some of us stood guard through the night, while the others slept, according to the advice of the friendly chief. Next morning we commenced our march at early dawn, and by dint of hard travelling through the prairies, we arrived about sunset, on the main Platte, where we joined Mr. Pratte and his company. We felt, and expressed gratitude to the pilot, who, by his knowledge of the country, had conducted us by the shortest and easiest route. We did not forget the substantial expression of our good will, in paying him. He started for his own village the same evening, accompanying us here, and returning, on foot, although he could have had a horse for the journey.

At this encampment, on the banks of the Platte, we remained four days, during which time we killed some antelopes and deer, and dressed their skins to make us moccasins. Among our arrangements with Mr. Pratte, one was, that my father should take the command of this company, to which proposition my father and our associates consented. The honor of this confidence was probably bestowed upon him, in consequence of most of the company having served under him, as rangers, during the late war. Those who had not, had been acquainted with his services by general report.

In conformity with the general wish, my father immediately entered upon his command, by making out a list of the names of the whole company, and dividing it into four messes; each mess having to furnish two men, to stand guard by reliefs, during the night. The roll was called, and the company was found to be a hundred and sixteen. We had three hundred mules, and some horses. A hundred of them were packed with goods and baggage. The guard was posted as spies, and all the rest were ordered to commence the arrangements of packing for departure. The guard was detached, to keep at some distance from the camp, reconnoitre, and discover if any Indians were lurking in the vicinity. When on the march, the guards were ordered to move on within sight of our flank, and parallel to our line of march. If any Indians were descried, they were to make a signal by raising their hats; or if not in sight of us, to alarm us by a pistol shot. These arrangements gave us a chance always to have some little time to make ready for action.

It may be imagined, that such a caravan made no mean figure, or inconsiderable dust, in moving along the prairies. We started on the morning of the 6th of August, travelling up the main Platte, which at this point is more than a hundred yards wide, very shallow, with a clean sand bottom, and very high banks. It is skirted with a thin belt of cotton-wood and willow trees, from which beautiful prairie plains stretch out indefinitely on either side. We arrived in the evening at a village of the Pawnee Loups. It is larger than the village of the Republican Pawnees, which we had left behind us. The head chief of this village received us in the most affectionate and hospitable manner, supplying us with such provisions as we wanted. He had been all the way from these remote prairies, on a visit to the city of Washington. He informed us, that before he had taken the journey, he had supposed that the white people were a small tribe, like his own, and that he had found them as numberless as the spires of grass on his prairies. The spectacle, however, that had struck him with most astonishment, was bullets as large as his head, and guns of the size of a log of wood. His people cultivate corn, beans, pumpkins and watermelons.

Here we remained five days, during which time Mr. Pratte purchased six hundred Buffalo skins, and some horses. A Pawnee war party came in from an expedition against a hostile tribe of whom they had killed and scalped four, and taken twenty horses. We were affected at the sight of a little child, taken captive, whose mother they had killed and scalped. They could not account for bringing in this child, as their warfare is an indiscriminate slaughter, of men, women and children.

A day or two after their arrival, they painted themselves for a celebration of their victory, with great labor and care. The chiefs were dressed in skins of wild animals, with the hair on.—These

skins were principally those of the bear, wolf, panther and spotted
or ring tailed panther. They wore necklaces of bear's and panther's
claws. The braves, as a certain class of the warriors are called, in
addition to the dress of the other chiefs, surmounted their heads
with a particular feather from a species of eagle, that they call the
war eagle. This feather is considered worth the price of ten ordinary horses. None but a brave is permitted to wear it as a badge.
A brave, gains his name and reputation as much by cunning and
dexterity in stealing and robbing, as by courage and success in murdering. When by long labor of the toilette, they had painted and
dressed themselves to their liking, they marched forth in the array
of their guns, bows, arrows and war clubs, with all the other ap-
pendages of their warfare. They then raised a tall pole, on the top
of which were attached the scalps of the foes they had killed. It
must be admitted, that they manifested no small degree of genius
and inventiveness, in making themselves frightful and horrible.
When they began their triumphal yelling, shouting, singing and
cutting antic capers, it seemed to us, that a recruit of fiends from
the infernal regions could hardly have transcended them in genuine diabolical display. They kept up this infernal din three days.
During all this time, the poor little captive child, barely fed to sustain life, lay in sight, bound hand and foot. When their rage at
length seemed sated, and exhausted, they took down the pole, and
gave the scalps to the women.

We now witnessed a new scene of yells and screams, and infuriated gestures; the actors kicking the scalps about, and throwing them from one to the other with strong expressions of rage
and contempt. When they also ceased, in the apparent satisfaction
of gratified revenge; the men directed their attention to the little
captive. It was removed to the medicine lodge, where the medicine
men perform their incantations, and make their offerings to the
Great Spirit. We perceived that they were making preparations to
burn the child. Alike affected with pity and horror, our party appealed, as one man, to the presiding chief, to spare the child. Our
first proposition was to purchase it. It was received by the chief
with manifest displeasure. In reply to our strong remonstrances, he

gravely asked us, if we, seeing a young rattlesnake in our path, would allow it to move off uninjured, merely because it was too small and feeble to bite? We undertook to point out the want of resemblance in the circumstances of the comparison, observing that the child, reared among them, would know no other people, and would imbibe their habits and enmities, and become as one of them. The chief replied, that he had made the experiment, and that the captive children, thus spared and raised, had only been instrumental, as soon as they were grown, of, bringing them into difficulties. 'It is' said he, 'like taking the eggs of partridges and hatching them; you may raise them ever so carefully in a cage; but once turn them loose, and they show their nature, not only by flying away, but by bringing the wild partridges into your corn fields: eat the eggs, and you have not only the food, but save yourself future trouble. We again urged that the child was too small to injure them, and of too little consequence to give them the pleasure of revenge in its destruction. To enforce our arguments, we showed him a roll of red broad cloth, the favorite color with the Indians. This dazzled and delighted him, and he eagerly asked us, how much we would give him. We insisted upon seeing the child, before we made him an offer. He led us to the lodge, where lay the poor little captive, bound so tight with thongs of raw hide, that the flesh had so swelled over the hard and dried leather, that the strings could no longer be perceived. It was almost famished, having scarcely tasted food for four days, and seemed rather dead than alive. With much difficulty we disengaged its limbs from the thongs, and perceiving that it seemed to revive, we offered him ten yards, of the red cloth. Expatiating upon the trouble and danger of his warriors in the late expedition, he insisted, that the price was too little. Having the child in our possession, and beginning to be indignant at this union of avarice and cruelty, our company exchanged glances of intelligence. A deep flush suffused the countenance of my father. 'My boys,' said he, 'will you allow these unnatural devils to burn this poor child, or practice extortion upon us, as the price of its ransom?' The vehemence and energy, with which these questions were proposed, had an effect, that may be easily imagined, in kindling the spirits of the rest of us. We carried it by acclamation, to take the child, and let them seek their own redress.

My father again offered the chief ten yards of cloth, which was refused as before. Our remark then was, that we would carry off the child, with, or without ransom, at his choice.—Meanwhile the child was sent to our encampment, and our men ordered to have their arms in readiness, as we had reason to fear that the chief would let loose his warriors upon us, and take the child by force. The old chief looked my father full in the face, with an expression of apparent astonishment. 'Do you think,' said he, 'you are strong enough to keep the child by force?' 'We will do it,' answered my father, 'or every man of us die in the attempt, in which case our countrymen will come, and gather up our bones, and avenge our death, by destroying your nation.' The chief replied with well dissembled calmness, that he did not wish to incur the enmity of our people, as he well knew, that we were more powerful than they; alledging, beside, that he had made a vow never to kill any more white men; and he added, that if we would give the cloth, and add to it a paper of vermillion, the child should be ours. To this we consented, and the contract was settled.

We immediately started for our encampment, where we were aware our men had been making arrangements for a battle. We had hardly expected, under these circumstances, that the chief would have followed us alone into a camp, where every thing appeared hostile. But he went on with us unhesitatingly, until he came to the very edge of it. Observing that our men had made a breast work of the baggage, and stood with their arms leaning against it ready for action, he paused a moment, as if faltering in his purpose to advance. With the peculiar Indian exclamation, he eagerly asked my father, if he had thought that he would fight his friends, the white people, for that little child? The reply was, that we only meant to be ready for them, if they had thought to do so. With a smiling countenance the chief advanced, and took my father's hand exclaiming, that they were good friends. 'Save your powder and lead,' he added, 'to kill buffaloes and your enemies.' So saying he left us for his own lodge.

This tribe is on terms of hostility with two or three of the tribes nearest their hunting grounds. They make their incursions on horseback, and often extend them to the distance of six or seven hundred miles. They chiefly engage on horseback, and their weapons, for the most part, consist of a bow and arrows, a lance and shield, though many of them at present have fire arms. Their commander stations himself in the rear of his warriors, seldom taking a part in the battle, unless he should be himself attacked, which is not often the case. They show no inconsiderable military stratagem in their marches, keeping spies before and behind, and on each flank, at the distance of a few days travel; so that in their open country, it is almost impossible to come upon them by surprise. The object of their expeditions is quite as often to plunder and steal horses, as to destroy their enemies. Each one is provided with the Spanish noose, to catch horses. They often extend these plundering expeditions as far as the interior of New Mexico. When they have reached the settled country, they lurk about in covert places, until an opportunity presents to seize on their prey. They fall upon the owner of a large establishment of cattle and horses, kill him during the night, or so alarm him as to cause him to fly, and leave his herds and family unprotected; in which case they drive off his horses, and secrete them in the mountains. In these fastnesses of nature they consider them safe; aware that the Mexicans, partly through timidity, and partly through indolence, will not pursue them to any great distance.

We left this village on the 11th of August, taking with us two of its inhabitants, each having a trap to catch, and a hoe to dig the beavers from their burrows. During this day's march we traversed a wide plain, on which we saw no game but antelopes and white wolves. At five in the evening, our front guard gave the preconcerted alarm by firing their pistols, and falling back a few moments afterwards, upon the main body.—We shortly afterwards discovered a large body of Indians on horseback, approaching us at full speed. When they were within hailing distance, we made them a signal to halt: they immediately halted. Surveying us a moment, and discovering us to be whites, one of them came towards us. We showed him the painted stick given us by the Pawnee Republican chief. He

seemed at once to comprehend all that it conveyed, and we were
informed, that this was a band of the Republican Pawnee warriors.
He carried the stick among them. It passed from hand to hand, and
appeared at once to satisfy them in regard to our peaceable intentions, for they continued their march without disturbing us. But
our two associate Indians, hearing their yells, as they rode off, took
them to be their enemies, from whom they had taken the child.
They immediately disappeared, and rejoined us no more. We travelled a few miles further, and encamped for the night on a small
stream, called Smoking river. It is a tributary stream of the main
Platte. On this stream a famous treaty had been made between the
Pawnees and Shienne; and from the friendly smoking of the calu-
met on this occasion, it received its name.

Next morning we made an early start, and marched rapidly all
day, in order to reach water at night. We halted at sunset to repose
ourselves, and found water for our own drinking, but none for our
mules and horses. As soon as the moon arose, we started again,
travelling hard all night, and until ten the next morning. At this
time we reached a most singular spring fountain, forming a basin
four hundred yards in diameter, in the centre of which the water
boiled up five or six feet higher, than it was near the circumference.
We encamped here, to rest, and feed our mules and horses, the remainder of the day, during which we killed some antelopes, that
came here to drink.

Near this place was a high mound, from which the eye swept
the whole horizon, as far as it could reach, and on this mound we
stationed our guard.

Next morning we commenced the toil of our daily march, pursuing a S. W. course, over the naked plains, reaching a small and,
as far as I know, a nameless stream at night, on the borders of which
were a few sparse trees, and high grass. Here we encamped for the
night. At twelve next day we halted in consequence of a pouring
rain, and encamped for the remainder of the day. This was the first
point, where we had the long and anxiously expected pleasure
of seeing buffaloes. We killed one, after a most animating sport in
shooting at it.

Next day we made an early start, as usual, and travelled hard all

day over a wide plain, meeting with no other incidents, than the
sight of buffaloes, which we did not molest. We saw, in this day's
march, neither tree nor rising ground. The plains are covered with
a short, fine grass, about four inches high, of such a kind, as to be
very injurious to the hoofs of animals, that travel over it. It seems
to me, that ours would not have received more injury from
travelling over a naked surface of rock. In the evening we reached
a small collection of water, beside which we encamped. We had to
collect our customary inconvenient substitute for fuel, not only
this evening, but the whole distance hence to the mountains.

On the morning of the 17th, we commenced, as usual, our early
march, giving orders to our advance guard to kill a buffaloe bull,
and make moccasins for some of our horses, from the skin, their
feet having become so tender from the irritation of the sharp grass,
as to make them travel with difficulty. This was soon accomplished,
furnishing the only incident of this day's travel. We continued the
next day to make our way over the same wearying plain, without
water or timber, having been obliged to provide more of our horses
with buffaloe skin moccasins. This day we saw numerous herds of
buffaloe bulls. It is a singular fact, in the habits of these animals,
that during one part of the year, the bulls all range in immense
flocks without a cow among them, and all the cows equally without
the bulls. The herd, which we now saw, showed an evident disposition to break into our caravan. They seemed to consider our horses
and mules, as a herd of their cows. We prevented their doing it, by
firing on them, and killing several.

This evening we arrived on one of the forks of the Osage, and
encamped. Here we caught a beaver, the first I had ever seen. On
the 20th, we started late, and made a short day's travel, encamping
by water. Next morning we discovered vast numbers of buffaloes,
all running in one direction, as though they were flying from some
sort of pursuit. We immediately detached men to reconoitre and
ascertain, whether they were not flying from the Indians. They
soon discovered a large body of them in full chase of these animals,
and shooting at them with arrows. As their course was directly towards our camp, they were soon distinctly in sight. At this moment
one of our men rode towards them, and discharged his gun. This

immediately turned their attention from the pursuit of the game, to us. The Indians halted a moment, as if in deliberation, and rode off in another direction with great speed. We regretted that we had taken no measures to ascertain, whether they were friendly or not. In the latter case we had sufficient ground to apprehend, that they would pursue us at a distance, and attack us in the night. We made our arrangements, and resumed our march in haste, travelling with great caution, and posting a strong guard at night.

The next day, in company with another, I kept guard on the right flank. We were both strictly enjoined not to fire on the buffaloes, while discharging this duty. Just before we encamped, which was at four in the afternoon, we discovered a herd of buffaloe cows, the first we had seen, and gave notice on our arrival at the camp. Mr. Pratte insisted, that we had mistaken, and said, that we were not yet far enough advanced into the country, to see cows, they generally herding in the most retired depths of the prairies. We were not disposed to contest the point with him, but proposed a bet of a suit of the finest cloth, and to settle the point by killing one of the herd, if the commander would permit us to fire upon it. The bet was accepted, and the permission given. My companion was armed with a musket, and I with a rifle. When we came in sight of the herd, it was approaching a little pond to drink. We concealed ourselves as they approached, and my companion requested me to take the first fire, as the rifle was surer and closer than the musket. When they were within shooting distance, I levelled one; as soon as it fell, the herd, which consisted of a thousand or more, gathered in crowds around the fallen one. Between us we killed eleven, all proving, according to our word, to be cows. We put our mules in requisition to bring in our ample supply of meat. Mr. Pratte admitted, that the bet was lost, though we declined accepting it.

About ten at night it commenced raining; the rain probably caused us to intermit our caution; for shortly after it began, the Indians attacked our encampment, firing a shower of arrows upon us. We returned their fire at random, as they retreated: they killed two of our horses, and slightly wounded one of our men; we found four Indians killed by our fire, and one wounded. The wounded

Indian informed our interpreter, that the Indians, who attacked us, were Arrickarees. We remained encamped here four days, attending our wounded man, and the wounded Indian, who died, however, the second day, and here we buried him.

We left this encampment on the 26th, and through the day met with continued herds of buffaloes and wild horses, which, however, we did not disturb. In the evening we reached a fork of the Platte, called Hyde Park. This stream, formerly noted for beavers, still sustains a few. Here we encamped, set our traps, and caught four beavers. In the morning we began to ascend this stream, and during our progress, we were obliged to keep men in advance, to affrighten the buffaloes and wild horses from our path. They are here in such prodigious numbers, as literally to have eaten down the grass of the prairies.

Here we saw multitudes of prairie dogs. They have large village establishments of burrows, where they live in society. They are sprightly, bold and self important animals, of the size of a Norwegian rat. On the morning of the 28th, our wounded companion was again unable to travel, in consequence of which we were detained at our encampment three days. Not wholly to lose the time, we killed during these three days 110 buffaloes, of which we saved only the tongues and hump ribs.

On the morning of the 31st, our wounded associate being somewhat recovered, we resumed our march. Ascending the stream, in the course of the day we came upon the dead bodies of two men, so much mangled, and disfigured by the wild beasts, that we could only discover that they were white men. They had been shot by the Indians with arrows, the ground near them being stuck full of arrows. They had been scalped. Our feelings may be imagined, at seeing the mangled bodies of people of our own race in these remote and unpeopled prairies. We consoled ourselves with believing that they died like brave men. We had soon afterwards clear evidence of this fact, for, on surveying the vicinity at the distance of a few hundred yards, we found the bodies of five dead Indians. The ground all around was torn and trampled by horse and footmen. We collected the remains of the two white men, and buried them. We then ascended the stream a few miles, and encamped. Find-

ing signs of Indians, who could have left the spot but a few hours
before, we made no fire for fear of being discovered, and attacked
in the night. Sometime after dark, ten of us started up the creek in
search of their fires. About four miles from our encampment, we
saw them a few hundred yards in advance. Twenty fires were distinctly visible. We counselled with each other, whether to fire on
them or not. Our conclusion was, that the most prudent plan was
to return, and apprize our companions of what we had seen. In
consequence of our information, on our return, sixty men were
chosen, headed by my father, who set off in order to surround their
camp before daylight. I was one of the number, as I should have
little liked to have my father go into battle without me, when it was
in my power to accompany him. The remainder were left in charge
of our camp, horses, and mules. We had examined our arms and
found them in good order. About midnight we came in sight of
their fires, and before three o'clock were posted all around them,
without having betrayed ourselves. We were commanded not to
fire a gun, until the word was given. As it was still sometime before
daylight, we became almost impatient for the command. As an Indian occasionally arose and stood for a moment before the fire, I in-
voluntarily took aim at him with the thought, how easily I could destroy him, but my orders with held me. Twilight at length came,
and the Indians began to arise. They soon discovered two of our
men, and instantly raising the war shout, came upon us with great
fury. Our men stood firm, until they received the order which was
soon given. A well directed and destructive fire now opened on
them, which they received, and returned with some firmness. But
when we closed in upon them they fled in confusion and dismay.
The action lasted fifteen minutes. Thirty of their dead were left on
the field, and we took ten prisoners, whom we compelled to bury
the dead. One of our men was wounded, and died the next day.
We took our prisoners to our encampment, where we questioned
them with regard to the two white men, we had found, and buried
the preceding day. They acknowledged, that their party killed them,
and assigned as a reason for so doing, that when the white men
were asked by the chief to divide their powder and balls with him,
they refused. It was then determined by the chief, that they should

be killed, and the whole taken. In carrying this purpose into effect, the Indians lost four of their best young men, and obtained but little powder and lead, as a compensation.

We then asked them to what nation they belonged? They answered the Crow. This nation is distinguished for bravery and skill in war. Their bows and arrows were then given them, and they were told, that we never killed defenceless prisoners, but that they must tell their brothers of us, and that we should not have killed any of their nation, had not they killed our white brothers; and if they did so in future, we should kill all we found of them, as we did not fear any number, they could bring against us. They were then allowed to go free, which delighted them, as they probably expected that we should kill them, it being their custom to put all their prisoners to death by the most shocking and cruel tortures. That they may not lose this diabolical pleasure by the escape of their prisoners, they guard them closely day and night. One of them, upon being released, gave my father an eagle's feather, saying, you are a good and brave man, I will never kill another white man.

We pursued our journey on the 1st of September. Our advance was made with great caution, as buffaloes were now seen in immense herds, and the danger from Indians was constant. Wandering tribes of these people subsist on the buffaloes, which traverse the interior of these plains, keeping them constantly in sight.

On the morning of the 2d, we started early. About ten o'clock we saw a large herd of buffaloes approaching us with great speed. We endeavored to prevent their running among our pack mules, but it was in vain. They scattered them in every direction over the plain; and although we rode in among the herd, firing on them, we were obliged to follow them an hour, before we could separate them sufficiently to regain our mules. After much labor we collected all, with the exception of one packed with dry goods, which the crowd drove before them. The remainder of the day, half our company were employed as a guard to prevent a similar occurrence. When we encamped for the night, sometime was spent in driving the buffaloes a considerable distance from our camp. But for this precaution, we should have been in danger of losing our horses and mules entirely.

The following morning, we took a S. S. W. course, which led us from the stream, during this day's journey. Nothing occured worthy of mention, except that we saw a great number of wolves, which had surrounded a small herd of buffaloe cows and calves, and killed and eaten several. We dispersed them by firing on them. We judged, that there were at least a thousand. They were large and as white as sheep. Near this point we found water, and encamped for the night.

On the morning of the 4th, a party was sent out to kill some buffaloe bulls, and get their skins to make moccasins for our horses, which detained us until ten o'clock. We then packed up and travelled six miles. Finding a lake, we encamped for the night. From this spot, we saw one of the most beautiful landscapes, that ever spread out to the eye. As far as the plain was visible in all directions, innumerable herds of wild horses, buffaloes, antelopes, deer, elk, and wolves, fed in their wild and fierce freedom. Here the sun rose, and set, as unobscured from the sight, as on the wastes of ocean. Here we used the last of our salt, and as for bread, we had seen none, since we had left the Pawnee village. I hardly need observe, that these are no small deprivations.

The next day we travelled until evening, nothing occurring, that deserves record. Our encampment was near a beautiful spring, called Bellefontaine, which is visited by the Indians, at some seasons of the year. Near it were some pumpkins, planted by the Indians. I cooked one, but did not find it very palateable: The next day we encamped without water. Late in the evening of the following day we reached a stream, and encamped. As we made our arrangements for the night, we came upon a small party of Indians. They ran off immediately, but we pursued them, caught four, and took them to the camp they had left, a little distant from ours. It contained between twenty and thirty women and children, beside three men. The women were frightened at our approach, and attempted to run. The Indians in our possession said something to them in their own language, that induced them to stop; but it was sometime, before they were satisfied, that we intended them no harm. We returned to our camp, and were attending to our mules and horses. Our little Indian boy was playing about the camp, as usual. Sud-

denly our attention was arrested by loud screams or cries; and
looking up, we saw our little boy in the arms of an Indian, whose
neck he was closely clasping, as the Indian pressed him to his
bosom, kissing him, and crying at the same time. As we moved towards the spot, the Indian approached us, still holding the child in
his arms; and falling on his knees, made us a long speech, which
we understood only through his signs. During his speech, he
would push the child from him, and then draw it back to him,
and point to us. He was the father of this boy, whom we saved from
being burnt by the Pawnees. He gave us to understand by his signs,
that his child was carried off by his enemies. When the paroxysm
of his joy was past, we explained, as well as we could, how we obtained the child. Upon hearing the name *Pawnee*, he sprang
upon his feet, and rushed into his tent. He soon came out, bringing
with him two Indian scalps, and his bow and arrows, and insisted,
that we should look at the scalps, making signs to tell us, that
they were Pawnee scalps, which he took at the time he lost his child.
After he finished this explanation, he would lay the scalps a short
distance from him, and shoot his arrows through them, to prove
his great enmity to this nation. He then presented my father a pair
of leggins and a pipe, both neatly decorated with porcupine quills;
and accompanied by his child, withdrew to his tent, for the night.
Just as the morning star became visible, we were aroused from our
slumbers, by the crying and shouting of the Indians in their tent.
We arose, and approached it, to ascertain the cause of the noise.
Looking in, we saw the Indians all laying prostrate with their faces
to the ground. We remained observing them, until the full light of
day came upon them.—They then arose, and placed themselves
around the fire. The next movement was to light a pipe, and begin
to smoke. Seeing them blow the smoke first towards the point
where the sun arose, and then towards heaven, our curiosity was
aroused, to know the meaning of what we had seen. The old chief
told us by signs, that they had been thanking the Great Spirit for
allowing them to see another day. We then purchased a few beaver
skins of them, and left them. Our encampment for the evening of
this day, was near a small spring, at the head of which we found a
great natural curiosity. A rock sixteen yards in circumference, rises

from eighty to ninety feet in height, according to our best judgment, from a surface upon which, in all directions, not the smallest
particle of rock, not even a pebble can be found. We were unable
to reach the top of it, although it was full of holes, in which the
hawks and ravens build their nests. We gave the spring the name
of Rock Castle spring. On the morning of the 9th, we left this spot,
and at night reached the foot of a large dividing ridge, which separates the waters of the Platte from those of the Arkansas. After
completing our arrangements for the night, some of us ascended
to the top of the ridge, to look out for Indians; but we saw none.

The succeeding morning we crossed the ridge, and came to
water in the evening, where we encamped. Here we killed a white
bear, which occupied several of us at least an hour. It was constantly
in chase of one or another of us, thus withholding us from shooting at it, through fear of wounding each other. This was the first,
I had ever seen. His claws were four inches long, and very sharp.
He had killed a buffaloe bull, eaten a part of it, and buried the remainder. When we came upon him, he was watching the spot,
where he had buried it, to keep off the wolves, which literally surrounded him.

On the 11th, we travelled over some hilly ground. In the course
of the day, we killed three white bears, the claws of which I saved,
they being of considerable value among the Indians, who wear them
around the neck, as the distinguishing mark of a brave. Those
Indians, who wear this ornament, view those, who do not, as their
inferiors. We came to water, and encamped early. I was one of
the guard for the night, which was rather cloudy. About the middle
of my guard, our horses became uneasy, and in a few moments
more, a bear had gotten in among them, and sprung upon one of
them. The others were so much alarmed, that they burst their fast-
enings, and darted off at full speed. Our camp was soon aroused,
and in arms, for defence, although much confused, from not knowing what the enemy was, nor from what direction to expect the attack. Some, however, immediately set off in pursuit of our horses.
I still stood at my post, in no little alarm, as I did not know with
the rest, if the Indians were around us or not. All around was
again stillness, the noise of those in pursuit of the horses being lost

in the distance. Suddenly my attention was arrested, as I gazed in the direction, from which the alarm came, by a noise like that of a struggle at no great distance from me. I espied a hulk, at which I immediately fired. It was the bear devouring a horse, still alive. My shot wounded him. The report of my gun, together with the noise made by the enraged bear, brought our men from the camp, where they awaited a second attack from the unknown enemy in perfect stillness.—Determined to avenge themselves, they now sallied forth, although it was so dark, that an object ten steps in advance could not be seen. The growls of the bear, as he tore up the ground around him with his claws, attracted all in his direction. Some of the men came so near, that the animal saw them, and made towards them. They all fired at him, but did not touch him. All now fled from the furious animal, as he seemed intent on destroying them. In this general flight one of the men was caught. As he screamed out in his agony, I, happening to have reloaded my gun, ran up to relieve him. Reaching the spot in an instant, I placed the muzzle of my gun against the bear, and discharging it, killed him. Our companion was litterally torn in pieces. The flesh on his hip was torn off, leaving the sinews bare, by the teeth of the bear. His side was so wounded in three places, that his breath came through the openings; his head was dreadfully bruised, and his jaw broken. His breath came out from both sides of his windpipe, the animal in his fury having placed his teeth and claws in every part of his body. No one could have supposed, that there was the slightest possibility of his recovery, through any human means. We remained in our encampment three days, attending upon him, without seeing any change for the worse or better in his situation. He had desired us from the first to leave him, as he considered his case as hopeless as ourselves did. We then concluded to move from our encampment, leaving two men with him, to each of whom we gave one dollar a day, for remaining to take care of him, until he should die, and to bury him decently.

On the 14th we set off, taking, as we believed, a final leave of our poor companion. Our feelings may be imagined, as we left this suffering man to die in this savage region, unfriended and unpitied. We travelled but a few miles before we came to a fine stream and some timber. Concluding that this would be a better place for our unfortunate companion, than the one where he was, we encamped with the intention of sending back for him. We despatched men for him, and began to prepare a shelter for him, should he arrive. This is a fork of Smoke Hill river, which empties into the Platte. We set traps, and caught eight beavers, during the night. Our companions with the wounded man on a litter, reached us about eight o'clock at night.

In the morning we had our painful task of leave taking to go through again. We promised to wait for the two we left behind at the Arkansas river. We travelled all day up this stream.—I counted, in the course of the day, two hundred and twenty white bears. We killed eight, that made an attack upon us; the claws of which I saved. Leaving the stream in the evening we encamped on the plain. A guard of twenty was relieved through the night, to prevent the bears from coming in upon us. Two tried to do it and were killed.

In the morning we began our march as usual: returning to the stream, we travelled until we came to its head. The fountain, which is its source, boils up from the plain, forming a basin two hundred yards in circumference, as clear as crystal, about five feet in depth. Here we killed some wild geese and ducks. After advancing some distance farther, we encamped for the night. Buffaloes were not so numerous, during this day's journey, as they had been some time previous, owing, we judged, to the great number of white bears.

On the 17th we travelled until sunset, and encamped near water. On the 18th we found no water, but saw great numbers of wild horses and elk. The succeeding morning we set off before light, and encamped at 4 o'clock in the afternoon by a pond, the water of which was too brackish to drink. On the 20th we found water to encamp by. In the course of the day I killed two fat buffaloe cows. One of them had a calf, which I thought I would try to catch alive. In order to do so, I concluded it would be well to be free from any unnecessary incumbrances, and accordingly laid aside my shot-pouch, guns and pistols. I expected it would run but instead of that, when I came within six or eight feet of it, it turned around, and ran upon me, butting me like a ram, until I was knocked flat upon my back. Every time I attempted to rise, it laid me down again. At last I caught by one of its legs, and stabbed it with my butcher knife, or I believe it would have butted me to death. I made up my mind, that I would never attempt to catch another buffaloe calf alive, and also, that I would not tell my companions what a capsizing I had had, although my side did not feel any better for the butting it had received. I packed on my horse as much meat as he could carry, and set out for the camp, which I reached a little after dark. My father was going in search of me, believing me either lost, or killed. He had fired several guns, to let me know the direction of the camp.

We travelled steadily on the 21st, and encamped at night on a small branch of the Arkansas. During the day, we had seen large droves of buffaloes running in the same direction, in which we travelled, as though they were pursued. We could, however, see nothing in pursuit. They appeared in the same confusion all night. On the 22d, we marched fast all day, the buffaloes still running before us. In the evening we reached the main Arkansas, and encamped. The sky indicating rain, we exerted ourselves, and succeeded in pitching our tents and kindling fires, before the rain began to fall. Our meat was beginning to roast, when we saw some Indians about half a mile distant, looking at us from a hill. We immediately tied our mules and horses. A few minutes after, ten Indians approached us with their guns on their shoulders. This open, undisguised approach made us less suspicious of them, than we should otherwise have been. When they were within a proper distance, they stopped, and called out *Amigo, Amigo*. One of our number understood them, and answered *Amigo,* which is friend, when they came up to us. They were Commanches, and one of them was a chief. Our interpreter understood and spoke their language quite well. The chief seemed bold, and asked who was our captain? My father was pointed out to him. He then asked us to go and encamp with him, saying that his people and the whites were good friends. My father answered, that we had encamped before we knew where they were, and that if we moved now, we feared that the goods would be wet. The chief said, this was very good; but that, as we now knew where his camp was, we must move to it. To this my father returned, that if it did not rain next morning, we would; but as before, that we did not wish to get the goods wet to night. The chief then said, in a surly manner, 'you don't intend then to move to my camp to night?' My father answered, 'No!' The chief said he should, or he would come upon us with his men, kill us, and take every thing we had. Upon this my father pushed the chief out of the tent, telling him to send his men as soon as he pleased; that we would kill them, as fast as they came. In reply the chief pointed his finger to the spot, where the sun would be at eight o'clock the next morning, and said, 'If you do not come to my camp, when the sun is there, I will set all my warriors upon you.' He then ran off through the rain to his own camp. We began, immediately, a kind of breastwork, made by chopping off logs, and putting them together. Confidently expecting an attack in the night, we tied our horses and mules in a sink hole between us and the river. It was now dark. I do not think an eye was closed in our camp that night; but the morning found us unmolested; nor did we see any Indians, before the sun was at the point spoken of. When it had reached it, an army of between six and eight hundred mounted Indians, with their faces painted a black as though they had come from the infernal regions, armed with fuzees and spears and shields appeared before us. Every thing had been done by the Indians to render this show as intimidating as possible. We discharged a couple of guns at them to show that we were not afraid, and were ready to receive them. A part advanced towards us; but one alone, approaching at full speed, threw down his bow and arrows, and sprang in among us, saying in broken English 'Commanches no good, me Iotan, good man.' He gave us to understand, that the Iotan nation was close at hand, and would not let the Commanches hurt us, and then started back, the Commanches fired some shots at us, but from such a distance, that we did not return them. In less than half an hour, we heard a noise like distant thunder. It became more and more distinct, until a band of armed Indians, whom we conjectured to be Iotans, became visible in the distance. When they had drawn near, they reined up their horses for a moment, and then rushed in between us and Commanches, who charged upon the Iotans. The latter sustained the charge with firmness. The discharge of their fire arms and the clashing of their different weapons, together with their war-yell, and the shrieks of the wounded and dying were fit accompaniments to the savage actors and scene. I do not pretend to describe this deadly combat between two Indian nations; but, as far as I could judge, the contest lasted fifteen minutes. I was too deeply interested in watching the event, to note it particularly. We wished to assist the Iotans, but could not distinguish them from the mass, so closely were the parties engaged. We withheld our fire through fear of injuring the Iotans, whom we considered our friends. It was not long before we saw, to our great satisfaction, the Commanches dismounted, which was the signal of their entire defeat. The Iotans then left the Commanches, and returned to their women and children, whom they had left some distance behind. They brought them to our camp, and pitched their own tents all around us, except that of the chief, which was placed in the centre with ours. A guard of warriors was then posted around the encampment, and an order given for the wounded Iotans to be brought into the tent of the chief. There were ten, two of whom died before night. A message was now sent to the chief of the Commanches, in obedience to which he came to the Iotan chief. A council then seemed to be held, and a peace was made, the terms of which were, that the Iotan chief should pay the Commanche chief two horses for every warrior, he had lost in the battle, over the number of Iotans killed. We gave the Iotan chief Goods to the amount of one hundred dollars, which pleased him exceedingly. He expressed himself perfectly satisfied with this recompense for the warriors he had lost in our defence. The knowledge, that a party as large as ours was traversing the country, had soon spread in all directions from the reports of Indians, who had met with us, and we became to these savage tribes a matter of interest, as a source of gain to be drawn from us by robbing, kindness or trade.—Our movements were observed. The Commanches determined to possess themselves of their object by force; and the Iotans interfered in our defence, that they might thus gain their point by extortion from friends."

Not a single Commanche was allowed to enter our camp, as arrangements were making for the Iotans to trade with us. All, who had any beaver skins, or dressed deer skins, were sent for. A guard was placed around in a circle, inside of which the skins were thrown down. Each Indian then inquired for the article he wanted. In this way we exchanged with them butcher knives, paint, and powder and ball, for beaver and deer skins, to the amount of fifteen hundred dollars, allowing them what we considered the value of the skins.

The old Commanche chief came to the Iotan chief to ask permission to talk with us, but was forbidden; and we were told not to have any dealings with him. We did not. The Iotan chief then gave us the character of the Commanche chief. He seemed to be thinking some time before he began. 'I know,' said he, 'you must think it strange that I should fight with the Commanches, and then pay them for their warriors killed, over our own number lost, and make peace with them. I will give you my reasons for doing so. Four years ago, this Commanche chief with his followers, went in company with my father, who was a chief, and a few of his followers, went in company with my father, who was a chief, and a few of his followers, in search of buffaloes. After they had killed what they wanted, they divided the meat. The Commanche took all the best of it, leaving the remains for my father. The old man put up with it, and said nothing. On their return, close to this place they met a band of Nabahoes, a nation that had long been at war with ours, and killed a great number of our people. My father wanted to kill them, and began to fire upon them. The Commanches joined the Nabahoes, and together they killed my father and most of his men. He then paid for the lives he had taken, in horses, giving twenty for my father, and four for each warrior. I only give two horses for a warrior. I am now happy. I have killed three times as many of them, as they did of us, and paid less for it. I know they can never get the upper hand of me again. This Commanche chief is a mean man, for whenever he has power, he makes others do as he pleases, or he kills them, and takes all they have. He wanted to act in this way with you; but I do not think he could, for you know how to shoot better than he does; and you would not give up, as long as you had powder and ball and one man alive.' My father as commander, said, 'his men were all good soldiers, and knew how to get the advantage in fighting; and that we had plenty of ammunition and good guns, and were not in the least afraid of being beaten by them.' 'I think so,' replied the chief; 'But I thank the Great Spirit, that it happened as it did. I have taken revenge for the death of my father, and his people, and gained, I hope, at the same time the love of a good and brave people by defending them.' We assured him that he had, expressing our thanks for his aid, and regret for those who had been killed in our defence. 'Yes,' said the chief, 'they were brave men; but they loved my father, whom they have now gone to see, where they will have plenty to eat, and drink, without having to fight for it.' These were his thoughts, as near as I can express them.

The Commanche chief made a second application for permission to talk with us, which was now granted. His object in conversing with us, was, as he said, to make friends with us, and induce us to give him some powder and ball. We told him that we would willingly make peace with him; but not give him any thing, as we did not break the peace. He had threatened to kill us, and take our property without any provocation from us, and certainly, if any present was necessary, it must come from him. We did not, however, wish any present from him, and would make peace with him, provided he promised never to kill, or try to kill a white man. He answered, that he had neither done it, or intended to do it; that with regard to us, he only sought to frighten us, so that we should come to his camp, before the Iotans came up, whom he knew to be not far distant, in order that he might precede them in trading with us, adding that as he had been so disappointed, he thought we ought to give him a little powder and ball. Our answer was, that we had no more ammunition to spare; and that we could not depart from our resolution of not purchasing a treaty from him; but we would give him a letter of recommendation to the next company that came in this direction, by means of which he might trade with them, and obtain what he wanted of these articles. He consented to a treaty on these conditions, and lighting his pipes we smoked friends.

He then asked us if we came through the Pawnee village? We answered in the affirmative. His next question was, had they plenty of ammunition? Our reply was again, yes. We were then given to understand, that he was then at war with them, and had been for a number of years, and that he should soon either make peace with them, or have a general engagement. He would prefer peace, as they were at war with the Spaniards, as well as himself. By uniting forces, they could beat the Spaniards, though in case of a treaty or not, he intended to go against the Spaniards, as soon as he should return from the country of the Pawnees. He added, 'I suppose you are friends with the Spaniards, and are now going to trade with them.' Our commander replied, that we were going to trade with them, but not to fight for them. That, said the chief, is what I wanted to know. I do not want war with your people, and should we accidentally kill any of them, you must not declare war against us, as we will pay you for them in horses or beaver skins. We did not express our natural feeling, that the life of one man was worth more than all the horses or beaver skins, his nation could bring forth; but told him, that we would not injure his people, unless they did ours, on purpose. He returned, apparently satisfied, to his camp. We were detained here until the fourth of November by our promise of awaiting the arrival of the two men, we had left with our wounded companion. They came, and brought with them his gun and ammunition. He died the fifth day, after we had left him, and was buried as decently, as the circumstances would allow.

On the 5th of November we again set off in company with a party of Iotans. The Arkansas is here wide and shallow, like the Platte; and has wide but thinly timbered bottoms on both sides. Extending from the bottom ten or twelve miles on the south side, are low hills composed principally of sand. We found travelling upon them very fatiguing, particularly as we met with no water. Late in the evening we reached water, and encamped.

The next morning we resumed our journey. We were exceedingly diverted, during the day, to see the Iotan Indians in company with us, chase the buffaloes on horseback. They killed them with their arrows. The force, with which they shoot these arrows, is astonishing. I saw one of them shoot an arrow through a buffaloe bull, that had been driven close to our camp. We were again upon level plains, stretching off in all directions beyond the reach of the eye. The few high mounds scattered over them could not but powerfully arrest the curiosity. From the summit of one I again looked down upon innumerable droves of wild animals, dotting the surface, as they seemed to forget their savage natures, and fed, or reposed in peace. I indulged the thoughts natural to such a position and scene. The remembrance of home, with its duties and pleasures, came upon my mind in strong contrast with my actual circumstances. I was interrupted by the discharge of guns, and the screams and yells of Indians. The Iotans had found six Nabahoes a half a mile from us, and were killing them. Three were killed. The others, being well mounted, made their escape. The Iotans came to our camp with their scalps, leaving the bodies to be eaten by wild animals. My father sent men to bury them. The Iotans danced around these scalps all night, and in the morning took up the bodies, we had buried, and cut them in pieces. They then covered themselves with the skins of bears and panthers, and, taking the hearts of the dead men, cut them into pieces of the size of a mouthful, and laid them upon the ground, and kneeling put their hands on the ground, and crawled around the pieces of hearts, growling as though they were enraged bears, or panthers, ready to spring upon them, and eat them. This is their mode of showing hatred to their enemies. Not relishing such detestable conduct, we so manifested our feelings, that these Indians went to their own camps.

We encamped the evening of the next day near water. Nothing worthy of record occurred during the journey of the four succeeding days, except that we came to a small creek called Simaronee. Here we encamped, and killed some buffaloes, and shod our horses. We travelled up this stream some distance, and left it on the 15th.

On the 16th we encamped on a creek, where we found four gentle mules, which we caught. I could not account for their being there. Nothing of importance occurred in the two last days.

From the 17th to the 20th, we journied without interruption. The latter day we came in view of a mountain covered with snow, called Taos mountain. This object awakened in our minds singular but pleasant feelings. On the 23d we reached its foot. Here Mr.

Pratte concealed a part of his goods by burying them in the ground. We were three days crossing this mountain.

On the evening of the 26th, we arrived at a small town in Tous, called St. Ferdinando, situated just at the foot of the mountain on the west side. The alcaide asked us for the invoice of our goods, which we showed him, and paid the customary duties on them. This was a man of a swarthy complexion having the appearance of pride and haughtiness. The door-way of the room, we were in, was crowded with men, women and children, who stared at us, as though they had never seen white men before, there being in fact, much to my surprize and disappointment, not one white person among them. I had expected to find no difference between these people and our own, but their language. I was never so mistaken. The men and women were not clothed in our fashion, the former having short pantaloons fastened below the waist with a red belt and buck skin leggins put on three or four times double. A Spanish knife is stuck in by the side of the leg, and a small sword worn by the side. A long jacket or blanket is thrown over, and worn upon the shoulders. They have few fire arms, generally using upon occasions which require them, a bow and spear, and never wear a hat, except when they ride. When on horse back, they face towards the right side of the animal. The saddle, which they use, looks as ours would, with something like an arm chair fastened upon it.

The women wear upon the upper part of the person a garment resembling a shirt, and a short petticoat fastened around the waist with a red or blue belt, and something of the scarf kind wound around their shoulders. Although appearing as poorly, as I have described, they are not destitute of hospitality; for they brought us food, and invited us into their houses to eat, as we walked through the streets.

The first time my father and myself walked through the town together, we were accosted by a woman standing in her own door-way. She made signs for us to come in. When we had entered, she conducted us up a flight of steps into a room neatly whitewashed, and adorned with images of saints, and a crucifix of brass nailed to a wooden cross. She gave us wine, and set before us a dish composed of red pepper, ground and mixed with corn meal, stewed

in fat and water. We could not eat it. She then brought forward
some tortillas and milk. Tortillas are a thin cake made of corn and
wheat ground between two flat stones by the women. This cake is
called in Spanish, *metate*. We remained with her until late in the
evening, when the bells began to ring. She and her children knelt
down to pray. We left her, and returned. On our way we met a bier
with a man upon it, who had been stabbed to death, as he was
drinking whiskey.

This town stands on a beautiful plain, surrounded on one side
by the Rio del Norte, and on the other by the mountain, of which
I have spoken, the summit being covered with perpetual snow.

We set off for Santa Fe on the 1st of November. Our course for
the first day led us over broken ground. We passed the night in a
small town, called Callacia, built on a small stream, that empties
into the del Norte. The country around this place presents but a
small portion of level surface.

The next day our path lay over a point of the mountain. We
were the whole day crossing. We killed a grey bear, that was exceedingly fat. It had fattened on a nut of the shape and size of a bean,
which grows on a tree resembling the pine, called by the Spanish,
pinion. We took a great part of the meat with us. We passed the
night again in a town called Albukerque.

The following day we passed St. Thomas, a town situated on
the bank of the del Norte, which is here a deep and muddy stream,
with bottoms from five to six miles wide on both sides. These bottoms sustain numerous herds of cattle. The small huts of the shepherds, who attend to them, were visible here and there. We reached
another town called Elgidonis, and stopped for the night. We kept
guard around our horses all night, but in the morning four of our
mules were gone. We hunted for them until ten o'clock, when two
Spaniards came, and asked us, what we would give them, if they
would find our mules? We told them to bring the mules, and we
would pay them a dollar. They set off, two of our men following
them without their knowledge and went into a thicket, where they
had tied the mules, and returned with them to us. As may be supposed, we gave them both a good whipping. It seemed at first, that
the whole town would rise against us in consequence. But when we

related the circumstances fairly to the people, the officer corresponding to our justice of the peace, said, we had done perfectly right, and had the men put in the stocks.

We recommenced our journey, and passed a mission of Indians under the control of an old priest. After crossing a point of the mountain, we reached Santa Fe, on the 5th. This town contains between four and five thousand inhabitants. It is situated on a large plain. A handsome stream runs through it, adding life and beauty to a scene striking and agreeable from the union of amenity and cultivation around, with the distant view of the snow clad mountains. It is pleasant to walk on the flat roofs of the houses in the evening, and look on the town and plain spread below. The houses are low, with flat roofs as I have mentioned. The churches are differently constructed from the other buildings and make a beautiful show. They have a great number of large bells, which, when disturbed, make a noise, that would almost seem sufficient to awaken the dead.

We asked the governor for permission to trap beaver in the river Helay. His reply was that, he did not know if he was allowed by the law to do so; but if upon examination it lay in his power, he would inform us on the morrow, if we would come to his office at 9 o'clock in the morning. According to this request, we went to the place appointed, the succeeding day, which was the 9th of November. We were told by the governor, that he had found nothing, that would justify him, in giving us the legal permission, we desired. We then proposed to him to give us liberty to trap upon the condition, that we paid him five per cent on the beaver we might catch. He said, he would consider this proposition, and give us an answer the next day at the same hour. The thoughts of our hearts were not at all favorable to this person, as we left him.

About ten o'clock at night an express came from the river Pacus, on which the nobles have their country seats and large farming establishments, stating, that a large body of Indians had come upon several families, whom they had either robbed, or murdered. Among the number two Americans had been killed, and the wife of one taken prisoner, in company with four Spanish women, one of whom was daughter of the former governor, displaced because

he was an European. The drum and fife and French horn began
to sound in a manner, that soon awakened, and alarmed the whole
town. The frightened women, and the still more fear-stricken men,
joining in a full chorus of screams and cries, ran some to where the
drum was beating in the public square, and others to our quarters.
Upon the first sound of alarm we had prepared to repel the enemy,
whatever it might be, provided it troubled us. When this group
came rushing towards us, the light of the moon enabled us to discern them with sufficient clearness to prevent our doing them any
injury. We did not sleep any more that night, for the women, having got the wrong story, as most women do in a case of the kind,
told us that the Commanches were in town, killing the people. We
awaited an attack, without, however, hearing any sound of fire
arms. Our conclusion was, that they were skulking around, dealing
out death in darkness and silence with their arrows; and in the feelings, which were its natural result, the remainder of the night
passed. The first light of morning showed us a body of four hundred men ready to mount their horses. At sunrise the governor
came to us to ask, if we would aid in the attempt to recapture the
prisoners taken by the Commanches, relating to us the real cause
of the alarm of the preceding night. We complied readily with
his request, as we were desirous of gaining the good will of the people. Our arrangements were soon made, and we set off in company
with the troops I have mentioned.

The 12th was spent in travelling. We stopped for the night at St.
John's, a small town. On the 13th we reached the spot, where the
murders and robbery were committed. Here we took the course the
Indians had marked in their retreat, stopping only for refresh-
ments. We pressed on all night, as we found their fires still
smoking. At eight on the morning of the 15th, the trail being fresh,
we increased our speed, and at twelve came in sight of them, as
they advanced toward a low gap in the mountains. We now halted,
and counselled together with regard to the next movements. The
commander of the Spaniards proposed, that my father should
direct the whole proceedings, promising obedience on his own
part and that of his troops.

The gap in the mountains, of which I spake, was made by a

stream. The Indians were now entering it. My father formed a plan immediately, and submitted it to the Spanish commander, who promised to aid in carrying it into effect. In conformity to it, the Spaniards were directed to keep in rear of the Indians, without being seen by them. We took a circuitous route, screened from sight by the highland, that lay between us and the Indians, in order to gain unobserved a hollow in advance of them, in which we might remain concealed, until they approached within gunshot of us. Our main object was to surprize them, and not allow them time to kill their captives, should they be still alive. The party in the rear were to close in, upon hearing the report of our guns, and not allow them to return to the plain. Our plan seemed to assure us success. We succeeded in reaching the hollow, in which we placed ourselves in the form of a half circle, extending from one side of it to the other, our horses being tied behind us. Every man was then ordered to prime, and pick his gun afresh. The right flank was to fire first, the left reserving theirs to give a running fire, that should enable the right to re-load. The Indians, surrounding the prisoners, were to be taken as the first aim, to prevent the immediate murder of them by their captors. My post was in the centre of the line. We waited an hour and a half behind our screens of rocks and trees, before our enemies made their appearance. The first object, that came in sight, were women without any clothing, driving a large drove of sheep and horses. These were immediately followed by Indians. When the latter were within thirty or forty yards of us, the order to fire was given. The women ran towards us the moment they heard the report of our guns. In doing this they encountered the Indians behind them, and three fell pierced by the spears of these savages. The cry among us now was, 'save the women!' Another young man and myself sprang forward, to rescue the remaining two. My companion fell in the attempt. An Indian had raised his spear, to inflict death upon another of these unfortunate captives, when he received a shot from one of our men, that rendered him incapable of another act of cruelty. The captives, one of whom was a beautiful young lady, the daughter of the governor before spoken of, both reached me. The gratitude of such captives, so delivered, may be imagined. Fears, thanks and exclamations in

Spanish were the natural expression of feeling in such a position. My companions aided me in wrapping blankets around them, for it was quite cold; and making the best arrangements in our power for their comfort and safety. This was all done in less time, than is required to relate it, and we returned to our post.

The Indians stood the second fire, and then retreated. We pursued keeping up a quick fire, expecting every moment to hear the Spaniards in the rear following our example to check them in their retreat; but we could discover the entrance upon the plain, before we heard any thing from our Spanish muskets. The Indians then began to yell; but the Spaniards, after one discharge from their fire arms fled. Being mounted on good horses the Indians did not pursue them, but satisfied as to our numbers, now that we were upon the plain, they rallied, and rushed upon us. Our commander now ordered us to retreat into the woods, and to find shelter behind trees, and take aim that every shot might tell, as it was of the utmost importance, not to waste ammunition, saying, 'stand resolute, my boys, and we make them repent, if they follow us, although those * * Spaniards have deserted us, when we came to fight for them. We are enough for these * * devils alone.' As they came near us, we gave them a scattering though destructive fire, which they returned bravely, still pressing towards us. It was a serious contest for about ten minutes, after they approached within pistol shot of us. From their yells, one would have thought that the infernal regions were open before them, and that they were about to be plunged in headlong. They finally began to retreat again, and we soon put them completely to flight. The Spaniards, though keeping a safe distance, while this was going forward, saw the state of affairs, and joined us in the pursuit, still taking especial care not to come near enough to the Indians, to hurt them, or receive any injury themselves. After the Indians rallied, we lost ten men, and my father received a slight wound in the shoulder.

We removed our horses and the rescued captives into the plain, and encamped. The Spaniards had killed an Indian already wounded, and were riding over the dead bodies of those on the ground, spearing them and killing any, who still breathed. My father commanded them to desist, or he would fire upon them, and

the Spanish officer added his order to the same effect. The latter
then demanded of us, the two women, whom we had rescued, with
as much assurance, as though himself had been the cause of their
deliverance. My father replied, by asking what authority or right
he had, to make such a request, when his cowardice withheld him
from aiding in their release? The officer became enraged, and said,
that he was unable to rally his men, and that he did not consider
the captives any safer in our hands than in those of the Indians, as
we were not christians. This insult, coupled with such a lame apol-
ogy, only made my father laugh, and reply, that if cowardice constituted a claim to christianity, himself and his men were prime
and undoubted christians. He added further, that if the rescued
women preferred to accompany him, rather than remain, until he
should have buried his brave comrades, who fell in their defence,
and accept his protection, he had nothing to say. The subjects of
our discussion, being present while it took place, decided the point
before they were appealed to. The youngest said, that nothing
would induce her to leave her deliverers, and that when they were
ready to go, she would accompany them, adding, that she should
pray hourly for the salvation of those, who had resigned their lives
in the preservation of hers. The other expressed herself willing to
remain with her, and manifested the same confidence and gratitude.
The enraged officer and his men set off on their return to Santa Fe.

The sun was yet an hour from its setting. We availed ourselves
of the remaining light to make a breastwork with the timber, that
had drifted down the stream, that we might be prepared for the Indians, in case they should return. We finished it, and posted our sentinels by sunset. The governor's daughter now inquired for the individual, who first met her in her flight from the Indians, and so
humanely and bravely conducted her out of danger, and provided
for her comfort. I cannot describe the gratitude and loveliness, that
appeared in her countenance, as she looked on me, when I was
pointed out to her. Not attaching any merit to the act, I had performed, and considering it merely as a duty, I did not know how
to meet her acknowledgments, and was embarrassed.

On the morning of the 16th we buried our dead. My father's
shoulder was a little stiff, and somewhat swollen. We saddled our

horses, and began our return journey. I gave up my horse to one of
the ladies, and made my way on foot. We drove the sheep, which
escaped the balls, before us. Our last look at the ground of our late
contest gave a view sufficiently painful to any one, who had a heart;
horses and their riders lay side by side. The bodies of robbers surrounded by the objects of their plunder would probably remain,
scattered as they were, unburied and exposed to the wild beasts.

We halted in the evening for the refreshment of ourselves and
horses. This done, we again set off travelling all night. The sheep
giving out, we were obliged to leave them. At twelve next day we
reached Pacus. Here we met the father of the youngest of the two
ladies accompanied by a great number of Spaniards. The old man
was transported almost to frenzy, when he saw his daughter. We remained here for the day. On the morning of the 18th we all set off
together, the old governor insisting, that my father and myself
must ride in the carriage with him; but we excused ourselves, and
rode by the side of it with the interpreter. The father carressed us
exceedingly, and said a great many things about me in particular,
which I did not think, I deserved.

The next day at two in the afternoon, we arrived at Santa Fe.
We were received with a salute, which we returned with our small
arms. The governor came in the evening, and invited my father
and the interpreter to sup with him. He ordered some fat beeves to
be killed for the rest of us. The father of Jacova, for that was the
name of the young lady, I had rescued, came, and invited us all to
go, and drink coffee at his son-in-law's, who kept a coffee-house. We
went, and when we had finished our coffee, the father came, and
took me by the hand, and led me up a flight of steps, and into a
room, where were his two daughters. As soon as I entered the room,
Jacova and her sister both came, and embraced me, this being the
universal fashion of interchanging salutations between men and
women among these people, even when there is nothing more, than
a simple introduction between strangers. After I had been seated
an hour, looking at them, as they made signs, and listening to their
conversation, of which I did not understand a syllable, I arose
with the intention of returning to my companions for the night.
But Jacova, showing me a bed, prepared for me, placed herself be-

tween me and the door. I showed her that my clothes were not clean. She immediately brought me others belonging to her brother-in-law. I wished to be excused from making use of them, but she seemed so much hurt, that I finally took them, and reseated myself. She then brought me my leather hunting shirt, which I had taken off to aid in protecting her from the cold, and begged the interpreter who was now present, to tell me, that she intended to keep it, as long as she lived. She then put it on, to prove to me that she was not ashamed of it.

I went to bed early, and arose, and returned to my companions, before any of the family were visible. At eight the governor and my father came to our quarters, and invited us all to dine with him at two in the afternoon. Accordingly we all dressed in our best, and went at the appointed time. A band of musicians played during dinner. After it was finished, and the table removed, a fandango was begun. The ladies flocked in, in great numbers. The instruments, to which the dancers moved, were a guitar and violin. Six men and six women also added their voices. Their mode of dancing was a curiosity to me. The women stood erect, moving their feet slowly, without any spring or motion of the body, and the men half bent, moved their feet like drum sticks. This dance is called *ahavave*. I admired another so much, that I attempted to go through it. It was a waltz, danced to a slow and charming air. It produces a fine effect, when twenty or thirty perform it together. The dancing continued, until near morning, when we retired to rest.

At eight the following morning we received a license, allowing us to trap in different parts of the country. We were now divided into small parties. Mr. Pratte added three to our original number, they making the company, to which my father and myself belonged, seven. On the 22d, we set off. Our course lay down the del Norte to the Helay, a river never before explored by white people. We left our goods with a merchant, until we should return in the spring. Our whole day's journey lay over a handsome plain covered with herds of the different domestic animals. We reached Picacheh a small town in the evening. Jacova and her father overtook us here, on their way home, which was eighty miles distant from Santa Fe.

In the morning we began our journey, together. During the day we passed several small villages and stopped for the night in one called St. Philip, situated on the banks of the del Norte, surrounded by large vineyards. Jacova's father insisted upon our drinking plentifully of the wine made at this place.

The morning of the 24th saw us again on our journey. Our companion, the old governor, was much amused at seeing us kill wild geese and prairie wolves with our rifles, the latter being abundant in this country. In the evening we reached another small town, called St. Louis. All these inconsiderable villages contain a church. The succeeding day we traversed the same beautiful plain country, which had made our journey so far, delightful. The same multitude of domestic animals still grazed around our path.

On the 27th, we arrived at the residence of Jacova and her father. It was a large and even magnificent building. We remained here until the 30th, receiving the utmost attention and kindness. At our departure, the kind old governor pressed a great many presents upon us; but we refused all, except a horse for each one of us, some flour and dried meat.

Seven hunters coming up with us, who were going in our direction, we concluded to travel with them, as our united strength would better enable us to contend with the hostile Indians, through whose country our course lay. We made our way slowly, descending the river bank, until we reached the last town or settlement in this part of the province, called Socoro. The population of the part of the country, through which we travelled was entirely confined to a chain of settlements along the bottoms of the del Norte, and those of some of the rivers, which empty into it. I did not see, during the whole of this journey, an enclosed field, and not even a garden.

After remaining one day here, in order to recruit our horses, we resumed our course down the river, Dec. 3d. The bottoms, through which we now passed, were thinly timbered, and the only growth was cotton-wood and willow. We saw great numbers of bears, deer and turkeys. A bear having chased one of our men into the camp, we killed it.

On the 7th we left the del Norte, and took a direct course for the Copper mines. We next travelled from the river over a very mountainous country four days, at the expiration of which time we reached this point of our destination. We were here but one night, and I had not leisure to examine the mode, in which the copper was manufactured. In the morning we hired two Spanish servants to accompany us; and taking a north-west course pursued our journey, until we reached the Helay on the 14th. We found the country the greater part of the two last days hilly and somewhat barren with a growth of pine, live oak, *pinion,* cedar and some small trees, of which I did not know the name. We caught thirty beavers, the first night we encamped on this river. The next morning, accompanied by another man, I began to ascend the bank of the stream to explore, and ascertain if beaver were to be found still higher, leaving the remainder of the party to trap slowly up, until they should meet us on our return. We threw a pack over our shoulders, containing a part of the beavers, we had killed, as we made our way on foot. The first day we were fatigued by the difficulty of getting through the high grass, which covered the heavily timbered bottom. In the evening we arrived at the foot of mountains, that shut in the river on both sides, and encamped. We saw during the day several bears, but did not disturb them, as they showed no ill feeling towards us.

On the morning of the 13th we started early, and crossed the river, here a beautiful clear stream about thirty yards in width, running over a rocky bottom, and filled with fish. We made but little advance this day, as bluffs came in so close to the river, as to compel us to cross it thirty-six times. We were obliged to scramble along under the cliffs, sometimes upon our hands and knees, through a thick tangle of grape-vines and under-brush. Added to the unpleasantness of this mode of getting along in itself, we did not know, but the next moment would bring us face to face with a bear, which might accost us suddenly. We were rejoiced, when this rough ground gave place again to the level bottom. At night we reached a point, where the river forked, and encamped on the point between the forks. We found here a boiling spring so near the main stream, that the fish caught in the one might be thrown into the other without leaving the spot, where it was taken. In six minutes it would be thoroughly cooked.

The following morning my companion and myself separated, agreeing to meet after four days at this spring. We were each to ascend a fork of the river. The banks of that which fell to my lot, were very brushy, and frequented by numbers of bears, of whom I felt fearful, as I had never before travelled alone in the woods. I walked on with caution until night, and encamped near a pile of drift wood, which I set on fire, thinking thus to frighten any animals that might approach during the night. I placed a spit, with a turkey I had killed upon it, before the fire to roast. After I had eaten my supper I laid down by the side of a log with my gun by my side. I did not fall asleep for some time. I was aroused from slumber stretched on the log by which I was lying, within six feet of me, I raised my gun gently to my face, and shot it in the head. Then springing to my feet, I ran about ten steps, and stopped to reload my gun, not knowing if I had killed the panther or not. Before I had finished loading my gun, I heard the discharge of one on the other fork, as I concluded, the two running parallel with each other, separated only by a narrow ridge. A second discharge quickly followed the first, which led me to suppose, that my comrade was attacked by Indians.

I immediately set out and reached the hot spring by day break, where I found my associate also. The report of my gun had awakened him, when he saw a bear standing upon its hind feet within a few yards of him growling. He fired his gun, then his pistol, and retreated, thinking, with regard to me, as I had with regard to him, that I was attacked by Indians. Our conclusion now was, to ascend one of the forks in company, and then cross over, and descend the other. In consequence we resumed the course, I had taken the preceeding day. We made two day's journey, without beaver enough to recompense us for our trouble, and then crossed to the east fork, trapping as we went, until we again reached the main stream. Some distance below this, we met those of our party we had left behind, with the exception of the seven, who joined us on the del Norte. They had deserted the expedition, and set off upon their return down the river. We now all hastened on to overtake them, but it was to no purpose. They still kept in advance, trapping clean as they went, so that we even found it difficult to catch enough to eat.

Finding it impossible to come up with them, we ceased to urge our poor horses, as they were much jaded, and tender footed beside, and travelled slowly, catching what beaver we could, and killing some deer, although the latter were scarce, owing, probably to the season of the year. The river here was beautiful, running between banks covered with tall cotton-woods and willows. This bottom extended back a mile on each side. Beyond rose high and rather barren hills.

On the 20th we came to a point, where the river entered a cavern between two mountains. We were compelled to return upon our steps, until we found a low gap in the mountains. We were three day's crossing, and the travelling was both fatiguing and difficult. We found nothing to kill.

On the 23d we came upon the river, where it emptied into a beautiful plain. We set our traps, but to no purpose, for the beavers were all caught, or alarmed. The river here pursues a west course. We travelled slowly, using every effort to kill something to eat, but without success.

On the morning of the 26th we concluded, that we must kill a horse, as we had eaten nothing for four day's and a half, except the small portion of a hare caught by my dogs, which fell to the lot of each of a party of seven. Before we obtained this, we had become weak in body and mind, complaining, and desponding of our success in search of beaver. Desirous of returning to some settlement, my father encouraged our party to eat some of the horses, and pursue our journey. We were all reluctant to begin to partake of the hors-flesh; and the actual thing without bread or salt was as bad as the anticipation of it. We were somewhat strengthened, however, and hastened on, while our supply lasted, in the hope of either overtaking those in advance of us, or finding another stream yet undiscovered by trappers.

The latter desire was gratified the first of January, 1825. The stream, we discovered, carried as much water as the Helay, heading north. We called it the river St. Francisco. After travelling up

its banks about four miles, we encamped, and set all our traps, and
killed a couple of fat turkies. In the morning we examined our
traps, and found in them 37 beavers! This success restored our spirits instantaneously. Exhilarating prospects now opened before us,
and we pushed on with animation. The banks of this river are for
the most part incapable of cultivation being in many places formed
of high and rugged mountains. Upon these we saw multitudes of
mountain sheep. These animals are not found on level ground, being there slow of foot, but on these cliffs and rocks they are so nim-
ble and expert in jumping from point to point, that no dog or wolf
can overtake them. One of them that we killed had the largest
horns, that I ever saw on animals of any description. One of them
would hold a gallon of water. Their meat tastes like our mutton.
Their hair is short like a deer's, though fine. The French call them
the *gros cornes,* from the size of their horns which curl around
their ears, like our domestic sheep. These animals are about the size
of a large deer. We traced this river to its head, but not without
great difficulty, as the cliffs in many places came so near the water's
edge, that we were compelled to cross points of the mountain,
which fatigued both ourselves and our horses exceedingly.

The right hand fork of this river, and the left of the Helay
head in the same mountain, which is covered with snow, and divides its waters from those of Red river. We finished our trapping
on this river, on the 14th. We had caught the very considerable
number of 250 beavers, and had used and preserved most of the
meat, we had killed. On the 19th we arrived on the river Helay, encamped, and buried our firs in a secure position, as we intended to
return home by this route.

On the 20th we began to descend the Helay, hoping to find in
our descent another beaver stream emptying into it. We had abandoned the hope of rejoining the hunters, that had left us, and been
the occasion of our being compelled to feed upon horse flesh. No
better was to be expected of us, than that we should take leave to
imprecate many a curse upon their heads; and that they might
experience no better fate, than to fall into the hands of the savages,
or be torn in pieces by the white bears. At the same time, so ready

are the hearts of mountain hunters to relent, that I have not a doubt that each man of us would have risqued his life to save any one of them from the very fate, we imprecated upon them.

In fact, on the night of the 22d, four of them, actually half starved, arrived at our camp, declaring, that they had eaten nothing for five days. Notwithstanding our recent curses bestowed upon them, we received them as brothers. They related that the Indians had assaulted and defeated them, robbing them of all their horses, and killing one of their number. Next day the remaining two came in, one of them severely wounded in the head by an Indian arrow. They remained with us two days, during which we attempted to induce them to lead us against the Indians, who had robbed them, that we might assist them to recover what had been robbed from them. No persuasion would induce them to this course. They insisted at the same time, that if we attempted to go on by ourselves, we should share the same fate, which had befallen them.

On the morning of the 25th, we gave them three horses, and as much dried meat as would last them to the mines, distant about 150 miles. Fully impressed, that the Indians would massacre us, they took such a farewell of us, as if never expecting to see us again.

In the evening of the same day, although the weather threatened a storm, we packed up, and began to descend the river. We encamped this night in a huge cavern in the midst of the rocks. About night it began to blow a tempest, and to snow fast. Our horses became impatient under the pelting of the storm, broke their ropes, and disappeared. In the morning, the earth was covered with snow, four or five inches deep. One of our companions accompanied me to search for our horses. We soon came upon their trail, and followed it, until it crossed the river. We found it on the opposite side, and pursued it up a creek, that empties into the Helay on the north shore. We passed a cave at the foot of the cliffs. At its mouth I remarked, that the bushes were beaten down, as though some animal had been browsing upon them. I was aware, that a bear had entered the cave. We collected some pine knots, split them with our tomahawks, and kindled torches, with which I proposed to my companion, that we should enter the cave together, and shoot the bear. He gave me a decided refusal, notwithstanding I reminded him, that I had, more than once, stood by him in a similar adventure; and notwithstanding I made him sensible, that a bear in a den is by no means so formidable, as when ranging freely in the woods. Finding it impossible to prevail on him to accompany me, I lashed my torch to a stick, and placed it parallel with the gun barrel, so as that I could see the sights on it, and entered the cave. I advanced cautiously onward about twenty yards, seeing nothing. On a sudden the bear reared himself erect within seven feet of me, and began to growl, and gnash his teeth. I levelled my gun and shot him between the eyes, and began to retreat. Whatever light it may throw upon my courage, I admit, that I was in such a hurry, as to stumble, and extinguish my light. The growling and struggling of the bear did not at all contribute to allay my apprehensions. On the contrary, I was in such haste to get out of the dark place, thinking the bear just at my heels, that I fell several times on the rocks, by which I cut my limbs, and lost my gun. When I reached the light, my companion declared, and I can believe it, that I was as pale as a corpse. It was sometime, before I could summon sufficient courage to re-enter the cavern for my gun. But having re-kindled my light, and borrowed my companions gun, I entered the cavern again, advanced and listened. All was silent, and I advanced still further, and found my gun, near where I had shot the bear. Here again I paused and listened. I then advanced onward a few strides, where to my great joy I found the animal dead. I returned, and brought my companion in with me. We attempted to drag the carcass from the den, but so great was the size, that we found ourselves wholly unable. We went out, found our horses, and returned to camp for assistance. My father severely reprimanded me for venturing to attack such a dangerous animal in its den, when the failure to kill it outright by the first shot, would have been sure to be followed by my death.

Four of us were detached to the den. We were soon enabled to drag the bear to the light, and by the aid of our beasts to take it to camp. It was both the largest and whitest bear I ever saw. The best proof, I can give, of the size and fatness is, that we extracted ten gallons of oil from it. The meat we dried, and put the oil in a trough, which we secured in a deep crevice of a cliff, beyond the reach of animals of prey. We were sensible that it would prove a treasure to us on our return.

On the 28th we resumed our journey, and pushed down the stream to reach a point on the river, where trapping had not been practised. On the 30th, we reached this point, and found the man, that the Indians had killed. They had cut him in quarters, after the fashion of butchers. His head, with the hat on, was stuck on a stake. It was full of the arrows, which they had probably discharged into it, as they had danced around it. We gathered up the parts of the body, and buried them.

At this point we commenced setting our traps. We found the river skirted with very wide bottoms, thick-set with the mosquito trees, which bear a pod in the shape of a bean, which is exceedingly sweet. It constitutes one of the chief articles of Indian subsistence; and they contrive to prepare from it a very palatable kind of bread, of which we all became very fond. The wild animals also feed upon this pod.

On the 31st we moved our camp ten miles. On the way we noted many fresh traces of Indians, and killed a bear, that attacked us. The river pursues a west course amidst high mountains on each side. We trapped slowly onward, still descending the river, and unmolested by the Indians. On the 8th of February, we reached the mouth of a small river entering the Helay on the north shore. Here we unexpectedly came upon a small party of Indians, that fled at the sight of us, in such consternation and hurry, as to leave all their effects, which consisted of a quantity of the bread mentioned above, and some robes made of rabbit skins. Still more; they left a small child. The child was old enough to distinguish us from its own people, for it opened its little throat, and screamed so lustily, that we feared it would have fits. The poor thing meanwhile made its best efforts to fly from us. We neither plundered nor molested their little store. We bound the child in such a manner, that it could not stray away, and get lost, aware, that after they deemed us sufficiently far off, the parents would return, and take the child away. We thence ascended the small river about four miles, and encamped. For fear of surprize, and apprehending the return of the savages, that had fled from us, and perhaps in greater force, we secured our camp with a small breast-work. We discovered very little encouragement in regard to our trapping pursuit, for we noted few signs of beavers on this stream. The night passed without bringing us any disturbance. In the morning two of us returned to the Indian camp. The Indians had re-visited it, and removed every thing of value, and what gave us great satisfaction, their child. In proof, that the feelings of human nature are the same every where, and that the language of kindness is a universal one; in token of their gratitude, as we understood it, they had suspended a package on a kind of stick, which they had stuck erect. Availing ourselves of their offer, we examined the present, and found it to contain a large dressed buck skin, an article, which we greatly needed for moccasins, of which some of us were in pressing want. On the same stick we tied a red handkerchief by way of some return.

We thence continued to travel up this stream four days in succession, with very little incident to diversify our march. We found the banks of this river plentifully timbered with trees of various species, and the land fine for cultivation. On the morning of the 13th, we returned to the Helay, and found on our way, that the Indians had taken the handkerchief, we had left, though none of them had shown any disposition, as we had hoped, to visit us. We named the stream we had left, the deserted fork, on account of having found it destitute of beavers. We thence resumed our course down the Helay, which continues to flow through a most beautiful country. Warned by the frequent traces of fresh Indian foot-prints, we every night adopted the expedient of enclosing our horses in a pen, feeding them with cotton-wood bark, which we found much better for them than grass.

On the 16th, we advanced to a point, where the river runs between high mountains, in a ravine so narrow, as barely to afford it space to pass. We commenced exploring them to search for a gap, through which we might be able to pass. We continued our expedition, travelling north, until we discovered a branch, that made its way out of the mountains. Up its ravine we ascended to the head of the branch. Its fountains were supplied by an immense snow bank, on the summit of the mountain. With great labor and fatigue we reached this summit, but could descry no plains within the limits of vision. On every side the peaks of ragged and frowning mountains rose above the clouds, affording a prospect of dreariness and desolation, to chill the heart. While we could hear the thunder burst, and see the lightning glare before us, we found an atmosphere so cold, that we were obliged to keep up severe and unremitting exercise, to escape freezing.

We commenced descending the western declivity of the mountains, amidst thick mists and dark clouds, with which they were enveloped. We pitied our horses and mules, that were continually sliding and falling, by which their limbs were strained, and their bodies bruised. To our great joy, we were not long, before we came upon the ravine of a branch, that wound its way through the vast masses of craggs and mountains. We were disappointed, however, in our purpose to follow it to the Helay. Before it mingled with that stream, it ingulfed itself so deep between the cliffs, that though we heard the dash of the waters in their narrow bed, we could hardly see them. We were obliged to thread our way, as we might, along the precipice, that constituted the banks of the creek. We were often obliged to unpack our mules and horses, and transport their loads by hand from one precipice to another. We continued wandering among the mountains in this way, until the 23d. Our provisions were at this time exhausted, and our horses and mules so worn out, that they were utterly unable to proceed further. Thus we were absolutely obliged to lie by two days. During this time, Allen and myself commenced climbing towards the highest peak of the mountains in our vicinity. It was night-fall, before we gained it. But from it we could distinctly trace the winding path of the river in several places; and what was still more cheering, could see smokes arising from several Indian camps. To meet even enemies, was more tolerable, than thus miserably to perish with hunger and cold in the mountains. Our report on our return animated the despair of our companions. On the morning of the 25th we resumed our painful efforts to reach the river. On the 28th, to our great joy, we once more found ourselves on its banks. A party of Indians, encamped there, fled at our approach. But fortunately they left a little mush prepared from the seeds of grass. Without scruple we devoured it with appetites truly ravenous. In the morning we took ten beavers in our traps, and Allen was detached with me to clear away a path, through which the pack horses might pass. We were obliged to cross the river twelve times in the course of a single day. We still discovered the fresh foot-prints of Indians, who had deserted their camps, and fled before us. We were continually apprehensive, that they would fire their arrows upon us, or overwhelm us with rocks, let loose upon us from the summits of the high cliffs, directly under which we were obliged to pass. The third day, after we had left our company, I shot a wild goose in the river. The report of my gun raised the screams of women and children. Too much alarmed to stop for my game, I mounted my horse, and rode toward them, with a view to convince them, or in some way, to show them, that we intended them no harm. We discovered them ahead of us, climbing the mountains, the men in advance of the women, and all fleeing at the top of their speed. As soon as they saw us, they turned, and let fly a few arrows at us, one of which would have despatched my companion, had he not been infinitely dextrous in dodging. Hungry and fatigued and by no means in the best humor, my companion returned them abundance of curses for their arrows. From words he was proceeding to deeds, and would undoubtedly have shot one of them, had I not caught his gun, and made him sensible of the madness of such a deed. It was clearly our wisdom to convince them, that we had no inclination to injure them. Some of them were clad in robes of rabbit skins, part of which they shed, in their hurry to clamber over the rocks.

Finding ourselves unable to overtake them, we returned to their camp, to discover if they had left any thing that we could eat. At no great distance from their camp, we observed a mound of fresh earth, in appearance like one of our coal kilns. Considering it improbable, that the Indians would be engaged in burning coal, we opened the mound, and found it to contain a sort of vegetable that had the appearance of herbage, which seemed to be baking in the ground, to prepare it for eating. I afterwards ascertained, that it was a vegetable, called by the Spanish, mascal, (probably maguey.) The Indians prepare it in this way, so as to make a kind of whiskey of it, tasting like crab-apple cider. The vegetable grows in great abundance on these mountains.

Next day we came to the point, where the river discharges its waters from the mountains on to the plains. We thence returned, and rejoined our company, that had been making their way onward behind us. March 3d, we trapped along down a small stream, that empties into the Helay on the south side, having its head in a south west direction. It being very remarkable for the number of its beavers, we gave it the name of Beaver river. At this place we collected 200 skins; and on the 10th continued to descend the Helay, until the 20th, when we turned back with as much fur, as our beasts could pack. As yet we had experienced no molestation from the Indians, although they were frequently descried skulking after us, and gathering up the pieces of meat, we had thrown away. On the morning of the 20th we were all prepared for an early start, and my father, by way of precaution, bade us all discharge our guns at the word of command, and then re-load them afresh, that we might, in case of emergency, be sure of our fire. We were directed to form in a line, take aim, and at the word, fire at a tree. We gave sufficient proofs, that we were no strangers to the rifle, for every ball had lodged close to the centre of our mark. But the report of our guns was answered by the yell of more than an hundred savages, above us on the mountains. We immediately marched out from under the mountains on to the plains, and beckoned them to come down, by every demonstration of friendship in our power. Nothing seemed to offer stronger enticement, than to hold out to them our red cloth. This we did, but without effect, for they either understood us not, or were reluctant to try our friendship. Leaving one of our number to watch their deportment, and to note if they followed us, we resumed our march. It would have been a great object to us to have been able to banish their suspicions, and make a treaty with them. But we could draw from them no demonstrations, but those of fear and surprize. On the 25th we returned to Beaver river, and dug up the furs that we had buried, or cashed, as the phrase is, and concluded to ascend it, trapping towards its head, whence we purposed to cross over to the Helay above the mountains, where we had suffered so much in crossing. About six miles up the stream, we stopped to set our traps, three being selected to remain behind in the camp to dry the skins, my father to make a pen for the horses, and I to guard them, while they were turned loose to feed in the grass. We had pitched our camp near the bank of the river, in a thick grove of timber, extending about a hundred yards in width. Behind the timber was a narrow plain of about the same width, and still further on was a high hill, to which I repaired, to watch my horses, and descry whatever might pass in the distance. Immediately back of the hill I discovered a small lake, by the noise made by the ducks and geese in it. Looking more attentively, I remarked what gave me much more satisfaction, that is to say, three beaver lodges. I returned, and made my father acquainted with my discovery. The party despatched to set traps had returned. My father informed them of my discovery, and told them to set traps in the little lake. As we passed towards the lake, we observed the horses and mules all crowded together. At first we concluded that they collected together in this way, because they had fed enough. We soon discovered, that it was owing to another cause. I had put down my gun, and stepped into the water, to prepare a bed for my trap, while the others were busy in preparing theirs. Instantly the Indians raised a yell, and the quick report of guns ensued. This noise was almost drowned in the fierce shouts that followed, succeeded by a shower of arrows falling among us like hail. As we ran for the camp leaving all the horses in their power, we saw six Indians stealthily following our trail, as though they were tracking a deer. They occasionally stopped, raised themselves, and surveyed every thing around them. We concealed ourselves behind a large cotton-wood tree, and waited until they came within a hundred yards of us. Each of us selected a separate Indian for a mark, and our signal to fire together was to be a whistle. The sign was given, and we fired together. My mark fell dead, and my companions' severely wounded. The other Indians seized their dead and wounded companions, and fled.

We now rejoined our company, who were busily occupied in dodging the arrows, that came in a shower from the summit of the hill, where I had stationed myself to watch our horses. Discovering that they were too far from us, to be reached by our bullets, we retreated to the timber, in hopes to draw them down to the plain. But they had had too ample proofs of our being marksmen, to think of returning down to our level, and were satisfied to remain yelling, and letting fly their arrows at random. We found cause both for regret and joy; regret, that our horses were in their power, and joy, that their unprovoked attack had been defeated with loss to themselves, and none to us.

At length they ceased yelling, and disappeared. We, on our part, set ourselves busily to work to fortify our camp for the night. Meanwhile our savage enemy devised a plan, which, but for the circumspection of my father, would have enabled them to destroy us. They divided themselves into two parties, the one party mounted on horses, stolen from us, and so arranged as to induce the belief, that they constituted the whole party. They expected that we would pursue them, to recover our horses. As soon as we should be drawn out from behind our fortification, they had a reserve party, on foot, who were to rush in, between us and our camp, and thus, between two fires, cut us all off together. It so happened, that I had retired a little distance from the camp, in the direction of the ambush party on foot. I met them, and they raised a general yell. My father, supposing me surrounded, ran in the direction of the yell, to aid me. He, too, came in direct contact with the foot party, who let fly a shower of arrows at him, from which nothing but good providence preserved him. He returned the fire with his gun and pistols, by which he killed two of them, and the report of which immediately brought his companions to his side. The contest was a warm one for a few minutes, when the Indians fled. This affair commenced about three in the afternoon; and the Indians made their final retreat at five; and the succeeding night passed without further molestation from them.

In the morning of the 26th, we despatched two of our men to bring our traps and firs. We had no longer any way of conveying them with us, for the Indians had taken all our horses. We, however, in the late contest, had taken four of their's, left behind in the haste of their retreat. As our companions were returning to camp with the traps, which they had taken up to bury, they discovered the Indians, sliding along insidiously towards our camp. We were all engaged in eating our breakfast in entire confidence. Our men cried out to us, that the enemy was close upon us. We sprang to our arms. The Indians instantly fled to the top of the hill, which we had named battlehill. In a few minutes they were all paraded on the horses and mules stolen from us. They instantly began to banter us in Spanish to come up to them. One of our number who could speak Spanish, asked them to what nation they belonged? They answered, *Eiotaro*. In return, they asked us, who we were? We answered *Americans*. Hearing this, they stood in apparent surprise and astonishment for some moments. They then replied, that they had thought us too brave and too good marksmen, to be Spaniards; that they were sorry for what they had done, under the mistake of supposing us Spaniards. They declared themselves ready to make a treaty with us, provided that we would return the four horses, we had taken from them, and bring them up the hill, where they promised us they would restore us our own horses in exchange. We were at once impressed, that the propsal was a mere trick, to induce us to place ourselves in their power. We therefore answered their proposal by another, which was, that they should bring down our horses, and leave them by the pen, where they had taken them, and we in return would let their horses loose, and make friendship with them. They treated our proposal with laughter, which would have convinced us, had we doubted it before, that their only purpose had been to ensnare us. We accordingly faced them, and fired upon them, which induced them to clear themselves most expeditiously.

We proceeded to bury our furs; and having packed our four horses with provisions and two traps, we commenced our march. Having travelled about ten miles, we encamped in a thicket without kindling a fire, and kept a strict guard all night. Next morning we made an early march, still along the banks of the river. Its banks are still plentifully timbered with cotton-wood and willow. The bottoms on each side afford a fine soil for cultivation. From these bottoms the hills rise to an enormous height, and their summits are covered with perpetual snow. In these bottoms are great numbers of wild hogs, of a species entirely different from our domestic swine. They are fox-colored, with their navel on their back, towards the back part of their bodies. The hoof of their hind feet has but one dew-claw, and they yield an odor not less offensive than our pole-cat. Their figure and head are not unlike our swine, except that their tail resembles that of a bear. We measured one of their tusks, of a size so enormous, that I am afraid to commit my credibility, by giving the dimensions. They remain undisturbed by man and other animals, whether through fear or on account of their offensive odor, I am unable to say. That they have no fear of man, and that they are exceedingly ferocious, I can bear testimony myself. I have many times been obliged to climb trees to escape their tusks. We killed a great many, but could never bring ourselves to eat them. The country presents the aspect of having been once settled at some remote period of the past. Great quantities of broken pottery are scattered over the ground, and there are distinct traces of ditches and stone walls, some of them as high as a man's breast, with very broad foundations. A species of tree, which I had never seen before, here arrested my attention. It grows to the height of forty or fifty feet. The top is cone shaped, and almost without foliage. The bark resembles that of the prickly pear; and the body is covered with thorns. I have seen some three feet in diameter at the root, and throwing up twelve distinct shafts.

On the 29th, we made our last encampment on this river, intending to return to it no more, except for our furs. We set our two traps for the last time, and caught a beaver in each.—We skinned the animals, and prepared the skins to hold water, through fear, that we might find none on our unknown route through the mountains to the Helay, from which we judged ourselves distant two hundred miles. Our provisions were all spoiled. We had nothing to carry with us to satisfy hunger, but the bodies of the two beavers which we had caught, the night before. We had nothing to sustain us in this disconsolate march, but our trust in providence; for we could not but foresee hunger, fatigue and pain, as the inevitable attendants upon our journey. To increase the depression of our spirits, our moccasins were worn out, our feet sore and tender, and the route full of sharp rocks.

On the 31st, we reached the top of the mountain, and fed upon the last meat of our beavers. We met with no traces of game. What distressed me most of all was, to perceive my father, who had already passed the meridian of his days, sinking with fatigue and weakness. On the morning of the first of April, we commenced

JAMES O. PATTIE 63

descending the mountain, from the side of which we could discern
a plain before us, which, however, it required two severe days travel
to reach. During these two days we had nothing either to eat or
drink. In descending from these icy mountains, we were surprised
to find how warm it was on the plains. On reaching them I killed
an antelope, of which we drank the warm blood; and however revolting the recital may be, to us it was refreshing, tasting like fresh
milk. The meat we put upon our horses, and travelled on until
twelve o'clock, before we found water.

Here we encamped the remainder of the day, to rest, and refresh
ourselves. The signs of antelopes were abundant, and the appearances were, that they came to the water to drink; from which we
inferred, that there was no other drinking place in the vicinity.
Some of our hunters went out in pursuit of the antelopes. From
the numbers of these animals, we called the place *Antelope Plain*.
The land lies very handsomely, and is a rich, black soil, with heavily
timbered groves in the vicinity.

On the morning of the 3d, though exceedingly stiff and sore, we
resumed our march, and reaching the opposite side of the plain, encamped at a spring, that ran from the mountain. Next day we ascended this mountain to its summit, which we found covered with
iron ore. At a distance we saw a smoke on our course. We were
aware that it was the smoke of an Indian camp, and we pushed
on towards it. In the evening we reached the smoke, but found it
deserted of Indians. All this day's march was along a country
abundant in minerals. In several places we saw lead and copper ore.
I picked up a small parcel of ore, which I put in my shot-pouch,
which was proved afterwards to be an ore of silver. The misfortune
of this region is, that there is no water near these mineral hills. We
commenced our morning march half dead with thirst, and pushed
on with the eagerness inspired by that tormenting appetite. Late in
the evening we found a little water, for our own drinking, in the
bottom of a rock. Not a drop remained for our four horses, that
evidently showed a thirst no less devouring than ours. Their feet
were all bleeding, and the moment we paused to rest ourselves,
the weary companions of our journey instantly laid down. It went
still more to my heart, to see my two faithful dogs, which had fol-

lowed me all the way from my father's house, where there was always *bread enough and to spare,* looking to me with an expression, which a hunter in the desert only can understand, as though begging food and water. Full gladly would I have explained to them, that the sterile wilderness gave me no means of supplying their wants.

We had scarcely commenced the next morning's march, when, at a little distance from our course, we saw a smoke. Supposing it an Indian camp, we immediately concluded to attack it. Adopting their own policy, we slipped onward in silence and concealment, until we were close by it. We found the persons women and children. Having no disposition to harm them, we fired a gun over their heads, which caused them instantly to fly at the extent of their speed. Hunger knows no laws; and we availed ourselves of their provision, which proved to be mascal, and grass seed, of which we made mush. Scanty as this nutriment was, it was sufficient to sustain life.

We commenced an early march on the 6th, and were obliged to move slowly, as we were bare-footed, and the mountains rough and steep. We found them either wholly barren, or only covered with a stinted growth of pine and cedar, live oak and barbary bushes. On the 8th, our provisions were entirely exhausted, and so having nothing to eat, we felt the less need of water. Our destitute and forlorn condition goaded us on, so that we reached the Helay on the 12th. We immediately began to search for traces of beavers, where to set our traps, but found none. On the morning of the 13th, we killed a raven, which we cooked for seven men. It was unsavory flesh in itself, and would hardly have afforded a meal for one hungry man. The miserable condition of our company may be imagined, when seven hungry men, who had not eaten a full meal for ten days, were all obliged to breakfast on this nauseous bird. We were all weak and emaciated. But I was young and able to bear hardships. My heart only ached for my poor father who was reduced to a mere skeleton. We moved on slowly and painfully, until evening, when we encamped. On my return from setting our two traps, I killed a buzzard, which, disagreeable as it was, we cooked for supper. In the morning of the 18th, I found one of the traps had caught an otter.

This served for breakfast and supper. It seemed the means of our present salvation, for my father had become so weak, that he could no longer travel. We therefore encamped early, and three of us went out to hunt deer among the hills. But in this sad emergency we could find none. When we returned, my father had prepared lots, that we should draw, to determine who of us should kill one of the dogs. I refused through fear that the lot would fall to me. These faithful companions of our sufferings were so dear to me, that I felt as though I could not allow them to be killed to save my own life; though to save my father, I was aware that it was a duty to allow it to be done.

We lay here until the 18th, my father finding the flesh of the dog both sweet, nutritive and strengthening. On the 18th, he was again able to travel; and on the 20th, we arrived at Bear creek, where we hid the bears oil, which we found unmolested. We lay here two days, during which time we killed four deer and some turkies. The venison we dried, and cased the skin of one of the deer, in which to carry our oil. We commenced an early march on the 23d, and on the 25th reached the river San Francisco, where we found our buried furs all safe. I suffered exceedingly from the soreness of my feet, giving me great pain and fever at night. We made from our raw deer skins a very tolerable substitute for shoes. The adoption of this important expedient enabled us to push on, so that we reached the Copper mines on the 29th.

The Spaniards seemed exceedingly rejoiced, and welcomed us home, as though we were of their own nation, religion and kindred. They assured us, that they had no expectation ever to see us again. The superintendent of the mines, especially, who appeared to me a gentleman of the highest order, received us with particular kindness, and supplied all our pressing wants. Here we remained, to rest and recruit ourselves, until the 2d of May. My father then advised me to travel to Santa Fe, to get some of our goods, and purchase a new supply of horses, with which to return, and bring in our furs. I had a horse, which we had taken from the Indians, shod with copper shoes, and in company with four of my companions, and the superintendent of the mines, I started for Santa Fe. The superintendent assured us, that he would gladly have furnished us horses; but the Appache Indians had recently made an incursion upon his establishment, stealing all his horses, and killing three men, that were herding them. This circumstance had suspended the working of the mines. Besides he was unable to procure the necessary coal, with which to work them, because the Appaches waylaid the colliers, and killed them, as often as they attempted to make coal.

We arrived at the house of the governor on the 12th. Jacova, his daughter, received us with the utmost affection; and shed tears on observing me so ill; as I was in fact reduced by starvation and fatigue, to skin and bone. Beings in a more wretched plight she could not often have an opportunity to see. My hair hung matted and uncombed. My head was surmounted with an old straw hat. My legs were fitted with leather leggins, and my body arrayed in a leather hunting shirt, and no want of dirt about any part of the whole. My companions did not shame me, in comparison, by being better clad. But all these repulsive circumstances notwithstanding, we were welcomed by the governor and Jacova, as kindly, as if we had been clad in a manner worthy of their establishment.

We rested ourselves here three days. I had left my more decent apparel in the care of Jacova, when we started from the house into the wilderness on our trapping expedition. She had had my clothes prepared in perfect order. I once more dressed myself decently, and spared to my companions all my clothes that fitted them. We all had our hair trimmed. All this had much improved our appearance. When we started on the 15th, the old gentleman gave each of us a good horse, enabling us to travel at our ease.

On the 18th we arrived at Santa Fe, where we immediately met some of our former companions. It hardly need be added, that the joy of this recognition was great and mutual. We found Mr. Pratte ill in bed. He expressed himself delighted to see me, and was still more desirous to see my father. He informed me, that four of the company that he had detached to trap, had been defeated by the Indians, and the majority of them killed. He had, also, despaired of ever seeing us again. I took a part of my goods, and started back to the mines on the 21st. None of my companions were willing to accompany me on account of the great apprehended danger from the Indians between this place and the mines. In consequence, I hired a man to go with me, and having purchased what horses I wanted, we two travelled on in company. I would have preferred to have purchased my horses of the old governor. But I knew that his noble nature would impel him to give them to me, and felt reluctant to incur such an obligation. When I left his house, he insisted on my receiving a gold chain, in token of the perpetual remembrance of his daughter. I saw no pretext for refusing it, and as I received it, she assured me that she should always make mention of my father and me in her prayers.

I left this hospitable place on the 24th, taking all my clothes with me, except the hunting shirt, which I had worn in the battle with the Commanches. This she desired to retain, insisting, that she wished to preserve this memorial to the day of her death. We arrived at the mines the first day of June, having experienced no molestation from the Indians. We continued here, making arrangements for our expedition to bring in the furs, until the 6th. The good natured commander gave us provisions to last us to the point where our furs were buried, and back again. Still more, he armed ten of his laborers, and detached them to accompany us. The company consisted of four Americans, the man hired at Santa Fe, and the commander's ten men, fifteen in all.

We left the mines on the 7th, and reached Battle-hill on Beaver river on the 22d. I need not attempt to describe my feelings, for no description could paint them, when I found the furs all gone, and perceived that the Indians had discovered them and taken them away. All that, for which we had hazarded ourselves, and suffered every thing but death, was gone. The whole fruit of our long, toilsome and dangerous expedition was lost, and all my golden hopes of prosperity and comfort vanished like a dream. I tried to convince myself, that repining was of no use, and we started for the river San Francisco on the 29th. Here we found the small quantity buried there, our whole compensation for a years toil, misery and danger. We met no Indians either going or returning.

We arrived at the mines the 8th of July, and after having rested two days proposed to start for Santa Fe. The commander, don Juan Unis, requested us to remain with him two or three months, to guard his workmen from the Indians, while pursuing their employment in the woods. He offered, as a compensation, a dollar a day. We consented to stay, though without accepting the wages. We should have considered ourselves ungrateful, after all the kindness, he had rendered us at the hour of our greatest need, either to have refused the request, or to have accepted a compensation. Consequently we made our arrangements to stay.

We passed our time most pleasantly in hunting deer and bears, of which there were great numbers in the vicinity. We had no other duties to perform, than to walk round in the vicinity of the workmen, or sit by and see them work. Most of my time was spent with don Juan, who kindly undertook to teach me to speak Spanish. Of him, having no other person with whom to converse, I learned the language easily, and rapidly. One month of our engagement passed off without any molestation from the Indians. But on the first day of August, while three of us were hunting deer, we discovered the trail of six Indians approaching the mines. We followed the trail, and within about a mile from the mines, we came up with them. They fled, and we pursued close at their heels. Gaining upon them, one of them dodged us, into the head of a hollow. We surrounded him. As soon as he saw that we had discovered him, and that escape was impossible, he sprang on his feet, threw away his bow and arrows, and begged us most submissively not to shoot him. One of our men made up to him, while the other man and myself stood with our guns cocked, and raised to our faces, ready to shoot him, if he made the least motion towards his bow. But he remained perfectly still, crossing his hands, that we might tie them. Having done it, we drove him on before us. We had advanced about a hundred yards from the point where we took him, when he pointed out to us a hollow tree, intimating that there was another Indian concealed there. We bade him instruct his companion to make no resistance, and to surrender himself, or we would kill him. He explained our words to his companion in the tree. He immediately came forth from his concealment with his bow, and we tied his

hands in the same way as the other's. We marched them before us
to the mines, where we put them in prison. The Spaniards, exasperated with their recent cruelties and murders, would have killed
them. We insisted that they should be spared, and they remained in
prison until the next morning.

We then brought them out of prison, conversed with them, and
showed them how closely we could fire. We instructed one of them
to tell his chief to come in, accompanied by all his warriors, to
make peace. We retained one of the prisoners as a hostage, assuring
the other, that if his chief did not come in to make peace, we would
put the hostage to death. In regard to the mode of making it, we
engaged, that only four of our men should meet them at a hollow,
half a mile from the mine. We enjoined it on him to bring them
there within the term of four days. We readily discovered by the
tranquil countenance of our hostage, that he had no apprehensions
that they would not come in.

Afterwards, by way of precaution, my father put in requisition
all the arms he could find in the vicinity of the mines, with which
he armed thirty Spaniards. He then ordered a trench dug, at a hundred yard's distance from the point designated for the Indians to
occupy. This trench was to be occupied by our armed men, during
the time of the treaty, in case, that if the Indians should be insolent
or menacing, these men might be at hand to overawe them, or aid
us, according to circumstances.

On the 5th, we repaired to the place designated, and in a short
time, the Indians to the number of 80, came in sight. We had prepared a pipe, tobacco, and a council fire, and had spread a blanket,
on which the chief might sit down. As soon as they came near us,
they threw down their arms. The four chiefs came up to us, and we
all sat down on the blanket. We commenced discussing the subject,
for which they were convened. We asked them, if they were ready
to make a peace with us; and if not what were the objections? They
replied, that they had no objections to a peace with the Americans,
but would never make one with the Spaniards. When we asked
their reasons, they answered that they had been long at war with
the Spaniards, and that a great many murders had been mutually
inflicted on either side. They admitted, that they had taken a great

many horses from the Spaniards, but indignantly alleged, that a large party of their people had come in to make peace with the Spaniards, of which they pretended to be very desirous; that with such pretexts, they had decoyed the party within their walls, and then commenced butchering them like a flock of sheep. The very few who had escaped, had taken an unalterable resolution never to make peace with them. 'In pursuance,' they continued, 'of our purposes of revenge, great numbers of our nation went in among the Spaniards, and were baptized. There they remain faithful spies for us, informing us when and where there were favorable opportunities to kill, and plunder our enemies.'

We told them in reply, that if they really felt disposed to be at peace with the Americans, these mines were now working jointly by us and the Spaniards; that it was wrong in them to revenge the crimes of the guilty upon the innocent, and that these Spaniards had taken no part in the cowardly and cruel butchery, of which they had spoken; and that if they would not be peaceable, and allow us to work the mines unmolested, the Americans would consider them at war, and would raise a sufficient body of men to pursue them to their lurking places in the mountains; that they had good evidence that our people could travel in the woods and among the mountains, as well as themselves; and that we could shoot a great deal better than either they or the Spaniards, and that we had no cowards among us, but true men, who had no fear and would keep their word.

The chiefs answered, that if the mines belonged to the Americans, they would promise never to disturb the people that worked them. We left them, therefore, to infer that the mines belonged to us, and took them at their word. We then lit the pipe, and all the Indians gathered in a circle round the fire. The four chiefs, each in succession made a long speech, in which we could often distinguish the terms Americans, and Espanola. The men listened with profound attention, occasionally sanctioning what was said by a nod of the head. We then commenced smoking, and the pipe passed twice round the circle. They then dug a hole in the ground in the centre of the circle, and each one spat in it. They then filled it up with earth, danced round it, and stuck their arrows in the little mound. They then gathered a large pile of stones over it, and painted themselves red. Such are their ceremonies of making peace. All the forms of the ceremony were familiar to us, except the pile of stones, and spitting in the hole they had dug, which are not practised by the Indians on the American frontiers. We asked them the meaning of the spitting. They said, that they did it in token of spitting out all their spite and revenge, and burying their anger under the ground.

It was two o'clock before all these ceremonies were finished. We then showed them our reserve force in the trench. They evinced great alarm to see their enemies the Spaniards so close to them, and all ready for action. We explained to them, that we intended to be in good faith, if they were; and that these men were posted there, only in case they showed a disposition to violence. Their fears vanished and tranquility returned to their countenances. The chiefs laughed, and said to each other, these Americans know how to fight, and make peace too. But were they to fight us, they would have to get a company entirely of their own people; for that if they took any Spaniards into their company, they would be sure to desert them in the time of action.

We thence all marched to the mines, where we killed three beeves to feed the Indians. After they had eaten, and were in excellent humor, the head chief made a present to my father, of ten miles square of a tract of land lying on a river about three miles from the mines. It was very favorable for cultivation, and the Spaniards had several times attempted to make a crop of grain upon it; but the Indians had as often either killed the cultivators, or destroyed the grain. My father informed them, that though the land might be his, he should be obliged to employ Spaniards to cultivate it for him; and that, having made the land his, they must consider these cultivators his people, and not molest them. With a look of great firmness, the chief said 'that he was a man of truth, and had given his word, and that we should find that nothing belonging to the mines would be disturbed, for that he never would allow the treaty to be violated.' He went on to add, 'that he wanted to be at peace with us, because he had discovered, that the Americans never showed any disposition to kill, except in battle; that they had had a proof of this in our not killing the two prisoners we had taken; but had sent one of them to invite his people to come in, and make peace with us, and that he took pleasure in making known to us, that they were good people too, and had no wish to injure men that did not disturb or injure them.'

All this farce of bringing the Indians to terms of peace with this establishment was of infinite service to the Spaniards, though of none to us; for we neither had any interest in the mines, nor intended to stay there much longer. But we were glad to oblige don Juan who had been so great a benefactor to us. He, on his part, was most thankful to us; for he could now work the mines without any risk of losing men or cattle. He could now raise his own grain, which he had hitherto been obliged to pack 200 miles, not without having many of those engaged in bringing it, either killed or robbed. The Indians now had so much changed their deportment as to bring in horses or cows, that they found astray from the mines. They regularly brought in deer and turkies to sell, which don Juan, to keep alive their friendship, purchased, whether he needed the articles or not. Every day more or less Indians came into the settlement to go and hunt deer and bears with us. They were astonished at the closeness of our shooting; and nothing seemed to delight them so much, as our telling them, we would learn them to shoot our guns. My father had the honor to be denominated in their language, *the big Captain*.

Don Juan, apprehending that the truce with the Indians would last no longer than while we staid, and that after our departure, the Indians would resume their former habits of robbery and murder, was desirous to retain us as long as possible. We agreed to stay until December, when our plan was to commence another trapping expedition on the Helay, following it down to its mouth. With every disposition on the part of don Juan to render our stay agreeable, the time passed away pleasantly. On the 16th of September, the priest, to whose diocese the mines belonged, made a visit to the mines, to release the spirits of those who had died since his last visit, from purgatory, and to make Christians by baptising the little persons who had been born in the same time.

This old priest, out of a reverend regard to his own person, had fled from this settlement at the commencement of the Indian disturbances; and had not returned until now, when the Indians had made peace. A body of Indians happened to be in, when the priest came. We were exceedingly amused with the interview between the priest and an Indian chief, who, from having had one of his hands bitten off by a bear, was called *Mocho Mano*. The priest asked the one handed chief, why he did not offer himself for baptism? Mocho remained silent for some time, as if ruminating an answer. He then said, 'the Appache chief is a very big rogue now. Should he get his crown sprinkled with holy water, it would either do him no good at all, or if it had any effect, would make him a greater rogue; for that the priests, who made the water holy, and then went sprinkling it about among the people for money, were the biggest rogues of all.' This made the priest as angry as it made us merry.

When we had done laughing, Mocho asked us, how we baptised among our people? I answered that we had two ways of performing it; but that one way was, to plunge the baptised person under water. He replied promptly, 'now there is some sense in that;' adding that when a great quantity of rain fell from the clouds, it made the grass grow; but that it seemed to him that sprinkling a few drops of water amounted to nothing.

The priest, meanwhile, prophesied, that the peace between the Spaniards and Indians would be of very short duration. On the 18th, he left the mines, and returned to the place whence he had come. On the 20th, we started with some Indian guides to see a mountain of salt, that they assured us existed in their country. We travelled a northerly course through a heavily timbered country, the trees chiefly of pine and live oak. We killed a great number of bears and deer on the first day; and on account of their reverence for my father, they treated me as if I had been a prince. On the second we arrived at the salt hill, which is about one hundred miles north of the mines. The hill is about a quarter of a mile in length, and on the front side of it is the salt bluff, eight or ten feet in thickness. It has the appearance of a black rock, divided from the earthy matters, with which the salt is mixed. What was to me the most curious circumstance of the whole, was to see a fresh water spring boiling up within twenty feet from the salt bluff, which is a detached and solitary hill, rising out of a valley, which is of the richest and blackest soil, and heavily timbered with oak, ash and black walnut. I remained here two days, during which I killed fifteen deer, that came to lick salt.

An Indian woman of our company dressed all my deer skins, and we loaded two mules with the salt, and started back to the mines, where we arrived the first of October. Nothing could have been more seasonable or acceptable to don Juan, than the salt we brought with us. Having mentioned these mines so often, perhaps it may not be amiss, to give a few details respecting them. Within the circumference of three miles, there is a mine of copper, gold and silver, and beside, a cliff of load stone. The silver mine is not worked, as not being so profitable, as either the copper or gold mines.

We remained here to the last of December, when the settlement was visited by a company of French trappers, who were bound for Red river. We immediately made preparations to return with them, which again revived the apprehensions of don Juan, that the Indians would break in upon the settlement as soon as we were gone, and again put an end to the working of the mines. To detain us effectually, he proposed to rent the mines to us for five years, at a thousand dollars a year. He was willing to furnish provisions for the first year gratis, and pay us for all the improvements we should make on the establishment. We could not but be aware, that this was an excellent offer. My father accepted it. The writings were drawn, and my father rented the establishment on his own account, selecting such partners as he chose.

I, meanwhile, felt within me an irresistible propensity to resume the employment of trapping. I had a desire, which I can hardly describe, to see more of this strange and new country. My father suffered greatly in the view of my parting with him, and attempted to dissuade me from it. He strongly painted the dangers of the route, and represented to me, that I should not find these Frenchmen like my own country people, for companions. All was unavailing to change my fixed purpose, and we left the mines, January 2d, 1826.

We travelled down the river Helay, of which I have formerly

given a description, as far as the point where we had left it for Battle-hill. Here, although we saw fresh Indian signs, we met with no
Indians. Where we encamped for the night, there were arrows
sticking in the ground. We made an early start on the 16th, and at
evening came upon the self same party of Indians, that had robbed
us of our horses, the year past. Some of them had on articles of my
father's clothes, that he had left where we buried our furs. They
had made our beaver skins into robes, which we now purchased of
them. While this bargain was transacting, I observed one of the
Indians mounted on the self same horse, on which my father had
travelled from the States. My blood instantly boiled within me,
and, presenting my gun at him, I ordered him instantly to dis-
mount. He immediately did as I bade him, and at once a trepida-
tion and alarm ran through the whole party. They were but
twenty men, and they were encumbered with women and children.
We were thirteen, well mounted and armed. The chief of the party
came to me, and asked me, 'if I knew this horse?' I answered, that
'I did, and that it was mine.' He asked me again, 'if we were the
party, whose horses and furs they had taken the year before?' I answered, that I was one of them, and that if he did not cause my furs
and horses to be delivered up to me, we would kill them all on the
spot. He immediately brought me 150 skins and three horses, observing, that they had been famished, and had eaten the rest, and
that he hoped this would satisfy me, for that in the battle they had
suffered more than we, he having lost ten men, and we having
taken from them four horses with their saddles and bridles. I observed to him in reply, that he must remember that they were the
aggressors, and had provoked the quarrel, in having robbed us of
our horses, and attempting to kill us. He admitted that they were
the aggressors, in beginning the quarrel, but added, by way of apol-
ogy, that they had thought us Spaniards, not knowing that we were
Americans; but that now, when he knew us, he was willing to
make peace, and be in perpetual friendship. On this we lit the pipe
of peace, and smoked friends. I gave him some red cloth, with
which he was delighted. I then asked him about the different nations, through which our route would lead us? He named four nations, with names, as he pronounced them, sufficiently barbarous.

All these nations he described as bad, treacherous and quarrelsome. Though it was late in the evening, we resumed our march, until we had reached the point where the river runs between mountains, and where I had turned back the year before. There is here little timber, beside musqueto-wood, which stands thick. We passed through the country of the first two tribes, which the Indian chief had described to us, without meeting an individual of them. On the 25th, we arrived at an Indian village situated on the south bank of the river. Almost all the inhabitants of this village speak Spanish, for it is situated only three days journey from a Spanish fort in the province of Sonora, through which province this river runs. The Indians seemed disposed to be friendly to us. They are to a considerable degree cultivators, raising wheat, corn and cotton, which they manufacture into cloths. We left this village on the 25th, and on the 28th in the evening arrived at the Papawar village, the inhabitants of which came running to meet us, with their faces painted, and their bows and arrows in their hands. We were alarmed at these hostile appearances, and halted. We told them that we were friends, at which they threw down their arms, laughing the while, and showing by their countenances that they were aware that we were frightened. We entered the village and the French began to manifest their uncontrollable curiosity, by strolling about in every direction. I noted several crowds of Indians, collected in gangs, and talking earnestly. I called the leader of my French companions, and informed him that I did not like these movements of the Indians, and was fearful that they were laying a plan to cut us all up. He laughed at my fears, telling me I was a coward. I replied, that I did not think that to be cautious, and on our guard, was to show cowardice, and that I still thought it best for us to start off. At this he became angry, and told me that I might go when I pleased, and that he would go when he was ready.

I then spoke to a Frenchman of our number, that I had known for a long time in Missouri; I proposed to him to join me, and we would leave the village and encamp by ourselves. He consented, and we went out of the village to the distance of about 400 yards, under the pretext of going there to feed our horses. When the sun was about a half an hour high, I observed the French captain com-

ing out towards us, accompanied by a great number of Indians, all
armed with bows and arrows. This confirmed me in my conviction
that they intended us no good. Expressing my apprehensions to my
French companion, he observed in his peculiar style of English, that
the captain was too proud and headstrong, to allow him to receive
instruction from any one, for that he thought nobody knew any
thing but himself.

Agreeing that we had best take care of ourselves, we made us
a fire, and commenced our arrangements for spending the night.
We took care not to unsaddle our horses, but to be in readiness to
be off at a moments warning. Our French captain came and encamped within a hundred yards of us, accompanied by not less than
a hundred Indians. They were all exceedingly officious in helping
the party unpack their mules; and in persuading the captain, that
there was no danger in turning them all loose, they promised that
they would guard them with their own horses. This proposal delighted the lazy Frenchmen, who hated to go through the details
of preparing for encampment, and had a particular dislike to
standing guard in the night. The Indian chief then proposed to the
captain to stack their arms against a tree, that stood close by. To
this also, under a kind of spell of infatuation he consented. The Indian chief took a rope, and tied the arms fast to a tree.

As I saw this, I told the captain that it seemed to me no mark of
their being friendly, for them to retain their own arms, and persuade us to putting ours out of our power, and that one, who had
known Indians, ought to be better acquainted with their character, than to encamp with them, without his men having their own
arms in their hand. On this he flew into a most violent passion, calling me, with a curse added to the epithet, a coward, wishing to
God that he had never taken me with him, to dishearten his men,
and render them insubordinate. Being remarkable neither for forbearance, or failing to pay a debt of hard words, I gave him as good
as he sent, telling him, among other things no ways flattering, that
he was a liar and a fool, for that none other than a fool would dis-
arm his men, and go to sleep in the midst of armed savages in the
woods. To this he replied, that he would not allow me to travel any
longer in his company. I answered that I was not only willing, but

desirous to leave him, for that I considered myself safer in my own single keeping, than under the escort of such a captain, and that I estimated him only to have sense enough to lead people to destruction.

He still continued to mutter harsh language in reply, as I returned to my own camp. It being now dusk, we prepared, and ate our supper. We had just finished it, when the head chief of the village came to invite us to take our supper with them, adding, by way of inducement, that they had brought some fine pumpkins to camp, and had cooked them for the white people. We told him, we had taken supper; and the more he insisted, the more resolutely we refused. Like the French captain, he began to abuse us, telling us we had bad hearts. We told him, that when with such people, we chose rather to trust to our heads than our hearts. He then asked us to let some of his warriors come and sleep with us, and share our blankets, alleging, as a reason for the request, that the nights were cold, and his warriors too poor to buy blankets. We told him, that he could easily see that we were poor also, and were no ways abundantly supplied with blankets, and that we should not allow them to sleep with us. He then marched off to the French camp, evidently sulky and in bad temper. While roundly rating us to the French captain, he gave as a reason why we ought not to sleep by ourselves, that we were in danger of being killed in the night by another tribe of Indians, with whom he was at war.

The captain, apparently more calm, came to us, and told us, that our conduct was both imprudent and improper, in not conciliating the Indians by consenting to eat with them, or allowing them to sleep with us. My temper not having been at all sweetened by any thing that had occurred since we fell out, I told him, that if he had a fancy to eat, or sleep with these Indians, I had neither power nor the will to control him; but that, being determined, that neither he nor they should sleep with me, he had better go about his business, and not disturb me with useless importunity. At this he began again to abuse and revile me, to which I made no return. At length, having exhausted his stock of epithets, he returned to his camp.

As soon as we were by ourselves, we began to cut grass for our horses, not intending either to unsaddle, or let them loose for the night. My companion and myself were alike convinced, that some catastrophe was in reserve from the Indians, and seeing no chance of defending ourselves against an odds of more than twenty to one, we concluded, as soon as all should be silent in the camp, to fly. We packed our mules so as to leave none of our effects behind, and kept awake. We remained thus, until near midnight, when we heard a fierce whistle, which we instantly understood to be the signal for an attack on the French camp. But a moment ensued, before we heard the clashing of war clubs, followed by the shrieks and heavy groans of the dying French, mingled with the louder and more horrible yells of these treacherous and blood thirsty savages. A moment afterwards, we heard a party of them making towards us. To convince them that they could not butcher us in our defenceless sleep, we fired upon them. This caused them to retreat. Convinced that we had no time to lose, we mounted our horses, and fled at the extent of our speed. We heard a single gun discharged in the Indian camp, which we supposed the act of an Indian, who had killed the owner. We took our direction towards a high mountain on the south side of the river, and pushed for it as fast as we thought our horses could endure to be driven. We reached the mountain at day break, and made our way about three miles up a creek, that issued from the mountain. Here we stopped to refresh our horses, and let them feed, and take food ourselves. The passage of the creek was along a kind of crevice of the mountain, and we were strongly convinced that the Indians would not follow upon our trail further than the entrance to the mountain. One of us ascended a high ridge, to survey whatever might be within view. My companion, having passed nearly an hour in the survey, returned to me, and said he saw something on the plain approaching us. I ascended with him to the same place, and plainly perceived something black approaching us. Having watched it for some time, I thought it a bear. At length it reached a tree on the plain, and ascended it. We were then convinced, that it was no Indian, but a bear searching food. We could see the smokes arising from the Indian town, and had no doubt, that the savages were dancing at the moment around the scalps of the unfortunate Frenchmen, who had fallen the victims of their indolence and rash confidence in these faithless people. All anger for their abuse of me for my timely advice was swallowed up in pity for their fate. But yesterday these people were the merriest of the merry. What were they now? Waiting a few moments, we saw the supposed bear descend the tree, and advance directly to the branch on which we were encamped. We had observed that the water of this branch, almost immediately upon touching the plain, was lost in the arid sand, and gave no other evidence of its existence, than a few green trees. In a moment we saw buttons glitter on this object from the reflected glare of the sun's rays. We were undeceived in regard to our bear, and now supposed it an Indian, decorated with a coat of the unfortunate Frenchmen. We concluded to allow him to approach close enough to satisfy our doubts, before we fired upon him. We lay still, until he came within fair rifle distance, when to our astonishment, we discovered it to be the French captain! We instantly made ourselves known from our perch. He uttered an exclamation of joy, and fell prostrate on the earth. Fatigue and thirst had brought him to death's door. We raised him, and carried him to our camp. He was wounded in the head and face with many and deep wounds, the swelling of which had given him fever. I happened to have with me some salve, which my father gave me when I left the mines. I dressed his wounds. Having taken food, and sated his thirst, hope returned to him. So great was his change in a few hours, that he was able to move off with us that evening. In his present miserable and forlorn condition, I exercised too much humanity and forbearance to think of adverting to our quarrel of the preceding evening. Probably estimating my forbearance aright, he himself led to the subject. He observed in a tone apparently of deep compunction, that if he had had the good sense and good temper to have listened to my apprehensions and cautions, both he and his people might have been now gaily riding over the prairies. Oppressed with mixed feelings, I hardly knew what reply to make, and only remarked, that it was too late now to lament over what was unchangeable, and that the will of God had been done. After a silence of some time, he resumed the conversation, and related all the particulars of the terrible disaster, that had come to his knowledge. His own escape he owed to retaining a pocket pistol, when the rest of their arms were stacked. This he fired at an Indian approaching him, who fell, and thus enabled him to fly; not, however, until he had received a number of severe wounds from their clubs. I had not the heart to hear him relate what become of the rest of his comrades. I could easily divine that the treacherous savages had murdered every one. Feelings of deep and burning revenge arose in my bosom, and I longed for nothing so much as to meet with these monsters on any thing like terms of equality. About sunset we could distinctly discern the river bottom about five miles distant from us. When it became dark, we descried three fires close together, which we judged to be those of savages in pursuit of us. Like some white people, the Indians never forgive any persons that they have outraged and injured. We halted, and took counsel, what was to be done. We concluded that my companion and myself should leave our wounded companion to take care of the horses, and go and reconnoitre the camp, in which were these fires, and discover the number of the Indians, and if it was great, to see how we could be most likely to pass them unobserved. When we had arrived close to the fires, we discovered a considerable number of horses tied, and only two men guarding them. We crawled still closer, to be able to discern their exact number and situation.

In this way we arrived within fifty yards of their camp, and could see no one, but the two, any where in the distance. We concluded, that all the rest of the company were alseep in some place out of our view. We presumed it would not be long before some of them would awake, it being now ten at night. Our intention was to take aim at them, as they should pass between us and their fire, and drop them both together. We could distinctly hear them speaking about their horses. At length one of them called to the other, in English, to go and wake their relief guards. Words would poorly express my feelings, at hearing these beloved sounds. I sprang from my couching posture, and ran towards them. They were just ready to shoot me, when I cried *a friend, a friend!* One of them exclaimed, 'where in God's name did you spring from.' 'You seem to have come out of the earth.' The surprise and joy upon mutual recognition was great on both sides. I gave him a brief sketch of the recent catastrophe of our company, as we followed them to camp. The company was all roused and gathered around us, eagerly listening to the recital of our recent disaster. At hearing my sad story, they expressed the hearty sorrow of good and true men, and joined us in purposes of vengeance against the Indians.

We were now thirty-two in all. We fired twelve guns, a signal which the wounded captain heard and understood, for he immediately joined us. We waited impatiently for the morning. As soon as it was brightdawn, we all formed under a genuine American leader, who could be entirely relied upon. His orders were, that twenty should march in front of the pack horses, and twelve behind. In the evening we encamped within five miles of the Indian village, and made no fires. In the morning of the 31st, we examined all our arms, and twenty-six of us started to attack the village When we had arrived close to it, we discovered most fortunately, what we considered the dry bed of a creek, though we afterwards discovered it to be the old bed of the river, that had very high banks, and ran within a hundred yards of the village. In this bed we all formed ourselves securely and at our leisure, and marched quite near to the verge of the village without being discovered. Every man posted himself in readiness to fire. Two of our men were then ordered to show themselves on the top of the bank. They were immediately discovered by the Indians, who considered them, I imagine, a couple of the Frenchmen that they had failed to kill. They raised the yell, and ran towards the two persons, who instantly dropped down under the bank. There must have been at least 200 in pursuit. They were in a moment close on the bank. In order to prevent the escape of the two men, they spread into a kind of circle to surround them. This brought the whole body abreast of us. We allowed them to approach within twenty yards, when we gave them our fire. They commenced a precipitate retreat, we loading and firing as fast as was in our power. They made no pause in their village, but ran off, men, women and children, towards a mountain distant 700 yards from their village. In less than ten minutes, the village was so completely evacuated, that not a human being was to be found, save one poor old blind and deaf Indian, who sat eating his mush as unconcernedly as if all had been tranquil in the village. We did not molest him.

We appropriated to our own use whatever we found in the village that we judged would be of any service to us. We then set fire to their wigwams, and returned to our camp. They were paid a bloody price for their treachery, for 110 of them were slain. At twelve we returned to the village in a body, and retook all the horses of the Frenchmen, that they had killed. We then undertook the sad duty of burying the remains of the unfortunate Frenchmen. A sight more horrible to behold, I have never seen. They were literally cut in pieces, and fragments of their bodies scattered in every direction, round which the monsters had danced, and yelled. We then descended the river about a mile below the village, to the point where it enters the Helay from the north. It affords as much water at this point as the Helay.

In the morning of the 1st of February, we began to ascend Black river. We found it to abound with beavers. It is a most beautiful stream, bounded on each side with high and rich bottoms. We travelled up this stream to the point where it forks in the mountains; that is to say, about 80 miles from its mouth. Here our company divided, a part ascending one fork, and a part the other. The left fork heads due north, and the right fork north east. It was my lot to ascend the latter. It heads in mountains covered with snow, near the head of the left hand fork of the San Francisco. On the 16th, we all met again at the junction of the forks. The other division found that their fork headed in snow covered mountains, as they supposed near the waters of Red river. They had also met a tribe of Indians, who called themselves *Mokee*. They found them no ways disposed to hostility. From their deportment it would seem as if they had never seen white people before. At the report of a gun they fell prostrate on the ground. They knew no other weapon of war than a sling, and with this they had so much dexterity and power, that they were able to bring down a deer at the distance of 100 yards.

We thence returned down the Helay, which is here about 200 yards wide, with heavily timbered bottoms. We trapped its whole course, from where we met it, to its junction with Red river. The point of junction is inhabited by a tribe of Indans called Umene.

Here we encamped for the night. On the morning of the 26th, a great many of these Indians crossed the river to our camp, and brought us dried beans, for which we paid them with red cloth, with which they were delighted beyond measure, tearing it into ribbands, and tieing it round their arms and legs; for if the truth must be told, they were as naked as Adam and Eve in their birth day suit. They were the stoutest men, with the finest forms I ever saw, well proportioned, and as straight as an arrow. They contrive, however, to inflict upon their children an artificial deformity. They flatten their heads, by pressing a board upon their tender scalps, which they bind fast by a ligature. This board is so large and light, that I have seen women, when swimming the river with their children, towing them after them by a string, which they held in their mouth. The little things neither suffered nor complained, but floated behind their mothers like ducks.

At twelve we started up Red river, which is between two and three hundred yards wide, a deep, bold stream, and the water at this point entirely clear. The bottoms are a mile in general width, with exceedingly high, barren cliffs. The timber of the bottoms is very heavy, and the grass rank and high. Near the river are many small lakes, which abound in beavers.

March 1st we came among a tribe of Indians, called Cocomarecopper. At sight of us they deserted their wigwams, one and all, and fled to the mountains, leaving all their effects at our discretion. Of course we did not meddle with any thing. Their corn was knee high. We took care not to let our horses injure it, but marched as fast as we could from their village, to deprive them of their homes as little time as possible. About four miles above the town we encamped, and set our traps. About twelve next day it began to rain, and we pitched our tents.

We had scarce kindled our fires, when 100 Indians came to our camp, all painted red in token of amity. They asked fire, and when we had given it, they went about 20 yards from us, and as the rain had been heavy and the air cool, they made a great fire, round which they all huddled. We gave them the bodies of six large fat beavers, which they cooked by digging holes in the ground, at the bottom of which they kindled fires, and on the fires threw the beavers, which they covered with dirt. This dainty, thus prepared they greedily devoured, entrails and all. Next morning, fearful that our guns might have experienced inconvenience from the rain, we fired them off to load them afresh. They were amazed and alarmed, to see us make, what they called thunder and lightning. They were still more startled, to see the bullet holes in the tree, at which we had aimed. We made signs to them, that one ball would pass through the body of two men. Some of our men had brought with them some scalps of the Papawars, the name of the tribe where our French captain lost his company. They informed us that they were at war with that tribe, and begged some of the scalps to dance round. They were given them, and they began to cut their horrid anticks about it.

Our traps had taken thirty beavers the last night. We gave them the meat of twenty, with which present they were delighted, their gratitude inducing them to manifest affection to us. They ate and danced all day and most of the night. On the morning of the 3d, they left us, returning to their camps. We resumed our march, and on the 6th arrived at another village of Indians called Mohawa. When we approached their village, they were exceedingly alarmed. We marched directly through their village, the women and children screaming, and hiding themselves in their huts. We encamped about three miles above the village. We had scarcely made our arrangements for the night, when 100 of these Indians followed us. The chief was a dark and sulky looking savage, and he made signs that he wanted us to give him a horse. We made as prompt signs of refusal. He replied to this, by pointing first to the river, and then at the furs we had taken, intimating, that the river, with all it contained, belonged to him; and that we ought to pay him for what we had taken, by giving him a horse. When he was again refused, he raised himself erect, with a stern and fierce air, and discharged his arrow into the tree, at the same time raising his hand to his mouth, and making their peculiar yell. Our captain made no other reply, than by raising his gun and shooting the arrow, as it still stuck in the tree, in two. The chief seemed bewildered with this mark of close markmanship, and started off with his men. We had no small apprehensions of a night attack from these Indians.

We erected a hasty fortification with logs and skins, but sufficiently high and thick, to arrest their arrows in case of attack. The night, contrary to our fears, passed without interruption from them. On the morning of the 7th, the chief returned on horse back, and in the same sulky tone again demanded a horse. The captain bade him be off, in a language and with a tone alike understood by all people. He started off on full gallop, and as he passed one of our horses, that was tied a few yards from the camp, he fired a spear through the animal. He had not the pleasure to exult in his revenge for more than fifty yards, before he fell pierced by four bullets. We could not doubt, that the Indians would attempt to revenge the death of their chief. After due consideration, we saw no better place in which to await their attack, than the one we now occupied. On the rear we were defended by the river, and in front by an open prairie. We made a complete breastwork, and posted spies in the limbs of the tall trees, to descry the Indians, if any approached us, while still at a distance. No Indians approached us through the day, and at night a heavy rain commenced falling. We posted sentinels, and secured our horses under the river bank. We kindled no fires, and we passed the night without annoyance. But at day break, they let fly at us a shower of arrows. Of these we took no notice. Perhaps, thinking us intimidated, they then raised the war whoop, and made a charge upon us. At the distance of 150 yards we gave them a volley of rifle balls. This brought them to a halt, and a moment after to a retreat, more rapid than their advance had been. We sallied out after them, and gave them the second round, which induced all, that were not forever stopped, to fly at the top of their speed. We had killed sixteen of their number. We returned to our camp, packed, and started, having made a determination not to allow any more Indians to enter our camp. This affair happened on the 9th.

We pushed on as rapidly as possible, fearful that these red children of the desert, who appear to inherit an equal hatred of all whites, would follow us, and attack us in the night. With timely warning we had no fear of them by day, but the affair of the destruction of the French company, proved that they might become formidable foes by night. To prevent, as far as might be, such acci-

dents, we raised a fortification round our camp every night, until
we considered ourselves out of their reach, which was on the evening of the 12th. This evening we erected no breast-work, placed
no other guard than one person to watch our horses, and threw
ourselves in careless security round our fires. We had taken very
little rest for four nights, and being exceedingly drowsy, we had
scarcely laid ourselves down, before we were sound asleep. The Indians had still followed us, too far off to be seen by day, but had
probably surveyed our camp each night. At about 11 o'clock this
night, they poured upon us a shower of arrows, by which they
killed two men, and wounded two more; and what was most pro-
voking, fled so rapidly that we could not even give them a round.
One of the slain was in bed with me. My own hunting shirt had
two arrows in it, and my blanket was pinned fast to the ground by
arrows. There were sixteen arrows discharged into my bed. We extinguished our fires, and it may easily be imagined, slept no more
that night.

In the morning, eighteen of us started in pursuit of them, leaving the rest of the company to keep camp and bury our dead. We
soon came upon their trail, and reached them late in the evening.
They were encamped, and making their supper from the body of a
horse. They got sight of us before we were within shooting distance, and fled. We put spurs to our horses, and overtook them just
as they were entering a thicket. Having every advantage, we killed
a greater part of them, it being a division of the band that had attacked us. We suspended those that we had killed upon the trees,
and left their bodies to dangle in terror to the rest, and as a proof,
how we retaliated aggression. We then returned to our company,
who had each received sufficient warning not to encamp in the
territories of hostile Indians without raising a breast-work round
the camp. Red river at this point bears a north course, and affords
an abundance of the finest lands. We killed plenty of mountain
sheep and deer, though no bears. We continued our march until the
16th, without seeing any Indians. On that day we came upon a
small party, of whom the men fled, leaving a single woman. Seeing
herself in our power, she began to beat her breast, and cry *Cowera,*
*Cowera;* from which we gathered, that she belonged to that tribe.

We treated her kindly, and travelled on. On the 23d, we came to a village of the Shuena Indians. As we approached it, they came out and began to fire arrows upon us. We gave them in return a round of rifle balls. In the excitement of an attack, we laughed heartily to see these sons of the desert dodge, and skulk away half bent, as though the heavens were falling upon them. From their manner we inferred, that they were in fact wholly unacquainted with white people, or at least they never before heard the report of a gun. The whole establishment dispersed to the mountains, and we marched through the village without seeing any inhabitants, except the bodies of those we had killed. We had received more than one lesson of caution, and we moved on with great circumspection. But so much of our time was taken up in defence and attacks, and fortifying our camps, that we had little leisure to trap. In order that our grand object should not be wholly defeated, we divided our men into two companies, the one to trap and the other to keep guard. This expedient at once rendered our trapping very productive. We discovered little change in the face of the country. The course of the river still north, flowing through a rich valley, skirted with high mountains, the summits of which were white with snow.

On the 25th we reached a small stream, emptying into Red river through the east bank, up which we detached three men, each carrying a trap, to discover if beavers abounded in that stream. They were to return the next day, while we were engaged in shoeing our horses. The next day elapsed, but none returned. We became anxious about their fate; and on the 27th, started to see what had become of them. At mid-day we found their bodies cut in pieces, and spitted before a great fire, after the same fashion which is used in roasting beaver. The Indians who had murdered them, saw us as we came on, and fled to the mountains, so that we had no chance of avenging the death of our unfortunate companions. We gathered the fragments of their bodies together and buried them. With sadness in our hearts, and dejection on our countenances, we returned to our camp, struck our tents, and marched on. The temperature in this region is rather severe, and we were wretchedly clad to encounter the cold.

On the 28th, we reached a point of the river where the moun-

tains shut in so close upon its shores, that we were compelled to
climb a mountain, and travel along the acclivity, the river still in
sight, and at an immense depth beneath us.—Through this whole
distance, which we judged to be, as the river meanders, 100 leagues,
we had snow from a foot to eighteen inches deep. The river bluffs
on the opposite shore, were never more than a mile from us. It is
perhaps, this very long and formidable range of mountains, which
has caused, that this country of Red river, has not been more explored, at least by the American people. A march more gloomy and
heart-wearing, to people hungry, poorly clad, and mourning the
loss of their companions, cannot be imagined. Our horses had picked
a little herbage, and had subsisted on the bark of shrubs. Our
provisions were running low, and we expected every hour to see
our horses entirely give out.

April 10th, we arrived where the river emerges from these horrid mountains, which so cage it up, as to deprive all human beings
of the ability to descend to its banks, and make use of its waters.
No mortal has the power of describing the pleasure I felt, when I
could once more reach the banks of the river.—Our traps, by furnishing us beavers, soon enabled us to renew our stock of provisions. We likewise killed plenty of elk, and dressed their skins for
clothing. On the 13th we reached another part of the river, emptying into the main river from the north. Up this we all trapped two
days. During this excursion we met a band of hostile Indians, who
attacked us with an unavailing discharge of arrows, of whom we
killed four.

On the 11th, we returned to the banks of Red river, which is
here a clear beautiful stream. We moved very slowly, for our beasts
were too lean and worn down, to allow us to do otherwise. On the
16th we met with a large party of the Shoshonees, a tribe of Indians
famous for the extent of their wanderings, and for the number of
white people they had killed, by pretending friendship to them, until they found them disarmed, or asleep. One of our company
could speak their language, from having been a prisoner among
them for a year. They were warmly clad with buffaloe robes, and
they had muskets, which we knew they must have taken from the
white people. We demanded of them to give up the fire arms, which

they refused. On this we gave them our fire, and they fled to the
mountains, leaving their women and children in our power.—We
had no disposition to molest them. We learned from these women,
that they had recently destroyed a company of French hunters
on the head waters of the Platte. We found six of their yet fresh
scalps, which so exasperated us, that we hardly refrained from killing the women. We took from them all the beaver skins which they
had taken from the slain French, and five of their mules, and added
to our provisions their stock of dried buffaloe meat. We had killed
eight of their men, and we mortified the women excessively, by
compelling them to exchange the scalps of the unfortunate Frenchmen for those of their own people.

We resumed our march, and ascended the river to the point
where it forked again, neither fork being more than from twenty-
five to thirty yards wide. On the 19th, we began to ascend the right
hand fork, which pursues a N. E. course. On the 23d, we arrived
at the chief village of the Nabahoes, a tribe that we knew to be
friendly to the whites. We enquired of them, if we could cross the
Rocky Mountains best at the head of this fork or the other; and
they informed us, that the mountains were impassable, except by
following the left hand fork. Knowing that they were at war with
the Shoshonee, we let them know how many of them we had
killed. With this they were delighted, and gave us eight horses, one
for each man we had slain. They sent with us, moreover, ten Indians to point out to us the route, in which to cross the mountains.

On the 25th, we started up the left hand fork, and arrived on
the 30th, in the country of the Pewee tribe, who are friendly to the
Nabahoes. Their chief village is situated within two day's travel of
the low gap, at which we were to cross the mountains, at which
gap we arrived on the first of May. The crossing was a work, the
difficulty of which may be imagined from the nature of the case and
the character of the mountains.—The passage occupied six days,
during which we had to pass along compact drifts of snow, higher
than a man on horseback. The narrow path through these drifts is
made by the frequent passing of buffaloes, of which we found
many dead bodies in the way. We had to pack cotton-wood bark
on the horses for their own eating, and the wood necessary to make

fires for our cooking. Nothing is to be seen among these mountains, but bare peaks and perpetual snow. Every one knows, that these mountains divide between the Atlantic and Pacific Oceans. At the point where we crossed them, they run in a direction a little north of west, and south of east, further than the eye can reach.

On the 7th, we struck the south fork of the Platte, near Long's Peak, and descended it five days. We then struck across the plain to the main Platte, on which we arrived on the 16th. In descending it we found the beavers scarce, for all these rivers had been thoroughly trapped. The river is skirted with only a few small willows, and the country is open prairie, entirely destitute of trees. We saw immense droves of elk, buffaloes, and white bears, which haunt the buffaloe range to prey upon those noble animals. We had the merriest sport imaginable, in chasing the buffaloes over these perfectly level plains, and shooting them with the arrows we had taken from the Indians we had killed. I have killed myself, and seen others kill a buffaloe, with a single shot of an arrow. The bows are made with ribs of buffaloes, and drive the arrows with prodigious force. On the 20th, we left this river and started for the Big Horn, a fork of the Yellow Stone, itself a considerable river of the Missouri. We reached the Big Horn on the 31st, and found but few beavers. June 2d, we struck over towards the main Yellow Stone, and on the 3d entered the country of the Flat Heads, who were entirely friendly. We purchased some furs of them. They are Indians of exceedingly handsome forms, were it not for the horrid deformity of their heads, which are transversely from ear to ear but a few inches in diameter, and in the other direction monstrous, giving them the appearance of wearing a military cap with all its plumage. This plumage is furnished by their matted tresses of hair, painted and skewered up to a high point. This monstrosity is occasioned by binding two pieces of board on each side of the head of the newborn infant, which is kept secure with bandages, until the child is three years old, at which time the head bones have acquired a firmness to retain their then shape during life.

On the 11th, we reached the Yellow Stone, and ascended it to its head; and thence crossed the ridges of the Rocky Mountains to Clarke's fork of the Columbia. But all these streams had been so much trapped, as to yield but few beavers. Clarke's fork is a hundred yards wide, a bold, clear, pleasant stream, remarkable for the number and excellence of its fish, and most beautiful country of fertile land on its shores. We ascended this river to its head, which is in Lang's Peak, near the head waters of the Platte. We thence struck our course for the head waters of the Arkansas, on which we arrived July 1st. Here we met a band of the Grasshopper Indians, who derive their name from gathering grasshoppers, drying them, and pulverizing them, with the meal of which they make mush and bread; and this is their chief article of food. They are so little improved, as not even to have furnished themselves with the means of killing buffaloes. At sight of us, these poor two-legged animals, dodged into the high grass like so many partridges.

We marched up this stream, trapping for the few beavers which it afforded. Its banks are scantily timbered, being only skirted with a few willows. On the 5th, we met a war party of the Black Foot Indians, all well mounted. As soon as they saw us, they came fiercely upon us, yelling as though the spirit of darkness had loaned them the voices of all his tenants. We dismounted, and as soon as they were within shooting distance, we gave them our fire, which they promptly returned. The contest was fierce for something more than 20 minutes, a part of the time not more than 50 yards apart. They then retreated, and we mounted our horses, and gave them chase, though unavailingly, for their horses were as fleet as the wind, compared with ours. We soon desisted from so useless a pursuit, and returned to the battle ground. We found sixteen Blackfeet dead, and with infinite anguish, counted four of our own companions weltering in their blood. We buried them with sorrowful hearts, and eyes full of tears. Ah! Among those who live at home, surrounded by numerous relations and friends, in the midst of repose, plenty and security, when one of the number droops, and dies with sickness or age, his removal leaves a chasm that is not filled for years. Think how we must have mourned these brave men, who had shared so many dangers, and on whose courage and aid we had every day relied for protection. Here on these remote plains, far from their friends, they had fallen by the bloody arrow or spear of these red, barbarous Ishmaelites of the desert, but neither unwept nor unrevenged. Having performed the sad task of depositing the bodies of these once warm hearted friends in the clay, we ascended to the head of this river, and crossed the mountain that separates its waters from those of the Rio del Norte, which river we struck on the 20th. We began to descend it, and on the 23d met a band of the Nabahoes, who accompanied us quite to their chief village. It will be seen, that all these streams upon which we have been trapping, rise from sources which interlock with each other, and the same range of peaks at very short distances from each other. These form the heads of Red river of the east, and the Colorado of the west, Rio del Norte, Arkansas, Platte, Yellow Stone, Missouri and Columbia. The village of these Indians is distant 50 miles from the Rio del Norte. We remained at it two days, and rested our horses, and refreshed ourselves. This tribe some years since had been at war with the Spanish, during which they plundered them of great numbers of horses, mules and cattle, which caused that they had now large stocks of these animals, together with flocks of sheep. They raise a great abundance of grain, and manufacture their wool much better than the Spanish. On the first of August we arrived at Santa Fe, with a fine amount of furs. Here disaster awaited us. The Governor, on the pretext that we had trapped without a license from him, robbed us of all our furs. We were excessively provoked, and had it not been from a sense of duty to our own beloved country, we would have redressed our wrongs, and retaken our furs with our own arms.

Here I remained until the 18th, disposing of a part of my goods, and reserving the remainder for a trip which I contemplated to the province of Sonora. I had the pleasure once more of receiving the affectionate greeting of Jacova, who gave me the most earnest counsels to quit this dangerous and rambling way of life, and settle myself down in a house of my own. I thanked her for her kindness and good counsel, and promised to follow it, after rambling another year in the wilderness.—Thence I went to the mines, where I had the inexpressible satisfaction again to embrace my dear father, whom I found in perfect health, and making money rapidly. I remained there three days, and, accompanied with one servant, arrived in Hanas on the first of September. This is a small town situated in the province of Biscay, between the province of Sonora and New Mexico, in a direction S. W. from the copper mines.

The country is generally of that character, denominated in Kentucky, barren. The soil is level and black. These people raise a great quantity of stock, such as horses, cows, sheep and goats. Their farming implements are clumsy and indifferent. They use oxen entirely in their agriculture. Their ploughs are a straight piece of timber, five feet long and eight inches thick, mortised for two other pieces of timber, one to be fitted to the beam, by which the oxen draw, and another to the handle, by which the man holds the plough. The point that divides the soil, is of wood, and hewed sloping to such a point, that a hollow piece of iron is fastened on it at the end. This is one inch thick, and three inches broad at top, and slopes also to a point.

Their hoes, axes and other tools are equally indifferent; and they are precisely in such a predicament, as might be expected of a people who have no saw mills, no labor saving machinery, and do every thing by dint of hard labor, and are withal very indolent and unenterprising.

I amused myself at times with an old man, who daily fell in my way, who was at once rich and to the last degree a miser; and yet devotedly attached to the priests, who were alone able to get a little money out of him. He often spoke to me about the unsafeness of my religion. Instead of meeting his remarks with an argument, I generally affronted him at once, and then diverted myself with his ways of showing his anger. I told him that his priest treated him as the Spanish hostlers do their horses. He asked me to explain the comparison. I observed, 'you know how the hostler in the first place throws his hasso over the mule's neck. That secures the body of the beast. Next the animal is blindfolded. That hinders his seeing where he is led. Next step he binds the saddle safe and fast. Then the holy father rigs his heels with spurs. Next come spur and lash, and the animal is now restive to no purpose. There is no shaking off the rider. On he goes, till the animal under him dies, and both go to hell together!' At this he flew into such a violent rage, as to run at me with his knife. I dodged out of his way, and appeased him by convincing him that I was in jest. The rich, in their way of living, unite singular contrasts of magnificence and meanness. For instance, they have few of the useful articles of our dining and tea sets, but a great deal of massive silver plate, and each guest a silver fork and spoon. The dining room is contiguous to the kitchen. A window is thrown open, and the cook hands a large dish through the window to a servant, who bears it to the table. The entertainer helps himself first, and passes the dish round to all the guests. Then another and another is brought on, often to the number of sixteen. All are savored so strong with garlic and red pepper, that an American at first cannot eat them. The meat is boiled to such a consistency that a spoon manages it better than a knife. At the close of the dinner they bring in wine and cigars, and they sit and smoke and drink wine until drowsiness steals upon them, and they go to bed for their siesta. They sleep until three in the afternoon, at which time the church bell tolls. They rise, take a cup of chocolate, and handle the wine freely. This short affair over, they return and sit down on the shaded side of the house, and chatter like so many geese till night, when they divide, a part to mass, and a part to the card table, where I have seen the poor, betting their shirts, hats and shoes. The village contains 700 souls.

On the 6th, I departed from this town, travelling a west course through a most beautiful country, the plains of which were covered with domestic animals running wild. On the 8th I arrived at the foot of the mountain, that divides the province of Sonora from Biscay. I slept at a country seat, where they were making whiskey of a kind of plantain, of which I have spoken before, which they call Mascal (Magney). Here were assembled great numbers of Spaniards and Indians. They were soon drunk, and as a matter of course, fighting with knives and clubs. In the morning, two Spaniards and one Indian were found dead. Late in the morning, a file of soldiers arrived, and took the suspected murderers to prison.

In the morning I commenced climbing the mountain before me, and in the evening arrived at a small town in Sonoro, called Barbisca; situated on the bank of a most beautiful little stream, called Iago, which discharges itself into the Pacific ocean, near the harbor of Ymus. Its banks are not much timbered, nor is the soil uncommonly good. The morning of the 9th was a great religious festival, or famous Saint's day, which collected a vast crowd of people. After breakfast and mass, the image of the virgin Mary was paraded round the public square in solemn procession, during which there was a constant crash of cannon and small arms. Then an old priest headed a procession, bearing the image of Christ, nailed to a cross. After these images were returned to their church, they brought into a square enclosure, strongly fenced for that purpose, a wild bull, which they threw down, tied and sharpened its horns. The tops of the houses were all covered with people to see the spectacle that was performing. The bull was covered with red cloth, and two men entered the enclosure, each holding in the right hand a bundle of sky rockets, and in the left a red handkerchief. The rockets were lashed to a stick a foot long, in the end of which was a small nail, a half an inch long, with a beard at the end, like that of a fish hook. They then untied the fierce animal. No sooner was he on his feet, than he sprang at one of his assailants, who avoided his attack, by dextrously slipping aside, and as the animal darted by him, stuck in his neck two small rockets, one on each side. The other assailant then gave a sharp whistle to draw the infuriated animal upon him. The bull snorted and dashed at him. He dodged the animal in the same manner, as the other had done, and left sticking in his forehead, as he passed, a garland of artificial flowers, made of paper, beautifully cut and painted, and large enough to cover his whole forehead. In this way they kept alternately driving him this way and that, sticking rockets in him as he dashed by them, until he was covered with eight or ten, clinging to his neck and shoulders. They then touched the crackers with a lighted match. Words would not paint the bull's expressions of rage and terror, as he bounded round the enclosure, covered with fire, and the rockets every moment discharging like fire arms. After this, a man entered with a small sword. The bull bellowed and darted at him. As the bull dropped his head to toss him, he set his feet upon the horns, and in a twinkling, thrust his sword between the shoulder blades, so as to touch the spinal marrow. The animal dropped as dead as a stone. The drum and fife then struck up, as a signal for the horsemen to come and carry off the dead animal, and bring in a fresh one. All this was conducted with incredible dispatch. In this way seven bulls were successively tortured to death, by foot-men.

After this, four men entered on horseback, equipped with spears in the shape of a trowel, and a handle four feet long. With this spear in the one hand, and a noose in the other, they gallopped round the bull. The bull immediately made at the horsemen pass-ing him, who moved just at such a pace, as not to allow the bull to toss the horse. The horseman then couched his spear backwards, so as to lay it on the bull's neck. The bull instantly reared and tossed, and in the act forced the spear between his fore shoulders, so as to hit the spinal marrow. If the spear is laid rightly, and the animal makes his accustomed motions, he drops instantly dead. But to do this requires infinite dexterity and fearlessness. If the man be clumsy, or of weak-nerves, he is apt to fail in couching the spear right, in which case, as a matter of course, the horse is gored, and it is ten to one that the man is slain. In this way fourteen bulls were killed, and with them, five horses and one man, during this festi-val. At night commenced gambling and card playing, and both as fiercely pursued as the bull fighting. This great feast lasted three days, during which, as the people were in a very purchasable hu-mor, I sold a number of hundred dollar's worth of my goods.

On the morning of the 12th, I left this place, and in the evening arrived at a small town called Vassarac, and remained there one day. The country in the vicinity is well timbered and very hilly. The woods are full of wild cattle and horses. On the 13th, I trav-elled through a fine rich country, abounding with cattle, and ar-rived in the evening at a town called Tepac, situated on a small creek, near a mountain, in which there is a gold mine worked by the Iago Indians, a nation formerly under the protection of an old priest. He attempted to practice some new imposition upon them, and they killed him some years ago. On this the Spaniards made war upon them, and the conflict was continued some years. They lost the best and bravest of their men, and the remnant were obliged to submit to such terms as the Spaniards saw fit to impose. They were either condemned to the mines, or to raise food for those who wrought them.

I remained in this town three days, and purchased gold in bars and lumps of the Indians, at the rate of ten dollars per ounce. The diggings seldom exceed twenty feet in depth. Most of the gold is found on the surface after hard rains. Their mode of extracting the gold from the earth with which it is mixed, or the stone in which it is imbedded, is this. The stone is pulverised or ground, still keeping the matter wet. It is carefully mixed with mercury, and kneaded with the hands, until the water is separated from the mass, and the mercury is perfectly incorporated with it. This process is repeated, until the water runs off perfectly clear. They then grind or triturate the mass anew until all the particles of earthy matter are washed away. The remaining matter is amalgam, of the color of silver, and the consistence of mush. They then put it into a wet deer skin, and strain the mercury by pressure through the pores of the skin. The gold is left, still retaining enough mercury to give it the color of silver. The coarse way of managing it afterwards, is to put it in the fire, and evaporate all the mercury from it, and it is then pure virgin gold. There is a more artificial way of managing it, by which the mercury is saved.

This province would be among the richest of the Mexican country, if it were inhabited by an enlightened, enterprising and industrious people. Nothing can exceed the indolence of the actual inhabitants. The only point, in which I ever saw them display any activity, is in throwing the lasso, and in horsemanship. In this I judge, they surpass all other people. Their great business and common pursuit, is in noosing and taming wild horses and cattle.

On the 15th, I left this place and travelled through a country well timbered and watered, though the land is too broken to be cultivated, and in the evening arrived in a town called Varguacha. This is a place miserably poor, the people being both badly fed and clothed. But their indolence alone is in fault. The land in the immediate vicinity of the town is good, and the woods teem with wild cattle. But they are too lazy to provide more meat than will serve them from day to day. On the 17th I continued my course through a beautiful country, thinly settled by civilized Indians, who raise sugar cane and abundance of stock. They are obviously more enterprising and industrious than the Spaniards. Approaching the shore of the great Pacific, I found the country more level and better settled. Some rich and noble sugar farms lay in my view.

On the 22d I arrived in Patoka, which is a considerable town, and the capital of this province. It is two day's travel hence to Ymus. The people here seemed to me more enlightened, and to have a higher air of civilization than any I had seen in the whole country. It probably results from the intercourse they have with foreigners, from their vicinity to the Pacific. Most of them are dressed in the stile of the American people. Their houses are much better furnished, and the farmers are supplied with superior farming utensils, compared with any thing I saw in the interior. The chief manufactures are soap and sugar, the latter of an inferior quality, I imagine, in consequence of the clumsy mode of manufacturing it. From the port of Ymus they also export considerable quantities of tallow and hides, for which the farmers are repaid in merchandize at an enormous advance. A great many horses and mules are driven from the interior to this port. Many also are taken to the American states. The price of mules in this province is from three to four dollars a head.

I remained here until I had disposed of all my goods. On the 26th, I left this town, and travelled on to port Ymus, at which I arrived on the 28th, and first saw the waters of the vast Pacific. I spent a day here on board an American ship, the master of which was surprised at the account I gave of myself, and would hardly believe that I had travelled to this place from the United States. I was equally amazed at hearing him relate the disasters which had befallen him at sea. On the 29th, I left this port, and travelled a N. W. course, through a country full of inhabitants, and abounding in every species of fruit. Snow never falls, although the general temperature is not so warm but that woollen garments may be worn. To add to its advantages, it is very healthy. On the 7th of October, I arrived at a town called Oposard. The population amounts to about 8000 souls. I here became acquainted with one of my own countrymen, married to a Spanish woman. He informed me, that he had been in this country thirty years, eight of which he had spent in prison. The sufferings he endured from the Spaniards were incredible; and I internally shuddered, as he related, lest I, in travelling through the country might fall into similar misfortunes. As some paliation of their cruelty, he observed, that he was made prisoner at the period when the revolution was just commencing in that country. At that time the Inquisition was still in force, and committed many a poor mortal to the flames, for his alleged heresy. He assured me, that he should have met the same fate, had he not become a member of their church. He afterwards married a lady, who had gained his affections by being kind to him in prison.

I remained with this man two days, and on the third resumed my journey, travelling an easterly course, and part of the time over a very rough country. I met no inhabitants, but Indians, who were uniformly friendly. On the 16th, I arrived at the mines of Carrocha, which were in the province of Chihuahua, situated between two mountains, and considered the richest silver mines in New Mexico. There are about 800 miners working this mine, and they have advanced under ground at least half a mile. On the 12th, I started for the capital, and reached it on the 16th, passing over great tracts of good and bad land, all untilled, and most of it an uninhabited wilderness. This city is the next largest in New Mexico. It is the largest and handsomest town I had ever seen, though the buildings are not so neat and well arranged as in our country. The roofs are flat, the walls well painted, and the streets kept very clean. Here they smelt and manufacture copper and silver, and several other metals. They have also a mint. The terms of their currency are very different from ours. They count eight rials, or sixteen four pence half pennies, to the dollar. Their merchandize is packed from Ymus, or Mexico.

I have heard much talk about the Splendid churches in this city. It is for others, who think much of such immense buildings, wrung from the labors of the poor, to describe them. For my part, having said it is a large and clean town, I present a result of their institutions and manners, which I considered the more important sort of information. During a stay of only three days here, ten dead bodies were brought into town, of persons who had been murdered in the night. Part of the number were supposed to have been killed on account of having been known to carry a great deal of money with them, and part to have had a quarrel about some abandoned women. This last is a most common occasion of night murders, the people being still more addicted to jealousy, and under still less restraints of law, than in old Spain, in the cities of which, assassination from this cause are notoriously frequent.

I asked my informant touching these matters, if there was no police in the city? He answered, that the forms of the law were complete, and that they had a numerous guard, and that it was quite as likely they committed the murders themselves, as not. I came to the same conclusion, for in a small and regular city like this, it was impossible that so many guards, parading the streets by night, should not be aware of the commission of such deeds, and acquainted with the perpetrators. No inquest of any sort was held over the bodies. They were, however, paraded through the streets to beg money to pay the priests for performing funeral rites at their burial. This excited in me still more disgust, than the murders. I expressed myself in consequence, with so much freedom, in regard to this sort of miserable imposition, as to give great offence to my host, who, like most of the people, was rigidly devoted to the religion of the church. On the evening of 16th, I left this city, and travelled through a fine country, thickly inhabited by shepherds, who live in small towns, and possess a vast abundance of stock. It is well watered, but thinly timbered. The most magnificent part of the spectacle is presented in the lofty snow covered mountains, that rise far in the distance, and have their summits lost in the clouds, glistening in indescribable brilliance in the rays of the rising and setting sun.

The road at this time was deemed to be full of robbers, and very dangerous. I was so fortunate as to meet with none. On the 18th, I arrived at a small town, called San Bueneventura, which is surrounded with a wall. In fact, most of the considerable villages are walled. They are called in Spanish, Presidio, the English of which is, a garrison. In the forenoon, I crossed a small river called Rio Grande, and travelled down this stream all day, the banks of which were thickly settled, and in high cultivation, with wheat, corn and barley. On the 22d, I arrived at a village called Casas Grandes, or the Great Houses. On the 23d, I pursued an east course towards Passo del Norte, situated on the banks of the Rio del Norte.

I travelled over a very rough country with some high mountains, inhabited by a wandering tribe of the Appache Indians, that live by seizing their opportunities for robbery and murder among the Spaniards riding off upon the stolen horses, to the obscure and almost inaccessible fastnesses of their mountains, where they subsist upon the stolen horseflesh.

I know not, whether to call the Passo del Norte, a settlement or a town. It is in fact a kind of continued village, extending eight miles on the river. Fronting this large group of houses, is a nursery of the fruit trees, of almost all countries and climes. It has a length of eight miles and a breadth of nearly three. I was struck with the magnificent vineyards of this place, from which are made great quantities of delicious wine. The wheat fields were equally beautiful, and the wheat of a kind I never saw before, the stalks generally yielding two heads each. The land is exceedingly rich, and its fertility increased by irrigation.

On the 28th, I started for the Copper mines, wrought by my father. This day my course led me up the del Norte, the bottoms of which are exceedingly rich. At a very short distance from the Passo, I began to come in contact with grey bears, and other wild animals. At a very little distance on either side are high and ragged mountains, entirely sterile of all vegetation. I had no encounter with the bears, save in one instance. A bear exceedingly hungry, as I suppose, came upon my horses as I was resting them at midday, and made at one of them. I repaid him for his impudence by shooting him through the brain. I made a most delicious dinner of the choice parts of his flesh. My servant would not touch it, his repugnance being shared by great numbers in his condition. It is founded on the notion, that the bear is a sort of degenerated man, and especially, that the entrails are exactly like those of human beings.

On the 30th, I struck off from the del Norte, and took my course for the Copper mines directly over the mountains, among which we toiled onward, subsisting by what we packed with us, or the product of the rifle, until the 11th of November, when I had once more the satisfaction of embracing my father at the Copper mines. He was in perfect health, and delighted to see me again. He urged me so earnestly to remain with him, though a stationary life was not exactly to my taste, that I consented from a sense of filial duty, and to avoid importunity. I remained here until the first of December, amusing myself sometimes by hunting, and sometimes by working in the gold mine, an employment in which I took much pleasure.

In a hunting excursion with a companion who was an American, he one morning saw fit to start out of bed, and commence his hunt while I was yet asleep in bed. He had scarcely advanced a league, before he killed a deer on the top of a high ridge. He was so inadvertent, as to commence skinning the animal, before he had re-loaded his rifle. Thus engaged, he did not perceive a bear with her cubs, which had advanced within a few feet of him. As soon as he saw his approaching companion, without coveting any farther acquaintance, he left deer and rifle, and ran for his life. He stopped not, until he arrived at the mines. The bear fell to work for a meal upon the deer, and did not pursue him. We immediately started back to have the sport of hunting this animal. As we approached the ridge, where he had killed the deer, we discovered the bear descending the ridge towards us. We each of us chose a position, and his was behind a tree, which he could mount, in case he wounded, without killing her. This most ferocious and terrible animal, the grizzly or grey bear, does not climb at all. I chose my place opposite him, behind a large rock, which happened to be near a precipice, that I had not observed. Our agreement was to wait until she came within 30 yards, and then he was to give her the first fire. He fired, but the powder being damp, his gun made long fire, whence it happened that he shot her too low, the ball passing through the belly, and not a mortal part. She made at him in terrible rage. He sprang up his tree, the bear close at his heels. She commenced biting and scratching the tree, making, as a Kentuckian would phrase it, *the lint fly*. But finding that she could not bite the tree down, and being in an agony of pain, she turned the course of her attack, and come growling and tearing up the bushes before her, towards me. My companion bade me lie still, and my own purpose was to wait until I could get a close fire. So I waited until the horrible animal was within six feet of me. I took true aim at her head. My gun flashed in the pan. She gave one growl and sprang at me with her mouth open. At two strides I leapt down the unperceived precipice. My jaw bone was split on a sharp rock, on which my chin struck at the bottom. Here I lay senseless. When I regained recollection, I found my companion had bled me with the point of his butcher knife, and was sitting beside me with his hat full of water, bathing my head and face. It was perhaps an hour, before I gained full recollection, so as to be able to walk. My companion had cut a considerable orifice in my arm with his knife, which I deemed rather supererrogation; for I judged, that I had bled sufficiently at the chin.

When I had come entirely to myself, my companion proposed that we should finish the campaign with the bear. I, for my part, was satisfied with what had already been done, and proposed to retreat. He was importunate, however, and I consented. We ascended the ridge to where he had seen the bear lie down in the bushes. We fixed our guns so that we thought ourselves sure of their fire. We then climbed two trees, near where the bear was, and made a noise, that brought her out of her lair, and caused her to spring fiercely towards our trees. We fired together, and killed her dead. We then took after the cubs. They were three in number. My companion soon overtook them. They were of the size of the largest rackoons. These imps of the devil turned upon him and made fight. I was in too much pain and weakness to assist him. They put him to all he could do to clear himself of them. He at length got away from them, leaving them masters of the field, and having acquired no more laurels than I, from my combat with my buffaloe calf. His legs were deeply bit and scratched, and what was worse, such was the character of the affair, he only got ridicule for his assault of the cubs. I was several weeks in recovering, during which time, I ate neither meat nor bread, being able to swallow nothing but liquids.

The country abounds with these fierce and terrible animals, to a degree, that in some districts they are truly formidable. They get into the corn fields. The owners hear the noise, which they make among the corn, and supposing it occasioned by cows and horses that have broken into the fields, they rise from their beds, and go to drive them out, when instead of finding retreating domestic animals, they are assailed by the grizzly bear. I have been acquainted with several fatal cases of that sort. One of them was a case, that intimately concerned me. Iago, my servant, went out with a man to get a load of wood. A bear came upon this man and killed him and his ass in the team. A slight flight of snow had fallen. Some Spaniards, who had witnessed the miserable fate of their companion, begged some of us to go and aid them in killing the bear. Four of us joined them. We trailed the bear to its den, which was a crevice in the bluff. We came to the mouth and fired a gun. The animal, confident in his fierceness, came out, and we instantly killed it. This occurred in New Mexico.

This stationary and unruffled sort of life had become unendurable, and with fifteen Americans, we arranged a trapping expedition on the Pacos. My father viewed my rambling propensities with stern displeasure. He had taken in a Spanish superintendant, who acted as clerk. This person had lived in the United States from the age of 18 to 30, and spoke English, French and Spanish. This man arranged the calculations, and kept the accounts of my father's concerns, and had always acted with intelligence and fidelity. The concern was on the whole prosperous; and although I felt deep sorrow to leave my father against his wishes, I had at least the satisfaction to know, that I was of no other use to him, than giving him the pleasure of my society.

On the 7th, our company arrived on the del Norte, and crossed it in the evening to the eastern shore. On the evening of the 8th, we struck the Pacos about twenty miles above its junction with the del Norte. This day's travel was through a wild and precipitous country, inhabited by no human being. We killed plenty of bears and deer, and caught some beavers. On the 9th, we began to ascend the river through a rich and delightful plain, on which are to be seen abundance of deserted sheep folds, and horse pens, where the Spanish vachers once kept their stock. The constant incursions of the Indians compelled this peaceful people to desert these fair plains. Their deserted cottages inspired a melancholy feeling. This river runs from N. E. to S. W. and is a clear, beautiful stream, 20 yards wide, with high and dry bottoms of a black and rich soil. The mountains run almost parallel to the river, and at the distance of eight or ten miles. They are thickly covered with noble pine forests, in which aspen trees are intermixed. From their foot gush out many beautiful clear springs. On the whole, this is one of the loveliest regions for farmers that I have ever seen, though no permanent settlements could be made there, until the murderous Indians, who live in the mountains, should be subdued.

We advanced slowly onward, until the 15th, without meeting any Indians. At day break of this day, our sentinels apprized us, that savages were at hand. We had just time to take shelter behind the trees, when they began to let their arrows fly at us. We returned them the compliment with balls, and at the first shot a number of them fell. They remained firm and continued to pour in their arrows from every side. We began to find it exceedingly difficult to dodge them, though we gave them some rounds before any one of our men was struck. At length one man was pierced, and they rushed forward to scalp him. I darted from behind my tree to prevent them. I was assailed by a perfect shower of arrows, which I dodged for a moment, and was then struck down by an arrow in the hip. Here I should have been instantly killed, had not my companions made a joint fire at the Indians, who were rushing upon me, by which a number of them were laid dead. But the agony of my pain was insupportable, for the arrow was still fast in my hip. A momentary cessation of their arrows enabled me to draw out the arrow from my hip, and to commence re-loading my gun. I had partly accomplished this, when I received another arrow under my right breast, between the bone and the flesh. This gave me less pain than the other shot, and finding I could not by any effort extract the arrow, I snapped it off, and finished loading my gun. The Indian nearest me fell dead, and I hobbled off, glad to be once more sheltered by a tree. My companions were not slow in making their rifles crack, and in raising mutual cheers of encouragement. The Indians were vastly our superiors in numbers, and we found it convenient to slip under the river bank. We were now completely sheltered from their arrows. After we had gained this security, they stood but a few shots more, before they fled, leaving their dead and wounded at our mercy. Truth is, we were too much exasperated to show mercy, and we cut off the heads of all, indiscriminately.

Our loss was one killed, and two wounded, another beside myself though neither of us dangerously. The Indians had 28 killed. Luckily our horses were on an island in the river, or we should have lost every one of them. Our only loss of property was a few blankets, which they took, as they fled by our camp. During the 20 minutes that the contest lasted, I had a fragment of an arrow fast in my breast, and the spike of the other in my hip. I suffered, it may be imagined, excruciating pain, and still severer pain during the operation of extraction. This operation, one of my companions undertook. He was some minutes in effecting it. The spike could not be entirely extracted from my hip, for being of flint, it had shivered against the bone.

The Indians that attacked us, were a tribe of the Muscallaros, a very warlike people, although they have no other arms except bows and arrows, which are, however, the most powerful weapons of the kind. They are made of an elastic and flexible wood, backed with the sinews of a buffaloe or elk. Their arrows are made of a species of reed grass, and are very light, though easily broken. In the end is stuck a hard piece of wood, which is pointed by a spike of flint an inch in length, and a quarter of an inch in width, and ground to the sharpest point. The men, though not tall, are admirably formed, with fine features and a bright complexion inclining to yellow. Their dress is a buckskin belt about the loins, with a shirt and moccasins to match. Their long black hair hangs in imbraided masses over their shoulders, in some cases almost extending to the heels. They make a most formidable appearance, when completely painted, and prepared for battle.

On the 16th, having made our arrangements for departure, I applied my father's admirable salve to my two severe wounds, and to my companion's slight wound in the arm, and we both felt able to join our companions in their march. We travelled all this day and the following night a west course, and the following day, without stopping longer than was necessary to take a little food. After this we stopped and rested ourselves and horses all night. I need not attempt to describe the bitter anguish I endured, during this long and uninterrupted ride. It will be only necessary to conceive my situation, to form a right conception of it. Our grand object had been to avoid another contest with the Muscallaros. In the evening we fell in with a party of the Nabahoes, who were now out on an expedition against the Muscallaros, who had recently killed one of their people, and against whom they had sworn immediate revenge. We showed the manifest proof of the chastisement they had received from us. Never had I seen such frantic leaps and gestures of joy. The screams and yells of exultation were such as cannot be imagined. It seemed as though a whole bedlam had broke loose. When we told them that we had lost but one man, their screams became more frantic still. Their medicine man was then called, and he produced an emollient poultice, the materials of which I do not know, but the effect was that the anguish of our wounds was at once assuaged. By the application of this same remedy, my wounds were quite healed in a fortnight.

The scalps, which some of our number had taken from the Muscallaros, were soon erected on a pole by the Nabahoes. They immediately commenced the fiercest dancing and singing I had yet seen, which continued without interruption three days and nights. During all this time, we endured a sort of worship from them, particularly the women. They were constantly presenting us with their favorite dishes, served in different ways, with dried berries and sweet vegetables, some of which, to people in our condition, were really agreeable.

In size and complexion these people resemble the Muscallaros, and their bows and arrows are similar; though some of the latter have fire arms, and their dress is much superior.—Part of their dress is of the same kind with that of the former, though the skins are dressed in a more workmanlike manner, and they have plenty of blankets of their own manufacturing, and constituting a much better article than that produced by the Spaniards. They dye the wool of different and bright colors, and stripe them with very neat figures. The women are much handsomer, and have lighter complexions than the men. They are rather small in stature, and modest and reserved in their behaviour. Their dress is chiefly com-

posed of skins made up with no small share of taste; and showily
corded at the bottom, forming a kind of belt of beads and porcupine quills.—They are altogether the handsomest women I have
seen among the red people, and not inferior in appearance to many
Spanish women. Their deportment to our people, was a mixture of
kindness and respect.

On the 21st, we started back to the river, accompanied by the
whole party of Nabahoes, who assured us that they would guard
us during the remainder of our hunt. We returned to the river
through a beautiful and level country, most of it well timbered and
watered. On our return we killed several bears, the talons of which
the Indians took for necklaces. On the 26th, we arrived at our battle ground. The view of the bodies of the slain, all torn in pieces
by wild beasts, inexpressibly disgusting to us, was equally a spectacle of pleasure to our red friends. We pointed out the grave of our
companion. They all walked in solemn procession round it, singing their funeral songs. As they left it, every one left a present on
the grave; some an arrow, others meat, moccasins, tobacco, war-
feathers, and the like, all articles of value to them. These simple
people believe that the spirit of the deceased will have immediate
use for them in the life to come. Viewing their offerings in this
light, we could not but be affected with these testimonies of kind
feeling to a dead stranger. They then gathered up the remains of
their slaughtered enemies, threw them in a heap, and cut a great
quantity of wood, which they piled over the remains. They then
set fire to the wood. We struck our tents, marched about five miles
up the river, set our traps, and encamped for the night. But the
Nabahoes danced and yelled through the night to so much effect,
as to keep all the beavers shut up in their houses, for, having been
recently trapped, they were exceedingly cautious.

On the morning of the 27th, we informed them why we had
taken no beavers, and during the following night they were perfectly quiet. We marched onward slowly, trapping as we went, until we reached the Spanish settlements on this river. On New Year's
eve, January 1st, 1827, the Spaniards of the place gave a fandango,
or Spanish ball. All our company were invited to it, and went. We
appeared before the Alcaide, clad not unlike our Indian friends;

that is to say, we were dressed in deer skin, with leggins, moccasins and hunting shirts, all of this article, with the addition of the customary Indian article of dress around the loins, and this was of red cloth, not an article of which had been washed since we left the Copper Mines. It may be imagined that we did not cut a particular dandy-like figure, among people, many of whom were rich, and would be considered well dressed any where. Notwithstanding this, it is a strong proof of their politeness, that we were civilly treated by the ladies, and had the pleasure of dancing with the handsomest and richest of them. When the ball broke up, it seemed to be expected of us, that we should each escort a lady home, in whose company we passed the night, and we none of us brought charges of severity against our fair companions.

The fandango room was about forty by eighteen or twenty feet, with a brick floor raised four or five feet above the earth. That part of the room in which the ladies sat, was carpetted with carpetting on the benches, for them to sit on. Simple benches were provided for the accommodation of the gentlemen. Four men sang to the music of a violin and guitar. All that chose to dance stood up on the floor, and at the striking up of a certain note of the music, they all commenced clapping their hands. The ladies then advanced, one by one, and stood facing their partners. The dance then changed to a waltz, each man taking his lady rather unceremoniously, and they began to whirl round, keeping true, however, to the music, and increasing the swiftness of their whirling. Many of the movements and figures seemed very easy, though we found they required practise, for we must certainly have made a most laughable appearance in their eyes, in attempting to practise them. Be that as it may, we cut capers with the nimblest, and what we could not say, we managed by squeezes of the hand, and little signs of that sort, and passed the time to a charm.

The village, in which was this ball, is called Perdido, or the lost town, probably from some circumstances in its history. It contains about 500 souls and one church. The bishop was present at this ball, and not only bestowed his worshipful countenance, but *danced before the Lord, like David, with all his might.* The more general custom of the ladies, as far as I observed, is to sit cross legged on the floor like a tailor. They are considerably addicted to the industry of spinning, but the mode has no resemblance to the spinning of our country. For a wheel, they have a straight stick about a foot long, rounded like the head of a spool. In the middle of the stick is a hole, through which the stick is fastened. Their mode of spinning with this very simple instrument reminded me strongly of the sport of my young days, spinning a top, for they give this spinning affair a twirl, and let it run on until it has lost its communicated motion to impart it anew. This shift for a spinning wheel they call necataro. They manufacture neither cotton nor wool into cloth, and depend altogether on foreign trade for their clothing. The greatest part of this supply comes over land from the United States. On the 2d, we started for San Tepec, through a country generally barren, though abounding in water. We saw plenty of bears, deer and antelope. Some of the first we killed, because we needed their flesh, and others we killed for the same reason that we were often obliged to kill Indians, that is, to mend their rude manners, in fiercely making at us, and to show them that we were not Spaniards, to give them the high sport of seeing us run. We arrived in the above named town on the 6th, and sold our furs. Here I met again some of the companions who came with me in the first instance from the United States. I enquired about others, whom I held in kind remembrance. Some had died by lingering diseases, and others by the fatal ball or arrow, so that out of 116 men, who came from the United States in 1824, there were not more than sixteen alive. Most of the fallen were as true men, and as brave as ever poised a rifle, and yet in these remote and foreign deserts found not even the benefit of a grave, but left their bodies to be torn by the wild beasts, or mangled by the Indians. When I heard the sad roll of the dead called over, and thought how often I had been in equal danger, I felt grateful to my Almighty Benefactor, that I was alive and in health. A strong perception of the danger of such courses as mine, as shown by the death of these men, came over my mind, and I made a kind of resolution, that I would return to my home, and never venture into the woods again. Among the number of my fallen companions, I ought not to forget the original leader of our company, Mr. Pratte, who died in his prime, of a lingering disease, in this place.

On the 10th, I commenced descending the Del Norte for the Copper Mines, in hopes once more to have the pleasure of embracing my father, and relate to him what I had suffered in body and mind, for neglecting to follow his wise and fatherly counsel. I now travelled slowly and by myself, and on the 12th, arrived at the house of my old friend the governor, who met me at his door, and gave me such an embrace, as to start the blood from my scarcely healed wound. I did not perceive at the moment, that his embrace had produced this effect, and entered the house, where I met Jacova, who received me with a partial embrace, and a manner of constrained politeness. She then sat down by me on the sopha, and began asking me many questions about my adventure since we had parted, often observing that I looked indisposed. At length she discovered the blood oozing through my waistcoat. She exclaimed, putting her hand on the wound, 'and good reason you have to look so, for you are wounded to death.' The look that accompanied this remark, I may not describe, for I would not be thought vain, and the stern character of my adventures forbids the intermixture of any thing of an entirely different aspect. I was not long, however, in convincing her that my wound was not really dangerous, and that I owed its present bleeding to the friendship of her father, a cause too flattering to be matter of regret. This drew from me a narrative of the occasion of my wound, which I related in the same simple terms and brief manner in which it is recorded in my journal. A long conversation of questions and replies ensued, of a nature and on subjects not necessary to relate. On the 10th, imploring God that we might meet again, we parted, and I resumed my journey, travelling slowly for my father's residence at the Copper Mines. I paused to rest and amuse myself in several of the small towns on my way. On the 26th, I had the high satisfaction once more to hold the hand of my father, and to find him in health and prosperity, and apparently with nowise abated affection for me, though I had rejected his counsels. This affection seemed to receive a warmer glow, when he heard my determination not to take to the woods again. I then in return wished to make myself acquainted with the true state of his affairs. He had established a vacherie on the river Membry where he kept stock. He had also opened a farm on the land which the old Appache chief had given him, which enabled him to raise grain for the use of his own establishment at the mines. He had actually a supply of grain in advance for the next year. He had made similar improvements upon every thing appertaining to the mines. The result of the whole seemed to be, that he was making money rapidly.

He still retained the Spaniard, of whom I have spoken before, as clerk and superintendent, believing him to be a man of real stability and weight of character, and placing the most entire reliance both upon his capacity and integrity. I was less sanguine, and had my doubts, though having seen no decided facts, upon which to ground them, I did not deem myself justified in honor to impart my doubts to my father.

On the 10th of February, my father requested me, on his account, to take a trip to Alopaz, to purchase for his establishment some wine and whiskey, which articles sell at the mines at a dollar and a half a pint. I started with one servant and six pack mules, each having a couple of small barrels fastened over their saddles, after the manner of our panniers. On the 16th, I reached the place, and purchased my cargo, but the weather was so inclement, that I thought it best not to return until it softened. I became acquainted with an American, married in this place. He was by pursuit a gunsmith, and had been up the upper Missouri with Col. Henry, and an old and noted trader on that river. The mutual story of what we two had seen and suffered, would probably appear incredible, and beyond the common order of things, to most people, except those who have hunted and trapped in the western parts of this continent, among the mountains and savages, and has nothing upon which to depend, but his own firmness of heart, the defence of his rifle, and the protection of the all present God. To such persons, the incidents which we mutually related, would all seem natural.

I remained here until the 1st of April. Spring in its peculiar splendor and glory in this country, had now wakened the fields and forests into life, and was extending its empire of verdure and flowers higher and higher up the mountains towards their snowy peaks. On this day I commenced my journey of return to the mines, with my servant and my cargo bestowed on my mules. Though the face of the country was all life and beauty, the roads so recently thawed, were exceedingly muddy and heavy. One of my mules in consequence gave out the second day. My servant packed the load of the tired mule upon his riding one, and walked on foot the remainder of the day. During the day we discovered fresh bear tracks in the wood, and my servant advised me to have my gun loaded. At this remark I put my hand in my shot pouch, and found but a single ball, and no lead with which to make more. At this discovery I saw at once the uselessness of self reproach of my own carelessness and neglect, though it will be easily imagined, what anxiety it created, aware that I had to travel through a long and dreary wilderness, replenished with grizzly bears and hostile Indians. Neither did I dare disclose a particle of what was passing in my mind to my servant, through fear that he would be discouraged, in which case, I knew his first step would be to turn back, and leave me to make the journey alone. It would have been impossible for me to do this, as we were both scarcely able to arrange the affairs of the journey. We advanced cautiously and were unmolested through the day. But I passed a most, uncomfortable night through fear of the bears, which, thawed out, were emerging from their winter dens with appetites rendered ravenous by their long winter fast. We and our mules would have furnished them a delicious feast, after the hunger of months. No sleep visited my eyes that night.

At ten o'clock of the 3d, we met a Spaniard on horse back. I accosted him in the usual terms, and asked if he had met any Indians on his way? He answered that he had, and that there was a body of friendly Appaches encamped near the road, at a distance of a little more than a league. I was delighted with this information, for I supposed I should be able to purchase a horse of them, on which I might mount my servant. While I was reflecting on this thought, my servant proposed to purchase his horse, and offered him a blanket in exchange. He instantly dismounted, took the blanket, and handed over the horse. Happy to see the poor fellow once more comfortably mounted, we bade the easy Spaniard adieu, and gaily resumed our journey. In a short time, according to his information, we saw the Indian camp near the road, from which their smokes were visible. We were solicitous to pass them unobserved and pushed on towards a stopping place, which we might reach at twelve o'clock. Here we stopped to enable our horses to rest, and eat, for the grass was fine. I ordered my servant to spancel the mules, and tether the horse to a shrub by a long rope. My gun reclined upon the packs. We ate a little ourselves, and afterwards I spread my blanket on the grass, close by the horses, and lay down to repose myself, though not intending to go to sleep. But the bright beams of the sun fell upon me in the midst of the green solitude, and I was soon in a profound sleep. A large straw hat on the side of my face shaded my head from the sun.

While enjoying this profound sleep, four of the Appaches came in pursuit of us. It seems our Spaniard had stolen his horse from them, a few hours before. They came upon us in possession of the horse, and supposed me the thief. One of them rode close to me, and made a dart at me with his spear. The stroke was aimed at my neck, and passed through my hat, nailing it to the ground just back of my neck, which the cold steel barely touched. It awakened me, and I sprang to my feet. Four Indians on horse back were around me, and the spear, which had been darted at me, still nailed my hat to the ground. I immediately seized the spear and elevated it towards the Indian, who in turn made his horse spring out of my reach. I called my servant, who had seen the Indians approaching me, and had hidden himself in the bushes. I then sprang to my gun, at the distance of ten or fifteen paces. When I had reached and cocked it, I presented it at an Indian who was unsheathing his fusil. As soon as he discovered my piece elevated, he threw himself from his horse, fell on his knees, and called for mercy. What surprized me, and arrested my fire, was to hear him call me by my Christian name. I returned my rifle to my shoulder and asked him who he was? He asked me, if I did not know Targuarcha? He smote his breast as he asked the question. The name was familiar. The others dismounted, and gathered round. An understanding ensued. When they learned the manner in which we came by the horse, their countenances were expressive of real sorrow. They had supposed me a

Spaniard, as they said, and the thief of their horse. They begged me not to be angry, with a laughable solicitude, offering me the horse as the price of friendship. Above all, they were anxious that I should not relate the affair to my father. They seemed to have an awe of him, resembling that due to the Supreme Being. This awe he had maintained by his steady deportment, and keeping up in their minds the impression, that he always had a large army at command, and was able, and disposed at the first insult, or breach of the treaty on their part, to bring it upon them to their utter destruction.

To all their apologies and kind words and excuses, I answered that I knew them as well as any other man, and that they were not to expect to atone for a dastardly attempt to take my life, and coming within a hair's breadth of taking it, by offering me a present, that I believed that they knew who I was, and only wanted an opportunity, when they could steal upon me unarmed, and kill me, as they had probably committed many other similar murders; that they were ready enough to cry pardon, as soon as they saw me handling my rifle, hoping to catch me asleep again, but that they would henceforward be sure to find me on my guard.

At this the Indian who had darted the spear at me, exclaimed that he loved me as a brother, and would at any occasion risk his life in my defence. I then distinctly recollected him, and that I had been two months with the band, to which he belonged, roving in the woods about the mines. Targuarcha had shown a singular kind of attachment to me, waiting upon me as if I had been his master. I was perfectly convinced that he had thrust his spear at me in absolute ignorance, that it was me. Still I thought it necessary to instil a lesson of caution into them, not to kill any one for an imagined enemy, until they were sure that he was guilty of the supposed wrong. Consequently I dissembled distrust, and told him, that it looked very little like friendship, to dart a spear at the neck of a sleeping man, and that to tell the plain truth, I had as little confidence in him, as a white bear. At this charge of treachery, he came close to me, and looking affectionately in my face, exclaimed in Spanish, 'if you think me such a traitor, kill me. Here is my breast. Shoot. At the same time he bared his breast with his hand, with such a profound expression of sorrow in his countenance, as no one was ever yet able to dissemble. I was softened to pity, and told him that I sincerely forgave him, and that I would henceforward consider him my friend, and not inform my father what he had done. They all promised that they would never attempt to kill any one again, until they knew who it was, and were certain that he was guilty of the crime charged upon him. Here we all shook hands, and perfect confidence was restored.

I now called again for my servant, and after calling till I was hoarse, he at length crawled from behind the bushes, like a frightened turkey or deer, and looking wild with terror. He had the satisfaction of being heartily laughed at, as a person who had deserted his master in the moment of peril. They are not a people to spare the feelings of any one who proves himself a coward by deserting his place. They bestowed that term upon him without mercy. All his reply was, sullenly to set himself to packing his mules.

Now arose a friendly controversy about the horse, they insisting that I should take it, as the price of our renewed friendship, and I, that I would not take it, except on hire or purchase. They were obstinate in persisting that I should take the horse along with me, and finally promised if I would consent, that they would return to camp and bring their families, and escort me to the mines. To this I consented, though I had first taken the precaution to procure some rifle balls of them. We then resumed our journey, and travelled on without incident till the 5th, when they overtook us, and we travelled on very amicably together, until we reached the Membry, which runs a south course, and is lost in a wide arid plain, after winding its way through prodigious high, craggy mountains. It affords neither fish nor beavers, but has wide and rich bottoms, of which as I have mentioned, they gave my father as much as he chose to cultivate.

From the point where the road crosses this river to the mines, is reckoned 15 miles. Here we met the chief of this band of the Appaches, with a great number of his people. They were all delighted to see us, and not the less so, when they discovered that we had spirituous liquors, of which they are fond to distraction. There was no evading the importunities of the chief to stay all night with him, he promising, if I would that he would go in next day with me to my father. I had scarcely arrived an hour, when I saw the Indian, that had darted his spear at me, come to the chief with shirt laid aside, and his back bare. He handed the chief a stout switch, asking him to whip him. The chief immediately flayed away about 50 lashes, the blood showing at every stroke. He then asked me, if the thing had been done to my satisfaction? I told him that I had no satisfaction to demand. The chief who had whipped him, was positively ignorant of the crime, for which he had suffered this infliction. But he said, when one of his men begged a flogging, he took it for granted, that it was not for the good deeds of the sufferer, and that he deserved it. When I learned that it was a voluntary penance for his offence to me on the road, I felt really sorry, and made him a present of a quart of whiskey, as an internal unction for the smart of his stripes, a medicine in high esteem among the Indians in such cases.

When we arrived at the mines, the old chief enquired what had been done to me on the road? As soon as he was informed, he sprang up, tore his hair, and seized a gun to shoot the poor culprit. I interposed between them, and convinced him, that Taguarcha had not been really to blame in any thing but his haste, and that if I had really been the thief, he would have done right to kill me, and get back his horse, and that not even my father would have thought the worst of him, but that we should both now like him better, as well as his people, for what had happened.

On the 15th, my father proposed to give me a sum of money, with which to go into the United States to purchase goods for the mines. The laborers much preferred goods, at the customary rate, to money, and the profit at that rate was at least 200 per cent on the cost. I was reluctant to do this, for my thoughts still detained me in that country. It was then concluded to send the before mentioned Spanish clerk on the commission, with sufficient money to pay for the goods, consigned to merchants in Santa Fe, to be purchased there, provided a sufficient quantity had recently arrived from the United States to furnish an assortment, and if not, he was recommended to merchants in St. Louis, to make the purchases there.

On the 18th, he started under these orders, under the additional one, that on his arriving at Santa Fe, and learning the state of things there, he should immediately write to the mines to that effect. In the customary order of things, this letter was to be expected in one month from the day he left the mines. After he was departed, he left none behind to doubt his truth and honor, nor was there the least suspicion of him, until the time had elapsed without a letter. A dim surmise began then to grow up, that he had run off with the money. We were still anxiously waiting for the intelligence. During this interval I had occupied the place of clerk in his stead. It was now insisted that I should go in search of the villain, who had obtained a good start of a month ahead of us, and 30,000 dollars value in gold bullion to expedite his journey. On the 20th, I started in the search, which I confess seemed hopeless, for he was a man of infinite ingenuity, who could enact Spaniard, which he really was, or Russian, Frenchman or Englishman, as he spoke the languages of these people with fluency. Still I pushed on with full purpose to make diligent and unsparing search.

On the 30th, I arrived at Santa Fe. I made the most anxious and careful enquiry for him, and gave the most accurate descriptions of him there. But no one had seen or heard of such a person. I sorrowfully retraced my steps down the Rio del Norte, now without a doubt of his treachery, and bitterly reflecting on myself for my heedless regard of my father's request. Had I done it, we had both secured an affluence. Now I clearly foresaw poverty and misfortune opening before us in the future. For myself I felt little, as I was young and the world before me; and I felt secure about taking care of myself. My grief was for my father and his companions, who had toiled night and day with unwearied assiduity, to accumulate something for their dear and helpless families, whom they had left in Missouri; and for the love of whom they had ventured into this rough and unsettled country, full of thieves and murderers. My father in particular, had left a large and motherless family, at a time of life to be wholly unable to take care of themselves, and altogether dependent on him for subsistence. There is no misery like self condemnation; and I suffered it in all its bitterness. The reflections that followed upon learning the full extent of the disaster, which I could but charge in some sense upon myself, came, as such reflections generally come, too late.

I arrived at the Passo del Norte on the 10th of May, and repeated the same descriptions and enquiries to no purpose.—Not a trace remained of him here; and I almost concluded to abandon the search in despair. I could imagine but one more chance. The owner of the mines lived at Chihuahua. As a forlorn hope I concluded to proceed to that city, and inform the governor of our misfortune. So I pushed to Chihuahua, where I arrived on the 23d.

I found the owner of the mines in too much anxiety and grief of mind on his own account, to be cool enough to listen the concerns of others. The President of the Mexican republic had issued orders, that all Spaniards born in old Spain, should be expelled from the Mexican country, giving them but a month's notice, in which to settle their affairs and dispose of their property. He being one of that class, had enough to think of on his own account. However, when he heard of our misfortune, he appeared to be concerned. He then touched upon the critical state of his own affairs. Among other things, he said he had all along hoped that my father was able and disposed to purchase those mines. He had, therefore, a motive personal to himself, to make him regret my father's loss and inability to make the purchase. He was now obliged to sell them at any sacrifice, and had but a very short time in which to settle his affairs, and leave the country. He requested me to be ready to start the next day in company with him to the mines.

Early on the 24th, we started with relays of horses and mules. As we travelled very rapidly we arrived at the mines on the 30th, where I found my father and his companions in the utmost anxiety to learn something what had happened to me. When they discovered the owner of the mines, whose name was Don Francisco Pablo de Lagera, they came forth in a body with countenances full of joy. That joy was changed to sadness, as soon as Don Pablo informed them the object of his visit. They perceived in a moment, that nothing now remained for them but to settle their affairs, and search for other situations in the country, or return to the United States in a worse condition than when they left it. My father determined at once not to think of this. Nothing seemed so feasible, and conformable to his pursuits, as a trapping expedition. With the pittance that remained to him, after all demands against the firm were discharged, and the residue according to the articles of agreement divided, he purchased trapping equipments for four persons, himself included. The other three he intended to hire to trap for him.

On the 1st of July, all these matters had been arranged, and my father and myself started for Santa Fe, with a view to join the first company that should start on a trapping expedition from that place. On the 10th, we arrived at Santa Fe, where we remained until the 22d, when a company of thirty men were about to commence an expedition of that sort down Red river. My father joined this company, and in the name of the companions made application for license of safe transit through the province of Chihuahua, and Sonora, through which runs the Red river, on which we meant to trap. The governor gave us a passport in the following terms:

Custom House of the frontier town of Santa Fe, in the teritory of New Mexico.

### Custom House Certificate

Allow Sylvester Pattie, to pursue his journey with certain beasts, merchandize and money, in the direction of Chihuahua and Sonora; to enter in beasts and money an amount equal to this invoice, in whatsoever place he shall appear, according to the rules of the Custom House, on his passage; and finally let him return this permit to the government of this city in            days. Do this under the established penalties.

Given at Santa Fe, in New Mexico.

RAMON ATTREN

*September 22d,* 1829

On the 23d, my father was chosen captain or commander of the company, and we started on our expedition. We retraced our steps down the del Norte, and by the mines to the river Helay, on which we arrived on the 6th of October, and began to descend it, setting our traps as we went, near our camp, whenever we saw signs of beavers. But our stay on this stream was short, for it had been trapped so often, that there were but few beavers remaining, and those few were exceedingly shy. We therefore pushed on to some place where they might be more abundant, and less shy. We left this river on the 12th, and on the 15th reached Beaver river. Here we found them in considerable numbers, and we concluded to proceed in a south course, and trap the river in its downward course. But to prevent the disagreement and insubordination which are apt to spring up in these associations, my father drew articles of agreement, purporting that we should trap in partnership, and that the first one who should show an open purpose to separate from the company, or desert it, should be shot dead; and that if any one should disobey orders, he should be tried by a jury of our number, and if found guilty should be fined fifty dollars, to be paid in fur. To this instrument we all agreed, and signed our names.

The necessity of some such compact had been abundantly discovered in the course of our experience. Men bound only by their own will and sense of right, to the duties of such a sort of partnership are certain to grow restless, and to form smaller clans, disposed to dislike and separate from each other, in parties of one by one to three by three. They thus expose themselves to be cut up in detail by the savages, who comprehend all their movements, and are ever watchful for an opportunity to show their hatred of the whites to be fixed and inextinguishable. The following are some of the more common causes of separation: Men of incompatible tempers and habits are brought together; and such expeditions call out innumerable occasions to try this disagreement of character. Men, hungry, naked, fatigued, and in constant jeopardy, are apt to be ill-tempered, especially when they arrive at camp, and instead of being allowed to throw themselves on the ground, and sleep, have hard duties of cooking, and keeping guard, and making breast-works assigned them. But the grand difficulty is the following. In a considerable company, half its numbers can catch as many beavers as all. But the half that keep guard, and cook, perform duties as necessary and important to the whole concern, as the others. It always happens too, in these expeditions, that there are some infinitely more dextrous and skilful in trapping and hunting than others. These capabilities are soon brought to light. The expert know each other, and feel a certain superiority over the inexpert. They know that three or four such, by themselves, will take as many beavers as a promiscuous company of thirty, and in fact, all that a stream affords. A perception of their own comparative importance, a keen sense of self interest, which sharpens in the desert, the mere love of roving in the wild license of the forest, and a capacity to become hardened by these scenes to a perfect callousness to all fear and sense of danger, until it actually comes; such passions are sufficient to thicken causes of separation among such companions in the events of every day.

Sad experience has made me acquainted with all these causes of disunion and dissolution of such companies. I have learned them by wounds and sufferings, by toil and danger of every sort, by wandering about in the wild and desolate mountains, alone and half starved, merely because two or three bad men had divided our company, strong and sufficient to themselves in union, but miserable, and exposed to almost certain ruin in separation. Made painfully acquainted with all these facts by experience, my father adopted this expedient in the hope that it would be something like a remedy for them.

But notwithstanding this, and the prudence and energy of my father's character, disunion soon began to spring up in our small party. Almost on the outset of our expedition, we began to suffer greatly for want of provisions. We were first compelled to kill and eat our dogs, and then six of our horses. This to me was the most cruel task of all. To think of waiting for the night to kill and eat the poor horse that had borne us over deserts and mountains, as hungry as ourselves, and strongly and faithfully attached to us, was no easy task to the heart of a Kentucky hunter. One evening, after a hard day's travel, my saddle horse was selected by lot to be killed. The poor animal stood saddled and bridled before us, and it fell to my lot to kill it. I loved this horse, and he seemed to have an equal attachment for me. He was remarkably kind to travel, and easy to ride, and spirited too. When he stood tied in camp among the rest, if I came any where near him, he would fall neighing for me. When I held up the bridle towards him, I could see consent and good will in his eye. As I raised my gun to my face, all these recollections rushed to my thoughts. My pulses throbbed, and my eyes grew dim. The animal was gazing me, with a look of steady kindness, in the face. My head whirled, and was dizzy, and my gun fell. After a moment for recovery, I offered a beaver skin to any one who would shoot him down. One was soon found at this price, and my horse fell! It so happened that this was the last horse we killed. Well was it for us that we had these surplus horses. Had it been otherwise, we should all have perished with hunger.

It was now the 15th of November, and while the horse flesh lasted, we built a canoe, so that we could trap on both sides of the river; for it is here too broad and deep to be fordable on horseback. One of our number had already been drowned, man and horse, in attempting to swim the river. A canoe is a great advantage, where the beavers are wild; as the trapper can thus set his traps along the shore without leaving his scent upon the ground about it.

On the 17th, our canoe was finished, and another person and myself took some traps in it, and floated down the river by water, while the rest of the company followed along the banks by land. In this way, what with the additional supply which the canoe enabled our traps to furnish, and a chance deer or wolf that Providence sometimes threw in our way, with caution and economy we were tolerably supplied with provisions; and the company travelled on with a good degree of union and prosperity, until the 26th.

Here the greater part of the company expressed disinclination to following our contemplated route any longer. That is, they conceived the route to the mouth of the Helay, and up Red river of California too long and tedious, and too much exposed to numerous and hostile Indians. They, therefore, determined to quit the Helay, and strike over to Red river by a direct route across the country. My father reminded them of their article. They assured him they did not consider themselves bound by it, and that they were a majority, against which nothing could be said. My father and myself still persevered in following the original plan. Two of the men had been hired on my father's account. He told them he was ready to pay them up to that time, and dismiss them, to go where they chose. They observed, that now that the company had commenced separating, they believed that in a short time, there would be no stronger party together than ours; that they had as good a disposition to risk their lives with us, as with any division of our number, and that they would stay by us to the death. After this speech four others of the company volunteered to remain with us, and we took them in as partners.

On the 27th, we divided the hunt, and all expressing the same regret at the separation, and heartily wishing each other all manner of prosperity, we shook hands and parted! We were now reduced to eight in number. We made the most solemn pledges to stand by each other unto death, and adopted the severest caution, of which we had been too faithfully taught the necessity. We tied our horses every night, and encamped close by them, to prevent their being stolen by the Indians. Their foot-prints were thick and fresh in our course, and we could see their smokes at no great distance north of us. We were well aware that they were hostile, and watching their opportunity to pounce upon us, and we kept ourselves ready for action, equally day and night. We now took an ample abundance of beavers to supply us with meat, in consequence of our reduced numbers. Our horses also fared well, for we cut plenty of cotton-wood trees, the bark of which serves them for food nearly as well as corn. We thus travelled on prosperously, until we reached the junction of the Helay with Red river.—Here we found the tribe of Umeas, who had shown themselves very friendly to the company in which I had formerly passed them, which strongly inspired confidence in them at present. Some of them could speak the Spanish language. We made many inquiries of them, our object being to gain information of the distance of the Spanish settlements. We asked them where they obtained the cloth they wore around their loins? They answered, from the Christians on the coast of the California. We asked if there were any Christians living on Red river? They promptly answered yes. This information afterwards proved a source of error and misfortune to us, though our motive for inquiry at this time was mere curiosity.

It was now the 1st of December; and at mid-day we began to see the imprudence of spending the remainder of the day and the ensuing night with such numbers of Indians, however friendly in appearance. We had a tolerable fund of experience, in regard to the trust we might safely repose in the red skins; and knew that caution is the parent of security. So we packed up, and separated from them. Their town was on the opposite shore of Red river. At our encampment upwards of two hundred of them swam over the river and visited us, all apparently friendly. We allowed but a few of them to approach our camp at a time, and they were obliged to lay aside their arms. In the midst of these multitudes of fierce, naked, swarthy savages, eight of us seemed no more than a little patch of snow on the side of one of the black mountains. We were perfectly aware how critical was our position, and determined to intermit no prudence or caution.

To interpose as great a distance as possible between them and us, we marched that evening sixteen miles, and encamped on the banks of the river. The place of encampment was a prairie, and we drove stakes fast in the earth, to which we tied our horses in the midst of green grass, as high as a man's head, and within ten feet of our own fire. Unhappily we had arrived too late to make a pen for our horses, or a breast work for ourselves. The sky was gloomy. Night and storm were settling upon us, and it was too late to complete these important arrangements. In a short time the storm poured upon us, and the night became so dark that we could not see our hand before us. Apprehensive of an attempt to steal our horses, we posted two sentinels, and the remaining six lay down under our wet blankets, and the pelting of the sky, to such sleep as we might get, still preserving a little fire. We were scarcely alseep before we were aroused by the snorting of our horses and mules. We all sprang to our arms, and extinguished our little fire. We could not see a foot before us, and we groped about our camp feeling our way among the horses and mules. We could discover nothing; so concluding they might have been frightened by the approach of a bear or some other wild animal, some of us commenced rekindling our fires, and the rest went to sleep. But the Indians had crawled among our horses, and had cut or untied the rope by which each one was bound. The horses were then all loose. They then instantly raised in concert, their fiendish yell. As though heaven and earth were in concert against us, the rain began to pour again, accompanied with howling gusts of wind, and the fiercest gleams of lightning, and crashes of thunder. Terrified alike by the thunder and the Indians, our horses all took to flight, and the Indians repeating yell upon yell, were close at their heels. We sallied out after them, and fired at the noises, though we could see nothing. We pursued with the utmost of our speed to no purpose, for they soon

reached the open prairie, where we concluded they were joined
by other Indians on horseback, who pushed our horses still faster;
and soon the clattering of their heels and the yells of their accursed
pursuers began to fade, and become indistinct in our ears.

Our feelings and reflections as we returned to camp were of the
gloomiest kind. We were one thousand miles from the point whence
we started, and without a single beast to bear either our property
or ourselves. The rain had past. We built us a large fire. As we stood
round it we discussed our deplorable condition, and our future al-
ternatives. Something was to be done. We all agreed to the
proposition of my father, which was, early in the morning to
pursue the trails of our beasts, and if we should overtake the
thieves, to retake the horses, or die in the attempt; and that, failing
in that, we should return, swim the river, attack their town, and
kill as many of the inhabitants as we could; for that it was better
to die by these Indians, after we had killed a good number of them,
than to starve, or be killed by Indians who had not injured us, and
when we could not defend ourselves.

Accordingly, early in the morning of the 2d, we started on the
trail in pursuit of the thieves. We soon arrived at a point where the
Indians, departing from the plain, had driven them up a chasm of
the mountains. Here they had stopped, and caught them, divided
them, and each taken a different route with his plundered horses.
We saw in a moment that it was impossible to follow them farther
to any purpose. We abandoned the chase, and returned to our camp
to execute the second part of our plan. When we arrived there, we
stopped for a leisure meal of beaver meat. When we had bestowed
ourselves to this dainty resort, a Dutchman with us broke the
gloomy silence of our eating, by observing that we had better stuff
ourselves to the utmost; for that it would probably, be the last
chance we should have at beaver meat. We all acquiesced in this observation, which though made in jest, promised to be a sober truth,
by eating as heartily as possible. When we had finished our meal,
which looked so likely to be the last we should enjoy together, we
made rafts to which we tied our guns, and pushing them onward
before us, we thus swam the river. Having reached the opposite
shore, we shouldered our rifles, and steered for the town, at which

we arrived about two in the afternoon. We marched up to the numerous assemblage of huts in a manner as reckless and undaunted
as though we had nothing to apprehend. In fact, when we arrived
at it, we found it to contain not a single living being, except one
miserable, blind, deaf, and decrepid old man, not unlike one that I
described in a hostile former visit to an Indian village. Our
exasperation of despair inclined us to kill even him. My father for-
bade. He apparently heard nothing and cared for nothing, as he saw
nothing. His head was white with age, and his eyes appeared to
have been gouged out. He may have thought himself all the while
in the midst of his own people. We discovered a plenty of their
kind of food, which consisted chiefly of acorn mush. We then set
fire to the village, burning every hut but that which contained the
old man. Being built of flags and grass, they were not long in reducing to ashes. We then returned to our camp, re-swimming the river,
and reaching the camp before dark.

We could with no certainty divine the cause of their having
evacuated their town, though we attributed it to fear of us. The occurrences of the preceding day strengthened us in this impression.
While they remained with us, one of our men happened to fire off
his gun. As though they never had heard such a noise before, they
all fell prostrate on the earth, as though they had all been shot.
When they arose, they would all have taken to flight, had we not
detained them and quieted their fears.

Our conversation with these Indians of the day before, now recurred to our recollections, and we congratulated ourselves on having been so inquisitive as to obtain the now important information,
that there were Spanish settlements on the river below us. Driven
from the resource of our horses, we happily turned our thoughts to
another. We had all the requisite tools to build canoes, and directly
around us was suitable timber of which to make them. It was
a pleasant scheme to soothe our dejection, and prevent our lying
down to the sleep of despair. But this alternative determined upon,
there remained another apprehension sufficient to prevent our enjoying quiet repose. Our fears were, that the unsheltered Indians,
horse-stealers and all, would creep upon us in the night, and mas-

sacre us all. But the night passed without any disturbance from them.

On the morning of the 3d, the first business in which we engaged, was to build ourselves a little fort, sufficient for defence against the Indians. This finished, we cut down two trees suitable for canoes, and accomplished these important objects in one day. During this day we kept one man posted in the top of a tall tree, to descry if any Indians were approaching us in the distance. On the morning of the fourth we commenced digging out our canoes, and finished and launched two. These were found insufficient to carry our furs. We continued to prepare, and launch them, until we had eight in the water. By uniting them in pairs by a platform, we were able to embark with all our furs and traps, without any extra burden, except a man and the necessary traps for each canoe. We hid our saddles, hoping to purchase horses at the settlements, and return this way.

We started on the 9th, floating with the current, which bore us downward at the rate of four miles an hour. In the evening we passed the burnt town, the ruins of which still threw up smouldering smoke. We floated about 30 miles, and in the evening encamped in the midst of signs of beavers. We set 40 traps, and in the morning of the 10th caught 36 beavers, an excellent night's hunt. We concluded from this encouraging commencement, to travel slowly, and in hunters phrase, trap the river clear; that is, take all that could be allured to come to the bait. The river, below its junction with the Helay, is from 2 to 300 yards wide, with high banks, that have dilapidated by falling in. Its course is west, and its timber chiefly cotton-wood, which in the bottoms is lofty and thick set. The bottoms are from six to ten miles wide. The soil is black, and mixed with sand, though the bottoms are subject to inundation in the flush waters of June. This inundation is occasioned by the melting of the snow on the mountains about its head waters.

We now floated pleasantly downward at our leisure, having abundance of the meat of fat beavers. We began in this short prosperity, to forget the loss of our horses, and to consider ourselves quite secure from the Indians. But on the 12th, at midday, by mere

accident, we happened, some way below us, to discover two
Indians perched in a tree near the river bank, with their bows and
arrows in readiness, waiting evidently until we should float close by
them, to take off some of us with their arrows. We betrayed no signs
of having seen them, but sat with our guns ready for a fair shot.
When we had floated within a little short of a hundred yards, my
father and another of the company gave them a salute, and brought
them both tumbling down the branches, reminding us exactly of
the fall of a bear or a turkey. They made the earth sound when
they struck it. Fearful that they might be part of an ambush, we
pulled our canoes to the opposite shore, and some of us climbed
trees, from which we could command a view of both shores. We
became satisfied that these two were alone, and we crossed over to
their bodies. We discovered that they were of the number that had
stolen our horses, by the fact, that they were bound round the waist
with some of the hemp ropes with which our horses had been tied.
We hung the bodies of the thieves from a tree, with the product of
their own thefts. Our thoughts were much relieved by the discovery of this fact, for though none of us felt any particular forbearance towards Indians under any circumstances, it certainly would
have pained us to have killed Indians that had never disturbed us.
But there could be no compunction for having slain these two
thieves, precisely at the moment that they were exulting in the
hope of getting a good shot at us. Beside they alarmed our false
security, and learned us a lesson to keep nearer the middle of the
river.

We continued to float slowly downwards, trapping beavers on
our way almost as fast as we could wish. We sometimes brought in
60 in a morning. The river at this point is remarkably circuitous,
and has a great number of islands, on which we took beavers. Such
was the rapid increase of our furs, that our present crafts in a few
days were insufficient to carry them, and we were compelled to stop
and make another canoe. We have advanced between 60 and 70 miles
from the point where we built the other canoes. We find the timber
larger, and not so thick. There are but few wild animals that belong
to the country farther up, but some deer, panthers, foxes and wild-
cats. Of birds there are great numbers, and many varieties, most

of which I have never before seen. We killed some wild geese and pelicans, and likewise an animal not unlike the African leopard, which came into our camp, while we were at work upon the canoe. It was the first we had ever seen.

We finished our canoe on the 17th, and started on the 20th. This day we saw ten Indians on a sand bar, who fled into the woods at the sight of us. We knew them to be different people from those who had stolen our horses, both by their size and their different manner of wearing their hair. The heads of these were shaved close, except a tuft, which they wore on the top of their head, and which they raised erect, as straight as an arrow. The Umeas are of gigantic stature from six to seven feet high. These only average five feet and a half. They go perfectly naked, and have dark complexions, which I imagine is caused by the burning heat of the sun. The weather is as hot here at this time, as I ever experienced. We were all very desirous to have a talk with these Indians, and enquire of them, how near we were to the Spanish settlements; and whether they were immediately on the bank, for we began to be fearful that we had pssed them.

Three days passed without our having any opportunity of conversation with them. But early on the morning of the 24th, we found some families yet asleep in their wigwams, near the water's edge. Our approach to them was so imperceptible and sudden, that they had no chance to flee. They were apparently frightened to insanity. They surrendered without making any further effort to escape. While they stared at us in terrified astonishment; we made them comprehend that we had no design to kill, or injure them. We offered them meat, and made signs that we wished to smoke with them. They readily comprehended us, and the ghastliness of terror began to pass from their countenances. The women and children were yet screaming as if going into convulsions. We made signs to the men to have them stop this annoying noise. This we did by putting our hands to our mouths. They immediately uttered something to the women and children which made them still. The pipe was then lit, and smoking commenced. They puffed the smoke towards the sky, pointed thither, and uttered some words, of course unintelligible to us. They then struck themselves on the breast, and afterwards on the forehead. We understood this to be a sort of religious appeal to the Supreme Being, and it showed more like reverence to him, than any thing we had yet seen among the Indians; though I have seen none but what admit that there is a master of life, whom they call by a name to that import, or that of Great Spirit.

When the smoking was finished, we began to enquire of them by signs, how far we were from the Spanish settlement? This we effected by drawing an image of a cow and sheep in the sand and then imitating the noise of each kind of domestic animals, that we supposed the Spaniards would have. They appeared to understand us, for they pointed west, and then at our clothes, and then at our naked skin. From this we inferred that they wished to say that farther to the west lived white people, as we were. And this was all we could draw from them on that subject. We then asked them, if they had ever seen white people before? This we effected by stretching open our eyes with our fingers, and pointing to them, and then looking vehemently in that direction, while we pointed west with our fingers. They shook their heads in the negative. Then stretching their own ears, as we had our eyes, striking themselves on the breast, and pointing down the river, they pronounced the word *wechopa*. This we afterwards understood implied, that their chief lived lower down the river, and that they had heard from him, that he had seen these people.

We gave the women some old shirts, and intimated to them as well as we could, that it was the fashion of the women to cover themselves in our country, for these were in a state of the most entire nudity. But they did not seem rightly to comprehend our wish. Many of the women were not over sixteen, and the most perfect figures I have ever seen, perfectly straight and symmetrical, and the hair of some hanging nearly to their heels. The men are exceedingly active, and have bright countenances, and quick apprehension. We gave them more meat, and then started. They followed our course along the bank, until night. As soon as we landed, they were very officious in gathering wood, and performing other offices for us. They showed eager curiosity in examining our arms, and appeared to understand their use. When my father struck fire with

his pistol, they gave a start, evidencing a mixture of astonishment
and terror, and then re-examined the pistol, apparently solicitous to
discover how the fire was made. My father bade me take my rifle,
and shoot a wild goose, that was sitting about in the middle of the
river. He then showed them the goose, and pointed at me, as I was
creeping to a point where I might take a fair shot. They all gazed
with intense curiosity, first at me, and then at the goose, until I fired.
At the moment of the reports some fell flat on the ground, and the
rest ran for the bushes, as though Satan was behind them. As soon
as the fallen had recovered from their amazement, they also fled.
Some of our company stopped them, by seizing some, and holding
them, and showing them that the goose was dead, and the manner
in which it had been killed. They gradually regained confidence
and composure, and called to their companions in the bushes. They
also came forth, one by one, and when the nature of the report of
the gun had been explained to them, they immediately swam into
the river and brought out the goose. When they carried it round
and showed it to their companions, carefully pointing out the ball
hole in the goose, it is impossible to show more expressive gestures,
cries and movements of countenances indicative of wonder and
astonishment, than they exhibited. The night which we passed with
them, passed away pleasantly, and to the satisfaction of all parties.
In the morning their attention and curiosity were again highly excited, when we brought in our beavers, which amounted in number to thirty-six. After we had finished skinning them, we left the
ample supply of food furnished by the bodies of the beavers, in
token of our friendship, to these Indians, and floated on. On the
27th, we arrived at the residence of the chief. We perceived that
they had made ready for our reception. They had prepared a feast
for us by killing a number of fatted dogs. As soon as we landed, the
chief came to us, accompanied by two subordinate chiefs. When
arrived close to us, he exclaimed, *wechapa,* striking himself on
the breast, pointing to our company, and repeating the same phrase.
We understood from this, that he wished to know who was our
captain? We all pointed to my father, to whom the chief immediately advanced, and affectionately embracing him, invited us to
enter his wigwam. We shouldered our rifles, and all followed this

venerable looking man to his abode. There he had prepared several earthen dishes, in which the flesh of young and fat dogs was served up, but without salt or bread. We all sat down. The pipe was lit, and we, and the thirty Indians present began to smoke. While we were smoking, they used many gesticulations and signs, the purport of which we could not make out, though, as they pointed often at us, we supposed we were the subjects of their gestures. The pipe was then taken away, and the chief arose, and stood in the centre of the circle which we formed by the manner in which we all sat around the fire. He then made a long harangue, and as we understood not a word, to us rather a tedious one. We took care to make as many gestures indicative of understanding it, as though we had comprehended every word.

The oration finished, a large dish of the choice dog's flesh was set before us, and signs were made to us to eat. Having learned not to be delicate or disobliging to our savage host, we fell to work upon the ribs of the domestic barkers. When we had eaten to satisfaction, the chief arose, and puffing out his naked belly, and striking it with his hand, very significantly inquired by this sign, if we had eaten enough? When we had answered in the affirmative, by our mode of making signs, he then began to enquire of us, as we understood it, who we were, and from whence we came, and what was our business in that country? All this we interpreted, and replied to by signs as significant as we could imagine. He continued to enquire of us by signs, if we had met with no misfortunes on our journey, calling over the names of several Indian tribes in that part of the country, among which we distinctly recognized the name of the Umeas? When he mentioned this name, it was with such a lowering brow and fierce countenance as indicated clearly that he was at war with them. He responded to these marks of dislike by an equal show of detestation by making the gesture of seeming desirous to shoot at them, and with the bitterest look of anger that we could assume; making him understand that they had stolen our horses. We made signs of intelligence that he comprehended us, and made us sensible of his deep hatred, by giving us to understand that they had killed many of his people, and taken many more prisoners; and that he had retaliated by killing and taking as many

Umeas. He pointed at the same time to two small children, and exclaimed Umea! We pointed at them with our guns, and gave him to understand, that we had killed two of them. Some of our people had brought their scalps along. We gave them to him, and he, looking first towards us, and then fiercely at them, seemed to ask if these were the scalps of his enemies? To which we replied, yes.— He then seized the hair of the scalps with his teeth, and shook them, precisely as I have seen a dog any small game that it had killed. He then gave such a yell of delight, as collected all his people round him in a moment, and such rejoicing, yelling, and dancing ensued from both men and women, as I shall forbear to attempt to describe. Their deportment on this occasion was in fact much nearer bestial than human. They would leave the dance round the scalps in turn, to come and caress us, and then return and resume their dance.

The remainder of this day and the ensuing night passed in being in some sense compelled to witness this spectacle. In the morning of the 28th, when we brought in the contents of our traps, we found we had taken twenty-eight beavers. When my father enquired this morning anew for the direction of the Spanish settlements, and how far they were distant, we could make out from the signs of the chief no information more exact than this. He still pointed to the west, and then back at us.—He then made a very tolerable imitation of the rolling and breaking of the surf on the sea shore. Below he drew a cow and a sheep. From this we were satisfied that there were Spanish settlements west of us; and our conclusion was, that they could not be very distant.

At mid-day we bade these friendly Indians farewell, and resumed our slow progress of floating slowly down the stream, still setting our traps, whenever we found any indications of beavers. We met with no striking incident, and experienced no molestation until January 1st, 1828. On this day we once more received a shower of arrows from about fifty Indians of a tribe called Pipi, of whom we were cautioned to beware by the friendly Indians we had last left. I forgot at the time to mention the name of that people, when speaking of them, and repeat it now. It is Cocopa. When the Pipi fired upon us, we were floating near the middle of the river. We immediately commenced pulling for the opposite shore, and were soon out of the reach of their arrows, without any individual having been wounded. As soon as our crafts touched the shore, we sprang upon the bank, took fair aim, and showed them the difference between their weapons and ours, by levelling six of them. The remainder fell flat, and began to dodge and skulk on all fours, as though the heavens had been loaded with thunder and mill stones, which were about to rain on them from the clouds.

We re-loaded our guns, and rowed over to the opposite, and now deserted shore. The fallen lay on the sand beach, some of them not yet dead. We found twenty three bows and the compliment of arrows, most of them belonging to the fugitives. The bows are six feet in length, and made of a very tough and elastic kind of wood, which the Spaniards call *Tarnio*. They polish them down by rubbing them on a rough rock. The arrows are formed of a reed grass, and of the same length with their bows, with a foot of hard wood stuck in the end of the cavity of the reed, and a flint spike fitted on the end of it.—They have very large and erect forms, and black skins. Their long black hair floats in tresses down their backs, and to the termination of each tress is fastened a snail shell. In other respects their dress consists of their birth-day suit; in other words, they are perfectly naked. The river seems here to run upon a high ridge; for we can see from our crafts a great distance back into the country, which is thickly covered with musquito and other low and scrubby trees. The land is exceedingly marshy, and is the resort of numerous flocks of swans, and blue cranes. The rackoons are in such numbers, that they cause us to lose a great many beavers, by getting into our traps and being taken instead of the true game. They annoy us too by their squalling when they are taken.

From the junction of the two rivers to this place, I judge to be about a hundred miles. We find the climate exceedingly warm, and the beaver fur, in accommodation to the climate, is becoming short. We conclude, in consequence, that our trapping is becoming of less importance, and that it is our interest to push on faster to reach the settlements. A great many times every day we bring our crafts to shore, and go out to see if we cannot discover the tracks of horses and cattle. On the 18th, we first perceived that we had arrived on

the back water of the tide; or rather we first attributed the deadness of the current to the entrance of some inundated river, swollen
by the melting of the snow on the mountains. We puzzled our
brains with some other theories, to account for the deadness of the
current. This became so entirely still, that we began to rig our oars,
concluding that instead of our hitherto easy progress of floating
gently onward, we had henceforward to make our head-way down
stream by dint of the machinery of our arms.

We soon were thoroughly enlightened in regard to the slack-
ness of the water. It began to run down again, and with the
rapidity of six miles an hour; that is, double the ordinary current
of the stream. We were all much surprised, for though I had seen
the water of the Pacific at Ymus, none of us had ever felt the influence of the tides, or been in a craft on the ocean waters before.
People of the same tribe, upon which we had recently fired, stood
upon the shore, and called loudly to us as we passed, to come
to land, making signs to us, that the motion of the water would cap-
size our crafts. They showed a great desire that we might come
to shore, we had no doubt, that they might rob and murder us. We
preserved such a distance from them, as to be out of the reach of
their arrows, and had no intention to fire upon them. Had we
wished for a shot, they were quite within rifle distance. We floated
on, having had a beautiful evening's run, and did not come to land,
until late; we then pitched our camp on a low point of land, unconscious, from our inexperience of the fact, that the water would
return, and run up stream again. We made our canoes fast to some
small trees, and all lay down to sleep, except my father, who took
the first watch. He soon aroused us, and called on us all to prepare
for a gust of wind, and a heavy rain, which he thought betokened
by a rushing noise he heard. We realized in a few moments, that it
was the returning tide. Still, so strongly impressed were we, that a
shower was approaching, that we made all the customary arrangements of preparation, by stretching our blankets to keep out the
water from above. But our enemy assailed us from another quarter.
Our camp was inundated from the river. We landsmen from the
interior, and unaccustomed to such movements of the water, stood
contemplating with astonishment the rush of the tide coming in

from the sea, in conflict with the current of the river. At the point of conflict rose a high ridge of water, over which came the sea current, combing down like water over a mildam. We all sprang to our canoes, which the rush of the water had almost capsized, though we held the fasts with our hands. In twenty minutes the place where we lay asleep, and even our fire place was three feet under water, and our blankets were all afloat. We had some vague and general ideas of the nature of the tide, but its particular operations were as much unknown to us, as though we never had heard of it at all. In the consternation of our ignorance, we paddled our crafts, as well as we could, among the timber, not dreaming that in the course of a few hours, the water would fall again. As it was, we gathered up our floating blankets, got into our canoes, and held fast to the brushes, until the water fell again, leaving us and our canoes high and dry. We were now assailed by a new alarm, lest the Indians, taking advantage of this new position in which we were placed, would attack and murder us.

In such apprehensions we passed the night, until the morning shone upon us with a bright and beautiful sun, which enabled us to dry all our wet things, and re-animated us with the confidence which springs from the view of a bright firmament and a free and full survey of our case. When the tide returned we got into our crafts, and descended with it, still expecting to find Spanish settlements. We continued in this way to descend, when the tide ran out, until the 28th, when the surf came up the river so strong that we saw in a moment, that our crafts could not live, if we floated them into this tumultuous commotion of the water.

Here we were placed in a new position, not the least disheartening or trying, among the painful predicaments, in which fortune had placed us. The fierce billows shut us in from below, the river current from above, and murderous savages upon either hand on the shore. We had a rich cargo of furs, a little independence for each one of us, could we have disposed of them, as we had hoped, among the Spanish people, whom we expected to have found here. There were no such settlements.—Every side on which we looked offered an array of danger, famine and death. In this predicament, what were furs to us? Our first thought was to commit our furs to the

waters, and attempt to escape with our lives. Our second resolve
was to ascend the river as far as we could, bury our furs, and start
on foot for some settlement. We saw that the chances were greatly
against us, that we should perish in the attempt; for the country
yielded little to subsist on, and was full of Indians who are to the
last degree savage and murderous, and whom nothing can subdue
to kindness and friendship. We had no idea of ever putting ourselves
in their power, as long as one of us could fire a pistol, or draw a
knife.

We now began to ascend with the tide, when it served us, and
lay by when it ran down, until we arrived at the point where
it ceased to flow. We then applied our oars, and with the help of set-
ting-poles, and at times the aid of a cordelle, we stemmed the current at the rate of one, and sometimes two miles an hour, until the
tenth of February, when we met a great rise of the river, and found
the current so strong, that we had no power to stem it in any way.
So we concluded to abandon our canoes, come to shore, bury our
furs, and make our way across the peninsula to the coast of
California, which we thought from the information of the Indians,
could not be very distant.

On the 16th, we completed the burying of our furs, and started
on foot with our packs on our backs. The contents of these packs
were two blankets for each man, a considerable quantity of dried
beaver meat, and a rifle with the ammunition. Our first day's
journey was through a country to the last degree trying to
our strength and patience. It was through the river bottom, which
was thick set with low, scrubby brush, interwoven with tall grass,
vines and creepers. The making our way through these was excessively slavish and fatiguing. We had a single alleviation. There was
plenty of fresh water to drink. We were so fatigued at night, that
sleep was irresistible. The weather was warm, and we kindled no
fire, through fear of the savages. We started on the morning of the
18th, all complaining much of stiffness and soreness of our limbs.
We had been unused to walking for a great length of time; and
this commencement was a rude experiment of resuming the habit.
At two in the afternoon, we reached the edge of a large salt plain,
which runs parallel with the river. Here we struck a north

west course, and travelled the remainder of this hot and fatiguing day without finding any water. We began to suffer severely from thirst. The earth, also, was so loose and sandy, that at every step we sank up to our ankles, the sun beaming down a fierce radiance the while; which made it seem as if the heavens and the earth were on fire. Our tongues became so parched, that not a particle of moisture flowed into our mouths. In this miserable and forlorn condition, abandoned by strength, courage and hope, we found some little alleviation of our misery, when the blaze of the sun was gone, and the cool night enabled us to throw down our weary and exhausted bodies under its dewy shade.

We made an early start in the morning, and pushed on as men, as thirsty as we were, naturally would, in the hope of finding water, until two in the afternoon. What a sight of joy! I have no words to express our delight at the sight of a little lake before us. We sprang greedily to it. The water was salt, too salt to be drank! Not the slightest indication of any other water course, or any omen of fresh water was any where in view. Far in the distance a snow-covered mountain glittered in the sun, and on the opposite shore of this salt lake, and at a distance of three or four miles from it, rose some hills of considerable height. We thought that from the summit of these hills we might possibly discover some water. We gathered dry flags, of which there was a great abundance about us, and made a kind of raft, on which each one of us put his pack, and swam the lake, pushing the little rafts that carried our packs, before us. The lake is about two hundred yards wide, and contains a great variety of fish. In length the lake stretches north and south, bounded on each shore with high, level and well timbered land, though apparently affording no fresh water.

When we reached the west shore of the lake, we saw fresh Indian foot-prints in the sand. This assured us, that there was water at no great distance. One of our company and myself started and ascended the highest peak of the hills in our view, we were not long in descrying a smoke in the south, at the distance of about ten miles. This sight gave us great courage and hope; for we felt assured that there must be water between us and the Indian camp. In a moment we started back with a vigorous step, to inform our companions, who were resting themselves under the shade of a tree. The information re-animated them, as it had us. We all shouldered our packs with a degree of alacrity, and pushed on toward the smoke.—We arrived about three in the afternoon on a small mound, within a quarter of a mile of the Indians. We could distnctly number them, and found them between forty and fifty in number, and their women and children were with them.

Here again was anxious ground of debate, what course we should pursue? should we attempt the long and uncertain course of conciliation, before the accomplishment of which we might perish with thirst? or should we rush among them, and buy the delicious element which we had full in view, at the hazard of our lives? Men as thirsty as we were, would be likely to fix upon the latter alternative, and we did so. We examined our arms to see that we were prepared to attack, or repel, according to circumstances, determined to fire upon them, if they showed either a disposition for fight, or to keep us from the water.

We were within a hundred and fifty yards of them before they perceived us. As soon as they saw us they all fled to the bushes, men, women and children, as though satan was behind them. We had no disposition to arrest them, but rushed forward to the water, and began to slake our burning thirst. My father immediately cautioned us against drinking too much, pointing out at the same time the hurtful consequences. But men have always proved themselves slow to resist their appetites at the command of their reason. Most of us overloaded our empty stomachs with water, and soon became as sick as death. After vomiting, however, we were relieved. My father told us that we had better stand to our arms; for that the Indians had probably only fled to hide their women and children, and prepare themselves to return and fight us.

Scarcely had he finished these remarks, when we discovered them bearing down upon us, painted as black as a thunder cloud, and yelling like so many fiends. Some of them were armed with clubs, some with bows and arrows. We all arranged ourselves to receive them, behind the top of a large fallen tree. When they were within rifle shot, we made signs to them to halt, or that otherwise we should fire upon them. They comprehended us, halted and ceased yelling, as though they wished to hear what we had to say. We made signs that we were friendly. At this they gazed in apparent confusion of thought, and seemed to be questioning each other, touching the meaning of our signs. These signs we continued to repeat. At length one of them called aloud in Spanish, and asked us who we were? How delightful were these sounds! We answered *Americans*. They repeated the name, asking us if we were friendly and Christians? To these questions we made a ready affirmative. They then proposed a treaty with us. Nothing could be more agreeable to us. At the same time we perceived that only eight of their people came to us, and the remainder of their company kept back. These eight that seemed to be their chief men, advanced to us, while the rest, with extreme anxiety painted upon their countenances, stood ready for action. We all sat down on the ground, and commenced talking. They enquired with great precision, who we were, whence we came, how we arrived here, what was our object, and whether we had met with any misfortunes? We answered these questions to their satisfaction; and soon the pipe was lit, and we commenced smoking. They then dug a hole in the ground, in which they buried their war axe, and professed to deposite all ill feelings with it. The Indian of their number, who spoke the Spanish language, was a fugitive from the Mission of St. Catherine.— Threatened with the punishment of some misdemeanor, he had fled from the establishment.

After we had finished smoking, they asked us if the remainder of their number might not come and converse with us. This we objected to, unless they would bring their women and children with them. To this order they expressed great reluctance. This reluctance by no means tended to allay our previous jealousy of their pretended friendship. We asked them their reasons for being unwilling to bring their women and children? They answered promptly that they did not feel it safe to put their women and children in our power, until they were more acquainted with us. There seemed reason in this. We observed, that their men might come, provided they would leave their arms behind. To this they readily assented, and called out to their men to come on, leaving their arms behind. A part of them seemingly much delighted, threw down their arms and came on. The remainder equally dissatisfied, wheeled about, and walked moodily away.

The new comers sat down in a circle round us. The pipe was again lit and circled round. Again the terms of the treaty were repeated, and they all expressed their satisfaction with them. They observed, that their head chief was absent, at the distance of two day's journey to the south, that in three or four days he would come and see us, desiring us to remain with them until he should come. Nothing could be more opportune for us, for we were all excessively fatigued, and needed a few days rest. After this they went and brought their women and children, who, like the other Indians we had seen, were all stark naked. At first they were excessively shy of us. This shyness wore off, and in the course of the day changed to an eager curiosity to examine us, and an admiration of our red flannel shirts, and the white skin *under them;* for little show of whiteness was to be seen in our faces. They soon ventured close to us, and with their own hands opened our bosoms, uttering exclamations of curiosity and admiration, especially on feeling the softness of our skins, in comparison of theirs. They certainly seemed to prefer our complexion to theirs, notwithstanding it had not the stamp of their fashion.

At length they made up to one of our companions, who was of a singularly light complexion, fair soft skin, and blue eyes. They wanted him to strip himself naked that they might explore him thoroughly, for they seemed to be doubtful of his being alike white in every part of his body. This, but as mildly as possible, he refused to do. They went off and brought a quantity of dried fish of excellent quality, and presented him. We persuaded him to oblige these curious and good natured women, by giving them a full view of his body. He was persuaded to strip to his skin. This delighted them, and they conversed and laughed among themselves, and they came one by one and stood beside him; so as to compare their bodies with his. After this, as long as we staid, they were constantly occupied in bringing us cooked fish and the vegetables and roots on which they are accustomed to feed. On the 25th, the head chief came. He was a venerable looking man, whom I judged to be about fifty years old. His countenance was thoughtful and serious, and his hair a little gray. At his return his people greeted him with an acclamation of yells, that made the wild desert echo. The pipe was lit, and we all sat down by him and smoked again. He was a man of but few words, but of sound judgment. After the smoking was finished, he asked us the same questions which had been asked us before. We made him similar answers, adding, that we wanted to travel to the Spanish settlements and purchase horses, upon which we might ride home to our country, and that we would pay him well if he would send some of his men to guide us to those settlements. He asked us in reply, what we had to give him? We showed him our blankets, and he expressed himself delighted with them, observing at the same time, that he would have preferred to have had red cloth. On this we pulled off our red shirts and stripped them into small pieces like ribbons, and distributed them among the people. They tied the strips round their legs, arms and heads, and seemed as much overjoyed with these small tatters of worn red flannel, as we should have been, to have brought our furs to a good market among our own people. In giving away our red shirts, we gave away, what in this warm climate was to us wholly unnecessary. To carry our blankets on our backs was a useless burden. We gave two of them to the chief. The two guides that he was to send with us we were to pay after our arrival at the Spanish settlements. These points of contract between us were settled to the mutual satisfaction of all.

We started on the 26th, with our two guides, neither of whom could speak Spanish, and of course we had nothing to do but follow them in silence. We struck off a south west course, which led in the direction of the snow covered mountain, which still loomed up in its brightness before us. Our guides made signs that we should arrive at the foot about midnight, though the distance appeared to us to be too great to be travelled over in so short a time. We were yet to learn, that we should find no water, until we drank that of the melted snow. We perceived, however, that their travelling gait, worn as we were, was more rapid than ours. We pushed on as fast as we could a league further, when we were impeded by a high hill in our way, which was about another league to the summit, and very precipitous and steep. When we reached the top of it we were much exhausted, and began to be thirsty. We could then see the arid salt plain stretching all the way from the foot of this hill to the snow covered mountains.

We thought it inexpedient to enquire of our guides, if there was no water to be found between us and the mountain. It appeared but too probable, that such was the fact. To know it to a certainty, would only tend to unnerve and dishearten us. If there was any, we were aware that we should reach it by travelling no more distance than as if we knew the fact. We found it best to encourage the little hope that remained, and hurried on through the drifted sand, in which we sank up to our ankles at every step. The cloudless sun poured such a blaze upon it, that by the scorching of our feet, it might have seemed almost hot enough to roast eggs in. What with the fierce sun and the scorching sand, and our extreme fatigue, the air seemed soon to have extracted every particle of moisture from our bodies. In this condition we marched on until nearly the middle of the day, without descrying any indication of water in any quarter. A small scrubby tree stood in our way, affording a tolerable shade. We laid ourselves down to get a few minutes rest. The Indians sternly beckoned us to be up and onward, now for the first time clearly explaining to us, that there was no water until we reached the mountains in view. This unseasonable and yet necessary information, extinguished the last remainder of our hope, and we openly expressed our fears that we should none of us ever reach it.

We attempted to chew tobacco. It would raise no moisture. We took our bullets in our mouths, and moved them round to create a moisture, to relieve our parched throats. We had travelled but a little farther before our tongues had become so dry and swollen, that we could scarcely speak so as to be understood. In this extremity of nature, we should, perhaps, have sunk voluntarily, had not the relief been still in view on the sides of the snow covered mountains. We resorted to one expedient to moisten our lips, tongue and throat, disgusting to relate, and still more disgusting to adopt. In such predicaments it has been found, that nature disburdens people of all conditions of ceremony and disgust. Every thing bends to the devouring thirst, and the love of life. The application of this hot and salt liquid seemed rather to enrage than appease the tortur-

ing appetite. Though it offered such a semblance of what would satisfy thirst, that we economized every particle. Our amiable Dutchman was of a sweetness of temper, that was never ruffled, and a
calmness and patience that appeared proof against all events. At another time, what laughter would have circulated through our
camp, to hear him make merry of this expedient! As it was, even
in this horrible condition, a faint smile circulated through our company, as he discussed his substitute for drink. 'Vell mine poys, dis
vater of mein ish more hotter as hell, und as dick as boudden, und
more zalter as de zeas. I can't drink him. For Cod's sake, gif me
some of yours, dat is more tinner.'

Having availed ourselves to the utmost of this terrible expedient, we marched on in company a few miles further. Two of our
companions here gave out, and lay down under the shade of a bush.
Their tongues were so swollen, and their eyes so sunk in their
heads, that they were a spectacle to behold. We were scarcely able,
from the condition of our own mouths, to bid them an articulate
farewell. We never expected to see them again, and none of us had
much hope of ever reaching the mountain, which still raised its
white summit at a great distance from us. It was with difficulty
that we were enabled to advance one foot before the other. Our
limbs, our powers, even our very resolutions seemed palsied. A circumstance that added to our distress, was the excessive and daz-
zling brightness of the sun's rays, so reflected in our eyes from the
white sand that we were scarcely able to see our way before us, or
in what direction to follow our guides. They, accustomed to go
naked, and to traverse these burning deserts, and be unaffected by
such trials, appeared to stand the heat and drought, like camels on
the Arabian sands. They, however, tried by their looks and gestures
to encourage us, and induce us to quicken our pace. But it was to
no purpose. However, we still kept moving onward, and had gained
a few miles more, when night brought us shelter at least from the
insupportable radiance of the sun, and something of coolness and
moisture.

But it was so dark, that neither we or our guides could discover
the course. We stopped, and made a large fire, that our companions, if yet living, and able to move, might see where we were, and

how to direct their own course to reach us. We also fired some guns, which, to our great relief and pleasure, they answered by firing off theirs. We still repeated firing guns at intervals, until they came up with us. They supposed that we had found water, which invigorated their spirits to such a degree, that it aroused them to the effort they had made. When they had arrived, and found that we had reached no water, they appeared to be angry, and to complain that we had disturbed their repose with false hopes, and had hindered their dying in peace. One of them in the recklessness of despair, drew from his package a small phial, half full of laudanum, and drank it off, I suppose in the hope of sleeping himself quietly to death. We all expected it would have that effect. On the contrary, in a few moments he was exhilarated, like a man in a state of intoxication. He was full of talk, and laughter, and gaiety of heart. He observed, that he had taken it in hopes that it would put him to sleep, never to wake again, but that in fact, it had made him as well, and as fresh, as in the morning when he started; but that if he had imagined that it would prove such a sovereign remedy for thirst, he would cheerfully have shared it with us. We scraped down beneath the burning surface of the sand, until we reached the earth that was a little cool. We then stripped off all our clothing and lay down. Our two Indians, also lay down beside us, covering themselves with their blankets. My father bade me lay on the edge of one of their blankets, so that they could not get up without awakening me. He was fearful that they would arise, and fly from us in the night. I implicitly conformed to my father's wish, for had this event happened, we should all undoubtedly have perished. But the Indians appear to have meditated no such expedient, at any rate, they lay quiet until morning.

As soon as there was light enough to enable us to travel we started, much refreshed by the coolness of the night, and the sleep we had taken. We began our morning march with renewed alacrity. At about ten in the forenoon we arrived at the foot of a sand hill about a half a mile in height, and very steep. The side was composed of loose sand, which gave way under our feet, so that our advancing foot steps would slide back to their former places. This soon exhausted our little remaining strength; though we still made many an unavailing effort to ascend. The sun was now so high, as to beam upon us with the same insufferable radiance of yesterday. The air which we inhaled, seemed to scald our lungs. We at length concluded to travel towards the north, to reach, if we might, some point where the hill was not so steep to ascend. At two in the afternoon we found a place that was neither so steep nor so high, and we determined here to attempt to cross the hill. With great exertions and infinite difficulty, a part of us gained the summit of the hill; but my father and another of our company, somewhat advanced in years, gave out below, though they made the most persevering efforts to reach the summit of the hill with the rest. Age had stiffened their joints, and laid his palsying hand upon their once active limbs, and vigorous frames. They could endure this dreadful journey no longer. They had become so exhausted by fruitless efforts to climb the hill, that they could no longer drag one foot after the other. They had each so completely abandoned the hope of ever reaching the water, or even gaining the summit of the hill, that they threw themselves on the ground, apparently convinced of their fate, and resigned to die. I instantly determined to remain with my father, be it for life or death. To this determination he would by no means consent, as he remarked it would bring my destruction, without its availing him. On the contrary, he insisted, that I should go on with the rest, and if I found any water near at hand, that I should return with my powder horn full. In this way he assured me, I might be instrumental in saving my own life, and saving him at the same time. To this I consented, and with much fatigue gained the summit of the hill, where my companions were seated waiting for us. They seemed undetermined, whether to advance onward, or wait for my father, until I related his determination. My purpose was to proceed onward only so far, as that, if the Almighty should enable us to reach water, I might be able to return with a powder horn full to him and Mr. Slover, (for that was the name of the elderly companion that remained with him.)

This resolution was agreed to by all, as a proper one. Being satisfied by our consciences as well as by the reasoning of my father and his companion, that we could render them no service by remaining with them, except to increase their sufferings by a view of ours; and aware, that every moment was precious, we pushed on once more for the mountain. Having descended this hill, we ascended another of the same wearying ascent, and sandy character with the former. We toiled on to the top of it. The Eternal Power, who hears the ravens when they cry, and provideth springs in the wilderness, had had mercy upon us! Imagine my joy at seeing a clear, beautiful running stream of water, just below us at the foot of the hill! Such a blissful sight I had never seen before, and never expect to see again. We all ran down to it, and fell to drinking. In a few moments nothing was to be heard among us, but vomiting and groaning. Notwithstanding our mutual charges to be cautious, we had overcharged our parched stomachs with this cold snow water.

Notwithstanding I was sick myself, I emptied my powder horn of its contents, filled it with water, and accompanied by one companion, who had also filled his powder horn, I returned towards my father and Mr. Slover, his exhausted companion, with a quick step. We found them in the same position, in which we had left them, that is, stretched on the sand at full length, under the unclouded blaze of the sun, and both fast asleep; a sleep from which, but for our relief, I believe they would neither of them ever have awakened. Their lips were black, and their parched mouths wide open. Their unmoving posture and their sunken eyes so resembled death, that I ran in a fright to my father, thinking him, for a moment, really dead. But he easily awakened, and drank the refreshing water. My companion at the same time bestowed his horn of water upon Mr. Slover. In the course of an hour they were both able to climb the hill, and some time before dark we rejoined the remainder of our company. They had kindled a large fire, and all seemed in high spirits. As for our two Indians, they were singing, and dancing, as it seemed to us, in a sort of worship of thankfulness to the Great Spirit, who had led them through so much peril and toil to these refreshing waters. We roasted some of our beaver meat, and took food for the first time in forty-eight hours, that is to say, from the time we left our Indian friends, until we reached this water. Our Dutchman insisted that the plain over which we passed, should be named the devil's plain, for he insisted, that it was more hotter as hell, and that none but teyvils could live upon it. In fact, it seemed a more fitting abode for fiends, than any living thing that belongs to our world. During our passage across it, we saw not a single bird, nor the track of any quadruped, or in fact any thing that had life, not even a sprig, weed or grass blade, except a single shrubby tree, under which we found a little shade. This shrub, though of some height, resembled a prickly pear, and was covered thick with thorns. The prickly pears were in such abundance, that we were often, dazzled as our eyes were with the sun's brightness, puzzled to find a path so as neither to torment our feet or our bodies with the thorns of these hated natives of the burning sands. This very extensive plain, the Sahara of California, runs north and south, and is bounded on each side by high barren mountains, some of which are covered with perpetual snow.

On the 28th, we travelled up this creek about three miles, and killed a deer, which much delighted our two Indian guides. At this point we encamped for the night. Here are abundance of palm trees and live oaks, and considerable of mascal. We remained until the 3d of March, when we marched up this creek, which heads to the south, forming a low gap in the mountain. On the 7th, we arrived at the point, and found some of the Christian Indians from the Mission of St. Catharine. They were roasting mascal and the tender inside heads of the palm trees for food, which, when prepared and cooked after their fashion, becomes a very agreeable food. From these Indians we learned that we were within four days' travel of the mission mentioned above.

Here we concluded to discharge our guides, and travel into the settlement with the Christian Indians. We gave them each a blanket, and they started back to their own people on the morning of the 8th. At the same time we commenced our journey with our new guides, and began to climb the mountain. This is so exceedingly lofty, as to require two days' travel and a half to gain its summit. During this ascent, I severely bruised my heel. We none of us wore any thing to shield our feet from the bare and sharp rocks, which composed almost the whole surface of this ascent, but thin deer skin moccasins. Obliged to walk on tip toe, and in extreme anguish, the severe fatigue of scrambling up sharp stones was any thing,

rather than agreeable. But I summoned patience and courage to
push on until the 12th. My leg then became so swollen and in-
flamed that it was out of my power to travel farther. The pain was
so severe as to create fever. I lay myself down on the side of a sharp
rock, resigning myself to my fate, and determined to make no effort to travel further, until I felt relieved. My companions all joined
with my father, in encouraging me to rise, and make an effort to
reach the mission, which they represented to be but three miles distant. It was out of the question for me to think of it, and they concluded to go to the settlement, and obtain a horse, and send out for
me. I kindled me a fire, for I suffered severe chills. The Indians gave
me the strictest caution against allowing myself to go to sleep in
their absence. The reason they assigned for their caution was a
substantial one. The grizzly bear, they said, was common on these
mountains, and would attack and devour me, unless I kept on my
guard. I paid little attention to their remarks at the time. But when
they were gone, and I was left alone, I examined the priming, and
picked the flints of my gun and pistol. I then lay down and slept,
until sometime in the early part of the night, when two Indians
came out from the settlement, and informed me that the corporal
of the guards at St. Catharines wished me to come in. Being fever-
ish, stiff, sore and withal testy, I gave them and their corporal no
very civil words. They said that the corporal only wanted me to
come in, because he was afraid the grizzly bears would kill me. I
asked them why they did not bring a horse for me? They informed
me, that the Mission had none at disposal at that time, but that
they would carry me on their backs. So I was obliged to avail myself of this strange conveyance, and mounted the back of one of
them while the other carried my arms. In this way they carried me
in, where I found my companions in a guard house. I was ordered
to enter with them by a swarthy looking fellow, who resembled a
negro, rather than a white.

I cannot describe the indignation I felt at this revolting breach
of humanity to people in suffering, who had thrown themselves on
the kindness and protection of these Spaniards. We related the reasons why we had come in after this manner. We showed them our
passport, which certified to them, that we were neither robbers,

murderers, nor spies. To all this their only reply was, how should
they know whether we had come clandestinely, and with improper
views, or not? Against this question, proposed by such people,
all reasonings were thrown away.—The cowardly and worthless
are naturally cruel. We were thrown completely in their power; and
instead of that circumstance exciting any generous desires to con-
sole and relieve us, their only study seemed to be to vex, degrade,
and torment us.

Here we remained a week, living on corn mush, which we received once a day; when a guard of soldiers came to conduct us
from this place. This mission is situated in a valley, surrounded
by high mountains, with beautiful streams of water flowing from
them. The natives raise sufficient corn and wheat to serve for the
subsistence of the mission. The mission establishment is built in a
quadrangular form; all the houses forming the quadrangle contiguous to each other; and one of the angles is a large church, adjoining
which are the habitations of the priests; though at this time there
happened to be none belonging to this at home. The number of Indians belonging to the mission at this time, was about five hundred. They were destitute of stock, on account of its having been
plundered from them by the free, wild Indians of the desert. The
air is very cool and temperate, and hard frosts are not uncommon.
This cool temperature of the atmosphere I suppose to be owing to
the immediate proximity of the snowy mountains.

On the 18th, we started under the conduct of a file of soldiers,
who led us two days' travel, over very high mountains, a south
west course, to another mission, called St. Sebastian, situated near
the sea coast, in a delightful valley, surrounded, like the other, by
lofty mountains, the sides of which present magnificent views of
the ocean. This mission contains six hundred souls. This mission
establishment, though much richer and neater than the other, is,
however, built on a precisely similar plan. Here they have rich vineyards, and raise a great variety of the fruits of almost all climates.
They also raise their own supplies of grain, and have a tolerable
abundance of stock, both of the larger and smaller kinds.

A serjeant has the whole military command. We found him of
a dark and swarthy complexion, though a man of tolerable infor-

mation. He seemed disposed to conduct towards us with some
courtesy and kindness. He saluted us with politeness, conducted us
to the guard house, and begged us to content ourselves, as well as
we could, until he could make some more satisfactory arrangements
for our comfort and convenience. To put him to the proof of his
professed kindness, we told him that we were very hungry. They
soon had a poor steer killed, that reeled as it walked, and seemed
sinking by natural decay. A part of the blue flesh was put boiling
in one pot, and a parcel of corn in the other. The whole process reminded me strongly of the arrangements which we make in Kentucky, to prepare a mess for a diseased cow. When this famous feast
was cooked, we were marched forth into the yard, in great ceremony, to eat it. All the men, women and children clustered round
us, and stood staring at us while we were eating, as though they
had been at a menagerie to see some wild and unknown animals.—
When we were fairly seated to our pots, and began to discuss the
contents, disgusted alike with the food, with them, and their behaviour, we could not forbear asking them whether they really took us
to be human beings, or considered us as brutes? They looked at
each other a moment, as if to reflect and frame an answer, and then
replied coolly enough, that not being Christians, they considered us
little superior to brutes. To this we replied, with a suitable mixture
of indignation and scorn, that we considered ourselves better Christians than they were, and that if they did not give us something to
eat more befitting men, we would take our guns, live where we
pleased, and eat venison and other good things, where we chose.
This was not mere bravado, for, to our astonishment, we were still
in possession of our arms. We had made no resistance to their treating us as prisoners, as we considered them nothing more than petty
and ignorant officers, whom we supposed to have conducted im-
properly, from being unacquainted with their duty. We were all
confident, that as soon as intelligence of our arrival should reach
the commanding officer of this station, and how we had been detained, and treated as prisoners, we should not only be released from
prison, but recompensed for our detention.

    This determination of ours appeared to alarm them. The in-
formation of our menaces, no doubt with their own comments,

soon reached the serjeant. He immediately came to see us, while we were yet at our pots, and enquired of us, what was our ground of complaint and dissatisfaction? we pointed to the pots, and asked him if he thought such food becoming the laws of hospitality to such people? He stepped up to the pots, and turning over the contents, and examining them with his fingers, enquired in an angry tone, who had served up such food to us? He added, that it was not fit to give a dog, and that he would punish those who had procured it. He comforted us, by assuring us that we should have something fit to eat cooked for us. We immediately returned quietly to the guard house. But a short time ensued before he sent us a good dish of fat mutton, and some tortillas. This was precisely the thing our appetites craved, and we were not long in making a hearty meal. After we had fed to our satisfaction, he came to visit us, and interrogated us in what manner, and with what views we had visited the country? We went into clear, full and satisfactory details of information in regard to every thing that could have any interest to him, as an officer; and told him that our object was to purchase horses, on which we might return to our own country; and that we wished him to intercede in our behalf with the commander in chief, that we might have permission to purchase horses and mules among them, for this purpose. He promised to do this, and returned to his apartment.

The amount of his promise was, that he would reflect upon the subject, and in the course of four days write to his commander, from whom he might expect an answer in a fortnight.—When we sounded him as to the probability of such a request being granted, he answered with apparent conviction, that he had no doubt that it would be in our favor. As our hopes were intensely fixed upon this issue, we awaited this answer with great anxiety. The commander at this time was at the port of San Diego. During this period of our suspense, we had full liberty to hunt deer in the woods, and gather honey from the blossoms of the Mascal, which grows plentifully on the sea shore. Every thing in this strange and charming country being new, we were continually contemplating curiosities of every sort, which quieted our solicitude, and kept alive the interest of our attention.

We used to station ourselves on the high pinnacles of the cliffs, on which this vast sea pours its tides, and the retreating or advancing tide showed us the strange sea monsters of that ocean, such as seals, sea otters, sea elephants, whales, sharks, sword fish, and various other unshapely sea dwellers. Then we walked on the beach, and examined the infinite variety of sea shells, all new and strange to us.

Thus we amused ourselves, and strove to kill the time until the 20th, when the answer of the commander arrived, which explained itself at once, by a guard of soldiers, with orders to conduct us to the port of San Diego, where he then resided. We were ordered to be in immediate readiness to start for that port. This gave us unmingled satisfaction, for we had an undoubting confidence, that when we should really have attained the presence of an officer whom we supposed a gentleman, and acting independently of the authority of others, he would make no difficulty in granting a request so reasonable as ours. We started on the 2d, guarded by sixteen soldiers and a corporal. They were all on horseback, and allowed us occasionally to ride, when they saw us much fatigued. Our first day's journey was a north course, over very rough mountains, and yet, notwithstanding this, we made twenty-five miles distance on our way.

At night we arrived at another mission, situated like the former, on a charming plain. The mission is called St. Thomas. These wise and holy men mean to make sure of the rich and pleasant things of the earth, as well as the kingdom of heaven. They have large plantations, with splendid orchards and vineyards. The priest who presides over this establishment, told me that he had a thousand Indians under his care. During every week in the year, they kill thirty beeves for the subsistence of the mission. The hides and tallow they sell to vessels that visit their coast, in exchange for such goods as they need.

On the following morning, we started early down this valley, which led us to the sea shore, along which we travelled the remainder of the day. This beautiful plain skirts the sea shore, and extends back from it about four miles. This was literally covered with horses and cattle belonging to the mission. The eye was lost beyond this handsome plain in contemplating an immeasurable range of mountains, which we were told thronged with wild horses and cattle, which often descend from their mountains to the plains, and entice away the domesticated cattle with them. The wild oats and clover grow spontaneously, and in great luxuriance, and were now knee high. In the evening we arrived at the port of Todos Santos, and there passed the night. Early on the 23d, we marched on. This day we travelled over some tracts that were very rough, and arrived at a mission situated immediately on the sea board, called St. Michael. Like the rest, it was surrounded with splendid orchards, vine yards and fields; and was, for soil, climate and position, all that could be wished. The old superintending priest of the establishment showed himself very friendly, and equally inquisitive. He invited us to sup with him, an invitation we should not be very likely to refuse. We sat down to a large table, elegantly furnished with various dishes of the country, all as usual highly seasoned. Above all, the supply of wines was various and abundant. The priest said grace at the close, when fire and cigars were brought in by the attendants, and we began to smoke. We sat and smoked, and drank wine, until 12 o'clock. The priest informed us that the population of his mission was twelve hundred souls, and the weekly consumption, fifty beeves, and a corresponding amount of grain. The mission possessed three thousand head of domesticated and tamed horses and mules. From the droves which I saw in the plains, I should not think this an extravagant estimation. In the morning he presented my father a saddle mule, which he accepted, and we started.

This day's travel still carried us directly along the verge of the sea shore, and over a plain equally rich and beautiful with that of the preceding day. We amused ourselves with noting the spouting of the huge whales, which seemed playing near the strand for our especial amusement. We saw other marine animals and curiosities to keep our interest in the journey alive. In the evening we arrived at a Ranch, called Buenos Aguos, or Good Water, where we encamped for the night.

We started early on the 25th, purchasing a sheep of a shepherd, for which we paid him a knife. At this Ranch they kept thirty thousand head of sheep, belonging to the mission which we had left.

We crossed a point of the mountain that made into the water's edge. On the opposite side of this mountain was another Ranch, where we staid the night. This Ranch is for the purposes of herding horses and cattle, of which they have vast numbers. On the 26th, our plain lay outstretched before us as beautiful as ever. In the evening we came in sight of San Diego, the place where we were bound. In this port was one merchant vessel, which we were told was from the United States, the ship Franklin, of Boston. We had then arrived within about a league of the port. The corporal who had charge of us here, came and requested us to give up our arms, informing us, it was the customary request to all strangers; and that it was expected that our arms would be deposited in the guard house before we could speak with the commander, or general. We replied, that we were both able and disposed to carry our arms to the guard house ourselves, and deposite them there if such was our pleasure, at our own choice. He replied that we could not be allowed to do this, for that we were considered as prisoners, and under his charge; and that he should become responsible in his own person, if he should allow us to appear before the general, bearing our own arms. This he spoke with a countenance of seriousness, which induced us to think that he desired no more in this request than the performance of his duty. We therefore gave him up our rifles, not thinking that this was the last time we should have the pleasure of shouldering these trusty friends. Having unburdened ourselves of our defence, we marched on again, and arrived, much fatigued, at the town at 3 o'clock in the evening. Our arms were stacked on the side of the guard house, and we threw our fatigued bodies as near them as we could, on the ground.

An officer was dispatched to the general to inform him of our arrival, and to know whether we could have an immediate audience or not? In a short time the officer returned with an answer for us, that we must remain where we were until morning, when the general would give us a hearing. We were still sanguine in seeing only omens of good. We forgot our past troubles, opened our bosom to hope, and resigned ourselves to profound sleep. It is true, innumerable droves of fleas performed their evolutions, and bit all their pleasure upon our bodies.—But so entire was our repose, that we

scarcely turned for the night. No dreams of what was in reserve
for us the following day floated across our minds; though in the
morning my body was as spotted as though I had the measles, and
my shirt specked with innumerable stains of blood, let by the ingen-
ious lancets of these same Spanish fleas.

On the 27th, at eight A.M., we were ushered into the general's
office, with our hats in our hands, and he began his string of inter-
rogations. The first question was, who we were? We answered,
Americans. He proceeded to ask us, how we came on the coast,
what was our object, and had we a passport? In answer to these
questions we again went over the story of our misfortunes. We then
gave him the passport which we had received from the governor of
Santa Fe. He examined this instrument, and with a sinister and
malicious smile, observed, that he believed nothing of all this, but
considered us worse than thieves and murderers; in fact, that he
held us to be spies for the old Spaniards, and that our business was
to lurk about the country, that we might inspect the weak and defenceless points of the frontiers, and point them out to the Spaniards, in order that they might introduce their troops into the
country; but that he would utterly detect us, and prevent our designs.—This last remark he uttered with a look of vengeance; and
then reperused the passport, which he tore in pieces, saying, it was
no passport, but a vile forgery of our own contrivance.

Though amazed and confounded at such an unexpected charge,
we firmly asserted our innocence in regard to any of the charges
brought against us. We informed him that we were born and bred
thorough and full blooded republicans; and that there was not a
man of us who would not prefer to die, rather than to be the spies
and instruments of the Spanish king, or any other king; and that
but a few years since, we had all been engaged in fighting the forces
of a king, allied with savages, and sent against the country of our
home; and that on this very expedition we had been engaged in
a great many battles with the Indians, hostile to his people, redeem-
ing their captives, and punishing their robberies and murders. In
distress, and in want of every thing from the robbery of these hostile Indians, we had taken refuge in his country, and claimed its
protection. We told him we considered it an unworthy return for

such general deportment, and such particular services to their country, that we should be viewed as spies, and treated as prisoners. He stopped us in the midst of our plea, apparently through fear that representations, which must have carried conviction to his prejudiced mind, might tend to soften his obdurate heart, and unnerve his purpose towards us. He told us he did not wish to hear any more of our long speeches, which he considered no better than lies; for that if we had been true and bona fide citizens of the United States, we should not have left our country without a passport, and the certificate of our chief magistrate. We replied that the laws of our country did not require that honest, common citizens, should carry passports; that it did not interfere with the individual business and pursuits of private individuals; that such persons went abroad and returned unnoted by the government; and in all well regulated states, sufficiently protected by the proof that they were citizens of the United States; but that there were in our country two classes of people, for whom passports were necessary, slaves and soldiers; that for the slave it was necessary to have one, to certify that he was travelling with the knowledge and permission of his master; and for the soldier, to show that he was on furlough, or otherwise abroad with the permission of his officer. As we spoke this with emphasis, and firmness, he told us that he had had enough of our falsehoods, and begged us to be quiet. He ordered us to be remanded to our prison, and was immediately obeyed.

As we were driven out of his office, my father, who was exceedingly exasperated, observed, 'my boys, as soon as we arrive in the guard house, let us seize our arms and redress ourselves, or die in the attempt; for it seems to me that these scoundrels mean to murder us.' We all unanimously agreed to this advice, and walked back with a willing mind, and an alert step. But our last hope of redressing ourselves, and obtaining our liberty was soon extinguished. On entering the guard house, our arms had been removed we knew not where. They had even the impudence to scarch our persons and to take from us even our pocket knives. The orderly sergeant then told us, that he was under the necessity of placing us in separate apartments. This last declaration seemed the death stroke to us all. Affliction and mutual suffering and danger had endeared us to each other, and this separation seemed like rending our hearts. Overcome by the suddenness of the blow, I threw my arms round the neck of my father, burst into tears, and exclaimed, 'that I foresaw, that the parting would be forever.' Though my father seemed subdued, and absorbed in meditation, he reproved this expression of my feelings, as weak and unmanly. The sergeant having observed my grief, asked me, pointing to him, if that was my father? When he learned that it was, he showed himself in some degree affected, and remarked, that it seemed cruel to separate father and child, and that he would go and explain the relationship to the general, and see if he could not obtain permission for us to remain together. On this he set off for the general's office, leaving me in the agony of suspense, and the rest gazing at each other in mute consternation and astonishment. The sergeant returned, informing me, that instead of being softened, the general had only been exasperated, and had in nothing relaxed his orders, which were, that we must immediately be put in separate confinement. He accordingly ordered some soldiers to assist in locking us up. We embraced each other, and followed our conductors to our separate prisons. I can affirm, that I had only wished to live, to sustain the increasing age and infirmities of my father. When I shook hands with him, and we were torn in sunder, I will say nothing of my feelings, for words would have no power to describe them. As I entered my desolate apartment, the sergeant seemed really affected, and assured me, that neither my companions nor myself should suffer any want of food or drink, as far as he could prevent it, for that he did not consider us guilty, nor worthy of such treatment.

My prison was a cell eight or ten feet square, with walls and floor of stone. A door with iron bars an inch square crossed over each other, like the bars of window sashes, and it grated on its iron hinges, as it opened to receive me. Over the external front of this prison was inscribed in capital letters *Destinacion de la Cattivo*. Our blankets were given us to lie upon. My father had a small package of medicines which he gave in charge to the sergeant, binding him on his word of honor not to part with it to any one. My door was locked, and I was left to reflect upon our position and my past misfortunes: and to survey the dreary walls of my prison. Here, I thought, was my everlasting abode. Liberty is dear to every one, but doubly dear to one, who had been from infancy accustomed to free range, and to be guided by his own will. Put a man, who has ranged the prairies, and exulted in the wilderness, as I have for years, in a prison, to let him have a full taste of the blessings of freedom, and the horror of shackles and confinement! I passed the remainder of the day in fierce walking backwards and forwards over my stone floor, with no object to contemplate, but my swarthy sentinel, through the grate. He seemed to be true to his office, and fitly selected for his business, for I thought I saw him look at me through the grate with the natural exultation and joy of a bad and malicious heart in the view of misery.

When the darkness of night came to this dreary place, it was the darkness of the grave. Every ray of light was extinct. I spread my blankets on the stone floor, in hopes at least to find, for a few hours, in the oblivion of sleep, some repose from the agitation of my thoughts. But in this hope I was disappointed. With every other friend and solace, sleep too, fled from me. My active mind ranged every where, and returned only to unavailing efforts to imagine the condition and feelings of my father, and what would be our ultimate fate. I shut my eyes by an effort, but nature would have her way, and the eyelids would not close.

At length a glimmer of daylight, through my grate, relieved this long and painful effort to sleep. I arose, went to my grate, and took all possible survey of what I could see. Directly in front of it was the door of the general's office, and he was standing in it. I gazed on him awhile. Ah! that I had had but my trusty rifle well charged to my face! Could I but have had the pleasure of that single shot, I think I would have been willing to have purchased it by my life. But wishes are not rifle balls, and will not kill.

The church bell told eight in the morning. The drum rolled. A soldier came, and handed me in something to eat. It proved to be dried beans and corn cooked with rancid tallow! The contents were about a pint. I took it up, and brought it within the reach of my nostrils, and sat it down in unconquerable loathing. When the soldier returned in the evening to bring me more, I handed him my morning ration untasted and just as it was. He asked me in a gruff tone why I had not eaten it? I told him the smell of it was enough, and that I could not eat it. He threw the contents of the dish in my face, muttering something which amounted to saying, that it was good enough for such a brute as I was. To this I answered, that if being a brute gave claims upon that dish, I thought he had best eat it himself. On this he flung away in a passion, and returned no more that night, for which I was not sorry. Had the food even been fit to eat, my thoughts were too dark and my mind too much agitated to allow me appetite. In fact, I felt myself becoming sick.

At night I was visited by the serjeant, who asked me about my health and spirits in a tone and manner, that indicated real kindness of feeling. I trusted in the reality of his sympathy, and told him, I was not well. He then questioned me, if I had eaten any thing? I told him no, and explained to him the double reason, why I had eaten nothing. He answered that he would remove one of the causes, by sending me something good. I then asked him if he had seen my father? He said he had, though he had been unable to hold any conversation with him, for want of his understanding Spanish. I thanked him for his manifestation of friendship, and he left me. In a short time he returned with two well cooked and seasoned dishes. I begged him to take it first to my father, and when he had eaten what he wished, he might bring the remainder to me, and I would share it among my companions. He assured me that my father was served with the same kind of food, and that my companions should not be forgotten in the distribution. While I was eating, he remained with me, and asked me, if I had a mother, and brothers, and sisters in my own country? My heart was full, as I answered him. He proceeded to question me, how long it had been since I had seen them or heard from them, and in what I had been occupied, during my long absence from my country? My misfortunes appeared to affect him. When I had finished eating, he enquired how I had passed the preceding night? In all his questions, he displayed true humanity and tenderness of heart. When he left me, he affectionately wished me good night. This night passed as sleepless and uncomfortable as the preceding one. Next day the kind serjeant brought my dinner again, though from anxiety and growing indisposition I was unable to eat. At night he came again

with my supper, and to my surprise accompanied by his sister, a
young lady of great personal beauty. Her first enquiry was that of
a kind and affectionate nature, and concerned my father. She enquired about my age, and all the circumstances that induced me to
leave my country? I took leave to intimate in my answer, my extreme anxiety to see my relatives, and return to my country, and
in particular, that it was like depriving me of life, in this strange
land, and in prison, to separate me from my old and infirm father.
She assured me that she would pray for our salvation, and attempt
to intercede with the general in our behalf, and that while we remained in prison, she would allow us to suffer nothing, which her
power, means or influence could supply. She then wished me a
good night, and departed. I know not what is the influence of the
ministration of a kind spirit, like hers, but this night my sleep was
sound and dreamless.

She frequently repeated these kind visits, and redeemed to the
letter all her pledges of kindness. For I suffered for nothing in regard to food or drink. A bed was provided for me, and even a
change of clothing. This undeviating kindness greatly endeared
her to me. About this time, Captain John Bradshaw, of the ship
Franklin, and Rufus Perkins, his supercargo, asked leave of the
general, to come and visit us. The general denied them. But Captain Bradshaw, like a true hearted American, disregarded the little
brief authority of this miserable republican despot, and fearless of
danger and the consequences, came to see me without leave. When
I spoke to him about our buried furs, he asked me about the chances
and the means we had to bring them in? And whether we were disposed to make the effort, and if we succeeded, to sell them to him?
The prisoners, as he separately applied to them, one and all assured
him, that nothing would give them more pleasure. He assured us,
that he would leave nothing in his power undone, in making efforts
to deliver us from our confinement. We thanked him for this proffered friendship, and he departed.

His first efforts in our favor were directed to gaining the friendship of the general, in order to soften his feelings in regard to us.
But in this he entirely failed. He then adopted an innocent stratagem, which was more successful. He informed the general that he

had business with a Spanish merchant in port, which he could not transact for want of some one who could speak the language fluently, who would interpret for him, that he understood that one of the American prisoners could speak the language perfectly well, and that if he would allow that prisoner to come and interpret for him a few hours, he would bind himself in a bond to any amount, that the prisoner at the expiration of his services, would return voluntarily to his prison. To this the general gave his consent. Captain Bradshaw came to my prison, and I was permitted by the general's order to leave my prison.

When I went abroad, Captain Bradshaw conducted me to the office of an old captain, who had charge of the arms. We begged him to intercede with the general to obtain his permission, that we might go out and bring in our furs. We informed him, that Captain Bradshaw and the supercargo, Rufus Perkins, would be our security in any amount, that the general was disposed to name, that we would return, and surrender ourselves to him, at the close of the expedition. He was at once satisfied of our honor and integrity, and that we were by no means those spies, whom the general took us for, and he promised to use all his influence with the general, to persuade him to dispatch us for our furs. We assured him, that in addition to our other proofs, that we were bonafide Americans, and true republicans, we had documents under the proper signature of the President of the United States, which we hoped, would be sufficient to satisfy him, and every one, who we were. He asked to see those papers, of which I spoke. I told him they were my father's commission of first lieutenant in the ranging service, during the late war with England, and an honorable discharge at the close of the war. He promised to communicate this information to the general, and departed, proposing to return in half an hour. During this interval, we walked to my father's cell, and I had the satisfaction of speaking with him through the grates. He asked me if I had been visited by a beautiful young lady? When I assented, he replied, that this charming young woman, as a ministering angel, had also visited his cell with every sort of kindness and relief, which she had extended to each one of our companions. I had the satisfaction afterwards, of speaking with each one of our companions. I need not add, how much delighted we were to speak with one another once more. From these visits I returned to the office of the captain of arms.

We found him waiting with the most painful intelligence. Nothing could move the general, to allow us to go out and bring in our furs. He expressed a wish, notwithstanding, to see the commission of which I had spoken, and that I should return to my cell. I gave the papers to Captain Bradshaw, requesting him to return them to my father, after the general should have examined them. This he promised, and I took my leave of him, returning to my dreary prison, less buoyant and more completely desponding of my liberty than ever.

In a few moments Captain Bradshaw and Perkins came again to my cell, and said that the general had no faith in our papers, and could not be softened by any entreaty, to give us our liberty. As he said this, the sentinel came up, and stopped him short in his conversation, and ordered them off affirming, that it was the general's express command, that he should not be allowed to see or speak with me again. They however pledged their honor as they left me, that whenever an occasion offered, they would yield us all the assistance in their power, and wishing me better fortune, they departed.

A fortnight elapsed in this miserable prison, during which I had no other consolation, than the visits of the young lady, and even these, such was the strictness of the general's orders, were like all angel visits, *few and far between*. At length a note was presented me by the serjeant, from my father. What a note! I appeal to the heart of every good son to understand what passed within me. This note was written on a piece of paste board torn from his hat. The characters were almost illegible, for they were written with a stick, and the ink was blood, drawn from his aged veins! He informed me that he was very ill, and without any hope of recovery, that he had but one wish on this side the grave, and that was, to see me once more before he died. He begged me to spare no entreaties, that the general would grant me permission to come and see him a last time; but, that if this permission could not be obtained, to be assured, that he loved me, and remembered me affectionately, in death.

This letter pierced me to the heart. O, could I have flown through my prison walls! Had I possessed the strength of the giants, how soon would I have levelled them, even had I drawn down destruction on my own head in doing it. But I could own nothing in my favour, but a fierce and self devouring will. In hopes that the heart of the general was not all adamant, I entreated the serjeant to go and inform him of my father's illness, and his desire to see me once more, and to try to gain permission that I might have leave to attend upon him, or if that might not be, to visit him once more, according to his wish. He went in compliance with my entreaties, and in a few minutes returned with a dejected countenance, from which I at once inferred what was the fate of my application. His voice faltered as he related that the general absolutely refused this request. Oh God! of what stuff are some hearts made! and this was a republican officer! What nameless tortures and miseries do not Americans suffer in foreign climes from those miserable despots who first injure and oppress, and then hate the victims of their oppression, as judging their hearts by their own, and thinking that their victims must be full of purposes of revenge.

The honest and kind hearted serjeant hesitated not to express manly and natural indignation, in view of this inhuman brutality of the general, in refusing a favor, called for by the simplest dictates of humanity, a favor too, in the granting which there could be neither difficulty nor danger. All he could do in the case he promised to do, which was to see that my father should want no sort of nourishment, or aid which he could render him. I tried to thank him, but my case was not of a kind to be alleviated by this sort of consolation. When I thought of our expectations of relief, when we threw ourselves in the power of these vile people, when I took into view our innocence of even the suspicion of a charge that could be brought against us, when I thought of their duplicity of disarming us, and their infamous oppression as soon as we were in their power, and more than all, when I thought of this last brutal cruelty and insult, my whole heart and nature rose in one mingled feeling of rage, wounded affection, and the indignation of despair. The image of my venerable father, suffering and dying unsolaced and unrelieved, and with not a person, who spoke his language, to close his eyes, and I so near him, was before me wherever I turned my eyes.

What a horrible night ensued at the close of this day! As the light was fading, the excellent young lady presented herself at my grate. She repeated all that her brother had related to me, in regard to the cruel refusal of the general. While she discussed this subject, the tears fell from her eyes, and I had the consolation to know, that one person at least felt real sympathy for my distress. She added, in faltering tones, that she was well aware that in a case like this words were of but little avail, but that I might be assured of the kindest attention to all the wants of my father, that she could relieve; and that if it was the will of God, to take him out of this world of sorrow and change, that he should be buried decently and as if he were her own father. Judge what I must have felt towards this noble minded and kind hearted young lady! As she withdrew, my prayers at this time were hearty, if never before, that God would reward her a thousand fold in all good things, for her sympathy with our sufferings.

Thus passed away these days of agony and suspense. The young lady visited me as often as it was understood the general's orders would permit, that is, once in two or three days, bringing me food and drink, of which in the present state of my thoughts, I had little need. In fact, I had become so emaciated and feeble that I could hardly travel across my prison floor. But no grief arrests the flight of time, and the twenty-fourth of April came, in which the serjeant visited me and in a manner of mingled kindness and firmness told me that my father was no more. At these tidings, simple truth calls on me to declare, my heart felt relieved. I am a hunter, and not a person to analyze the feelings of poor human nature. My father now was gone, gone where the voice of the oppressor is no more heard. Since the death of my mother, I have reason to think, that life had been to him one long burden. He had been set free from it all, and set free too, from the cruelty of this vile people, and the still viler general. I felt weak, and exhausted myself, and I expected to rejoin him in a few days, never to be separated from him. Life was a burden of which I longed to be relieved.

After I had given vent to natural feelings on this occasion, the serjeant asked me touching the manner in which we bury our dead in our country? I informed him. He then observed that the reason why he asked that question was, that his sister wished, that my father's body might be interred in a manner conformable to my wishes. I could only thank him for all this kindness and humanity to me, as he left me. I passed the remainder of this day in the indulgence of such reflections as I have no wish to describe, even had I the power.

At night the serjeant's sister again visited my prison. She seemed neither able nor disposed to enter upon the subject before us, and reluctant to call up the circumstance of my father's death to my thoughts. At length she presented me with a complete suit of black, and begged that I would wear it on the following day at my father's funeral. I observed, in astonishment, that she could not doubt what a melancholy satisfaction it would be to me to follow the remains of my father to the grave, but that between me and that satisfaction were the walls of my prison, through which I could not break. She remarked, that by dint of importunity, she had prevailed on the general to allow me to attend the funeral. The fair young lady then undertook the duties of minister and philosopher, counselling me not to grieve for that, for which there is no remedy, proving to me that it was the will of God, that he should thus obtain deliverance from prison, and all the evils of this transitory life, and abundance of common place language of this sort, very similar to what is held in my own country on like occasions. Having finished her kindly intended chapter of consolations, she wished me a good night and left me to my own thoughts. The night I spent in walking the floor of my prison.

At eight in the morning, a file of six soldiers appeared at the door of my prison. It was opened, and I once more breathed the fresh air! The earth and the sky seemed a new region.—The glare of light dazzled my eyes, and dizzied my head. I reeled as I walked. A lieutenant conducted the ceremonies: and when I arrived at the grave he ordered the crowd to give way, that I might see the coffin let down, and the grave filled. I advanced to the edge of the grave, and caught a glimpse of the coffin that contained the remains of the brave hunter and ranger. The coffin was covered with black. No prayers were said. I had scarce time to draw a second breath, before the grave was half filled with earth. I was led back to my prison, the young lady walking by my side in tears. I would gladly have found relief for my own oppressed heart in tears, if they would have flowed. But the sources were dried, and tears would not come to my relief. When I arrived at the prison, such a horrid revulsion came over me at the thoughts of entering that dreary place again, that I am sure I should have preferred to have been shot, rather than enter it again. But I recovered myself by reflecting that my health was rapidly declining, and that I should be able in a short time to escape from the oppressor and the prison walls, and rejoin my father, and be at rest.

This thought composed me, and I heard the key turn upon me with a calm and tranquilized mind. I lay down upon my bed, and passed many hours in the oblivion of sleep. The customary habit of sleep during the night returned to me; and my strength and appetite began to return with it. I felt an irresistible propensity to resume my former habit of smoking. I named my inclination to my friend the serjeant. He was kind enough to furnish me cigars. This was a new resource to aid me in killing the time. Apart from the soothing sensation of smoking, I amused myself for hours in watching the curling of my smoke from the cigar. Those who have always been free, cannot imagine the corroding torments of thoughts preying upon the bosom of the prisoner, who has neither friend to converse with, books to read, or occupation to fill his hours.

On the 27th of June, Captain Bradshaw's vessel was seized, on the charge of smuggling. There were other American vessels in this port at the same time, the names of the captains of which, as far as I can recollect, were Seth Rogers, Aaron W. Williams, and H. Cunningham. These gentlemen, jointly with their supercargoes, sent me five ounces of gold, advising me to keep this money secret from the knowledge of the Spaniards, and preserve it as a resource for my companions and myself, in case of emergencies.

About this time the general received several packages of letters in English, the contents of which, not understanding the language, he could not make out. There was no regular translator at hand; and he sent orders to the serjeant to have me conducted to the office for that purpose. When I entered the office he asked me if I could read writing? When I told him yes, he procured a seat, and bade me sit down. He then presented me a letter in English, requesting me to translate it into Spanish. Though I put forth no claims on the score of scholarship, I perfectly comprehended the meaning of the words in both languages. I accomplished the translation in the best manner in my power; and he was pleased entirely to approve it. He proceeded to ask me a great many questions relative to my travels through the Mexican country; how long I had been absent from my own country, and what had been my occupation, during that absence? To all which questions I returned satisfactory answers. When he bade the guard return me to prison, he informed me that he should probably call for me again.

I returned to my prison somewhat cheered in spirits. I foresaw that he would often have occasion for my services as a translator, and if I showed an obliging disposition, and rendered myself useful, I hoped to obtain enlargement for myself and my companions. As I expected, I was summoned to his office for several days in succession. On my entering the office he began to assume the habit of saluting me kindly, giving me a seat, enquiring after my health, and showing me the other customary civilities. When I found him in his best humor, I generally took occasion remotely to hint at the case of our being detained as prisoners. I tried, gently and soothingly, to convince him of the oppression and injustice of treating the innocent citizens of a sister republic, as if they were spies. He generally showed a disposition to evade the subject; or alleged as a reason for what he had done, that he regretted exceedingly that circumstances on our part seemed so suspicious, that, obliged as he was, to execute the laws of his country, he felt himself compelled to act as he had done; that it was far from his disposition to desire to punish any one unjustly, and without cause; and that he would be glad if we could produce any substantial evidence to acquit us from the suspicion of being spies.

Though, as a true and honest man, I knew that every word he

pronounced was a vile and deceitful lie, yet such is the power of the oppressor, I swallowed my rising words, and dissembled a sort of satisfaction. Waiving the further discussion of our imprisonment, I again recurred to the subject of permission to bring in our furs, persuading him, if he had any doubts about our good faith in returning to this place, to send soldiers to guard us; assuring him, that on obtaining our furs we would pay the soldiers, and indemnify him for any other expense he might incur on the occasion; and that, moreover, we would feel ourselves as grateful to him as if he had bestowed upon us the value of the furs in money. He heard me to the close, and listened with attention; and though he said he could not at present give his consent, he promised that he would deliberate upon the subject, and in the course of a week, let me know the result of his resolution. He then bade his soldiers remand me to prison. I begged him to allow me to communicate this conversation to my companions. This he refused, and I re-entered my prison.

From these repeated interviews, I began to acquaint myself with his interior character. I perceived, that, like most arbitrary and cruel men, he was fickle and infirm of purpose. I determined to take advantage of that weakness in his character by seeming submissive to his wishes, and striving to conform as far as I could to his capricious wishes; and more than all, to seize the right occasions to tease him with importunities for our liberty, and permission to bring in our furs. Four days elapsed before I had another opportunity of seeing him. During this time I had finished the translation of a number of letters, some of which were from Capt. Bradshaw, and related to the detention of his ship and cargo, and himself. When I had finished these translations, and was re-admitted to his presence, I asked him if he had come to any determination in regard to letting us go to bring in our furs? He answered in his surliest tone, no! How different were my reflections on returning to my prison from those with which I had left it! How earnestly I wished that he and I had been together in the wild woods, and I armed with my rifle!

I formed a firm purpose to translate no more letters for him. I found that I had gained nothing by this sort of service; nor even by dissembling a general disposition to serve him. I was anxious for another request to translate, that I might have the pleasure of refusing him, and of telling him to his face that though I was his prisoner, I was not his slave. But it was three days before he sent for me again. At their expiration I was summoned to his office, and he offered me a seat, according to former custom. When I was seated, with a smiling countenance he handed me a packet of letters, and bade me translate them. I took one, opened it, and carelessly perused a few lines, and returning the packet back, rose from my seat, and told him I wished to return to my prison; and bowing, I moved towards the door. He darted a glance at me resembling that of an enraged wild beast; and in a voice, not unlike the growl of a wounded, grizzly bear, asked me why I did not put myself to the translation of the letters? Assuming a manner and tone as surly as his own, I told him my reasons were, that I did not choose to labor voluntarily for an oppressor and enemy; and that I had come to the determination to do it no longer. At this he struck me over the head such a blow with the flat of his sword, as well nigh dropped me on the floor; and ordered the soldiers to return me to prison, where he said I should lay and rot. The moment I recovered from the stunning effect of the blow I sprang toward him; but was immediately seized by the guards, and dragged to the door; he, the while, muttered abundance of the curses which his language supplies. In return, I begged him to consider how much it was like an officer and gentleman to beat an unarmed prisoner in his power, but that if I only had a sword to meet him upon equal terms, I could easily kill as many such dastards as he was, as could come at me. He bade me be silent, and the soldiers to take me off. They shoved me violently on before them to prison. When it closed upon me I never expected to see the sun rise and set again.

Here I remained a week without seeing even the young lady, who was justly so dear to my heart. She was debarred by the general's orders not only from visiting me, but even sending me provisions! I was again reduced to the fare of corn boiled in spoiled tallow, which was brought me twice a day. At this juncture came on Capt. Bradshaw's trial. The declaration of the Captain, supercargo and crew was to be taken, and all the parties separately interrogated by a Spaniard. Not an individual of them could speak a word of Spanish, except the Captain, and he was not allowed to translate in his own case. The general supposed that by interrogating the parties separately, he should be able to gain some advantage from the contradictions of the testimony, and some positive proof of smuggling. Capt. Bradshaw being denied the privilege of interpreting for his crew, requested the general to procure some one who might be allowed to perform that office for him. The general told him that I was capable of the office, if I could be gained to the humor; but that he would as willingly deal with a devil, as with me, when out of humor. Capt. Bradshaw asked him if he might be allowed to converse with me on the subject? He consented, and Capt. B. came to my prison. In reference to the above information, he asked me what had taken place between me and the general which had so exasperated him against me? I related all the circumstances of our last interview. He laughed heartily at my defiance of the general. I was ready, of course, to render any service by which I could oblige Capt. B. He returned to the general, and informed him that I was ready to undertake to translate or interpret in his case.

In a short time my door was opened, and I was once more conducted to the office of the general. Capt. B. was sitting there in waiting. The general asked me if I had so far changed my mind, as to be willing to translate and interpret again? I told him I was always ready to perform that office for a *gentleman*. I placed such an emphasis on the word gentleman, as I purposed, should inform him, that I intended that appellation for the Captain, and not for him. Whether he really misunderstood me, or dissembled the appearance of misunderstanding me, I know not. He only named an hour, in which he should call on me for that service, cautioning me to act in the business with truth and good faith. I told him that my countrymen in that respect, had greatly the disadvantage of his people; for that it was our weakness, not to know how to say any thing but the truth. At this he smiled, ordering me back to prison, until I should be called for next day.

At eight the next morning, I was again summoned to his office, where he proceeded, through me, to question Captain B. touching the different ports at which he had traded, and what was his cargo, when he left the U. S.? He added a great many other questions in relation to the voyage, irrelevant to the purposes of this journal. The clerk on this occasion was an Indian, and a quick and elegant writer. Capt. B. produced his bill of lading, and the other usual documents of clearing out a ship; all which I was obliged to translate. They being matters out of the line of my pursuits, and I making no pretensions to accurate acquaintance with either language, the translation, of course, occupied no inconsiderable time. It was nearly twelve, when he bade us withdraw, with orders to meet him again at his office at two in the afternoon. Capt. B. accompanied me to prison, and as we went on, requested me to make the testimonies of his crew as nearly correspond, and substantiate each other, as possible; for that some of them were angry with him, and would strive to give testimony calculated to condemn him. I assured him that I would do any thing to serve him, that I could in honor. I entered my prison, and slept soundly, until the bells struck two.

I was then reconducted to the general's office; where he continued to interrogate Capt. B., until three. The Supercargo, Mr. R. Perkins, was then called upon to produce his manifesto, and cautioned to declare the truth, in relation to the subject in question. This manifesto differed in no essential respect from the account of the Captain. At sunset they were dismissed, and I remanded to my prison. Day after day the same task was imposed, and the same labors devolved upon me. I at length summoned courage to resume the old question of permission to go out and bring in our furs. To my surprise he remarked, that as soon as he had finished taking all the evidence in relation to Capt. Bradshaw's ship and cargo, he would not only allow us to go, but would send soldiers to prevent the Indians from molesting us. I informed him, that his intended kindness would be unavailing to us, if he did not allow us to depart before the month of August; for that in that month the melting of the snow on the mountains at the sources of Red river caused it to overflow, and that our furs were buried in the bottom, so that the river, in overflowing, would spoil them. He replied, that it was out of his power to grant the consent at this time, which was the 19th of July.

On the 28th he had finished taking all the depositions, and I

again asked him for permission to go and bring in our furs. He still
started delays, alleging that he had made no arrangements for that
purpose yet. Capt. B. was present, and asked him to allow me to
stay with him on board his vessel, promising that he would be ac-
countable for me. To my astonishment the general consented. I repaired to the house of the young lady, who had been so kind to me.
She received me with open arms, and manifested the most un-
equivocal delight. She congratulated me on being once more free
from my dismal prison, and asked me a thousand questions. The
Captain and myself spent the evening with her; and at its close, I
repaired with him on board his beautiful ship, the first sea vessel I
had ever been on board. It may be imagined what a spectacle of interest and eager curiosity the interior of this ship, the rigging,
masts, awning, in short, every thing appertaining to it, would be to
a person raised as I had been, and of a mind naturally inquisitive.
What a new set of people were the sailors! How amusing and
strange their dialect! They heartily shook me by the hand, and commenced describing the several punishments they would inflict
upon the general, if they had him in their power. Among the different inflictions purposed, none seemed to please them better, than
the idea of taring and feathering him, all which I would gladly have
seen him endure, but the worst of it was, after all, the general was
not in their power.

I spent the greater part of the night with the captain and supercargo, conversing about the oppressions and cruelties of the general, and the death of my father, for, during the time of his sickness,
Captain Bradshaw had sailed to Monte el Rey, and had not returned, until after his death. He intended, he said, if his vessel was
condemned, to slip his anchors, and run out of the harbor, at the
risk of being sunk, as he passed the fort. He promised me, if I would
take passage with him, that I should fare as he did, and that, when
we should arrive at Boston, he would obtain me some situation, in
which I could procure a subsistence. I thanked him for his very
kind offer, but remarked, that my companions had suffered a great
deal with me, that we had had many trials together, and had
hazarded our lives for each other, and that now I would suffer any
thing rather than desert them, and leave them in prison, prob-

ably, to have their sufferings enhanced, in consequence of my desertion.

In the morning we all three went on shore together, and took breakfast at the house of my friend, the brother of the young lady. We passed from breakfast, to the office of the general. I asked leave of him to visit my companions in prison. His countenance became red with anger, and he ordered the guard to search me, and take me to prison. I perceived that he thought I had arms concealed about me, and assured him I had none. This did not hinder the guard from searching me, before they put me in prison.

I heard no more from him, and remained shut up in prison until the 28th of August. On that day the general ordered me again to be conducted to his office, where, according to his request, I translated some letters for him. When I had finished, he asked me if I still had an inclination to go for my furs? I replied, that I had reason to suppose that they had been covered before this time, with the waters of Red river, and were all spoiled; but that nevertheless, I should be glad to be certain about it, and at least we should be able to bring in our traps. He asked me what adequate security I could give for our good behavior, and the certainty of our return, provided he should allow us the use of our arms for self defence? I replied, that I knew no one, who could give the security required, but that the soldiers he would send with us, would be his security for our return; but that it was out of the question to think of sending us on a trip, so dangerous under any circumstances, without allowing us to go armed. He remanded me to prison, saying, that he would reflect upon it, and let me know the result of his reflections in the morning. I reflected as I walked to prison, that I could have procured the security of Captain Bradshaw, merely for the asking. But I knew the character of my companions, and was so well aware, how they would feel when all should be once free again, and well armed, that I dared not bind any one in security for us. Such had been the extent of the injuries we had suffered, and so sweet is revenge, and so delightful liberty, when estimated by the bondage we had endured, that I was convinced that Mexico could not array force enough to bring us back alive. I foresaw that the general would send no more than ten or twelve soldiers with us. I knew that it would be no more than an amusement to rise upon them, take their horses for our own riding, flea some of them of their skins, to show them that we knew how to inflict torture, and send the rest back to the general on foot. Knowing that the temptation to some retaliation of this sort would be irresistible, I was determined that no one of my countrymen should be left amenable to the laws on our account. Such thoughts passed through my mind as I told the general, I could offer him no security.

Next morning, immediately after eight, I was allowed to walk to the general's office without being guarded. What a fond feeling came back to my heart with this small boon of liberty! How much I was exalted in my own thoughts, that I could walk fifty yards entrusted with my own safe keeping! When I entered the general's office, he saluted me with ceremoneous politeness. 'Buenas dias, don Santiago,' said he, and showed me to a seat. He proceeded to make known his pleasure, in respect to me and my companions. In the first place he told us, we were all to be allowed the use of our arms, in the next place, that he would send fifteen of his soldiers with us; and in the third place, that we should all be allowed a week, in which to exercise ourselves, before we set out on our expedition. All this good fortune delighted us, and was more almost, than we would have dared to wish. My companions, in an ecstacy of satisfaction, soon joined us from their prisons. We met with as much affection and gladness of heart, as if we had been brothers. They looked more like persons emancipated from the prison of the grave, than human beings; and I am perfectly aware, that my spectre like visage must have been equally a spectacle to them. We had the privilige of walking in the vicinity of the port, accompanied by a guard of soldiers. Our only immediate restriction was the necessity of returning to our guard house to sleep at night. In this way our time passed pleasantly.

On the 3d of September, the general sent for me to his office. When I entered, he presented me a note, and bade me accompany a soldier to a mission at the distance of thirty miles, where he stated I was to deliver this note to a priest, and that he perhaps would be able to furnish us with horses and mules for our expedition to bring in our furs. I started with the soldier, each of us well mounted. The

note was unsealed, and I read it of course. The contents were any
thing, rather than encouraging. It contained no demand for the
horses, as I had hoped. It simply stated to the priest, what sort
of person the general supposed me to be, that we had furs buried
on Red river, and wished horses on which to ride out and bring
them in, and that if the priest felt disposed to hire his horses to us,
he would send soldiers with us to bring us back.

Discouraging as the note was, we pushed ahead with it, and arrived at the priest's mission some time before night. I handed the
note to the old priest, who was a very grave looking personage. He
read the note, and then asked me to come in and take some wine
with him, of which they have great plenty. I followed him into a
large parlor, richly adorned with paintings of saints, and several
side boards, abundantly stored with wines, which I took it for
granted, were not unacceptable to the holy man. The glass ware,
the decorations of the parlor, and the arrangement of every thing
showed me at a glance, that this priest was a man of taste
and fashion. So I was on my guard not to let any of my hunting
phrases and back-wood's dialect escape me. He asked me a great
many questions about the circumstances of my passage across the
continent, to all which I responded in as choice and studied words
as I could command. He then asked me how many beasts we should
want? I replied that there were seven of us, and that we should each
need a pack mule, and a horse to ride upon, which would be fourteen in all. He then asked how many days it would require to go,
and return? I answered, that this was a point upon which I could
not pronounce with certainty, since I was unacquainted with the
road, and accidents might change the issue. He then proposed to
charge what was tantamount to 25 cents of our money a day for
each mule, that carried a saddle, during the expedition, longer or
shorter. To this I consented, and he drew an article of agreement
to that effect. He then wrote a note to send by me to the general, in
reply to his. By this time the sun was setting, and the church bells
began to strike. On this he knelt, and commenced his prayers. He
was repeating the Lord's prayer. According to the customs of his
church, when he had commenced a member of a sentence, I finished it, by way of response. Such are their modes of repeating

their prayers, when there are two or more in company. When we had finished, he turned to me, and asked me why I had prayed? I answered for the salvation of my soul. He said, that it had a christian appearance, but that he had been informed, that the people of our country did not believe that man had a soul, or that there is a Saviour. I assured him, that he had been entirely misinformed, for that we had churches on every side through all the land, and that the people read the Scriptures, and believed all that was taught in the Gospel, according to their understanding of it. But he continued, 'your people do not believe in the immaculate conception of the Virgin Mary.' I replied, that what the general faith of the people upon this point was, I could not say, and that for myself, I did not pretend to have sufficiently studied the Scriptures, to decide upon such points. My assumed modesty soothed him, and he told me, that it was evident, I had not studied the Scriptures, for that if I had, I could not be in doubt about such obvious articles of faith. I acquiesced in his supposition, that I had not studied the Scriptures, remarking, that I was aware that they contained many mysteries, about which the people in my country entertained various opinions. He said that he was truly sorry, that I was not more conversant with the Scriptures, for that if I had been, I could not have been led astray by the Protestants. His time, however, he added was now too limited to enlighten me, but he laughed, as he said he hoped to have the pleasure of baptising me on my return. To this I replied with a smile, for the truth was, I was fearful of disgusting him, and breaking off the bargain. Glad was I, when he dismissed this subject, and began to chat about other matters. We had an excellent supper, and I was shown to my bed.

In the morning I took my leave of the old father, and arrived on the following evening at San Diego. My companions were delighted with the apparent complete success of my mission. The general informed us, that we should have permission to start on the 6th, and that our beasts would be ready for an early start on that day. On the evening of the 5th, he called us to his office, and asked us, how many days we thought the expedition would require? We informed him, as near as we could conjecture. He then said, that he could not spare any soldiers to accompany us. We answered, that it was a point of indifference to us, whether he did or not. 'To insure your return however,' he rejoined, 'I shall retain one of you as a hostage for the return of the rest,' and pointing to me, he informed me, 'that I was the selected hostage,' and that I must remain in prison, during their absence, and that if they did not return, it would convince him, that we were spies, and that in consequence he would cause me to be executed.'

At this horrible sentence, breaking upon us in the sanguine rapture of confidence, we all gazed at each other in the consternation of despair. Some of our company remarked, that they had better abandon the expedition altogether, than leave me behind. Others stood in mute indecision. We had all in truth confidently anticipated never to return to this place again. My indignation, meanwhile, had mounted to such a pitch, as wholly to absorb all sense of personal danger, or care about myself. It seemed as if Providence had put the unrelenting seal of disappointment to every plan I attempted to devise. I told them to go, and not allow my detention to dishearten, or detain them, for that I had no fear of any thing, the general could inflict, that I had little left, but life to relinquish, and that their refusal to go, as things now were, would be taken for ample proofs, that we were spies, and would ensure our condemnation and the conviction, that we never had intended to return.

On this they all agreed to go, and began to pledge their honor and every thing sacred, that they would return, if life was spared them. I told them to follow their own inclinations, as to returning, for that I would as willingly be buried by the side of my father, as any one else; that, however, I did not believe the laws of the country would bear the general out, in putting me to death. The general now bade us arrange every thing to start early in the morning. I was again locked up in my prison, though my companions spent the greater part of the night in conversing with me. In the morning, when they were ready to start, they came and shook hands with me. When the Dutchman, as good hearted a fellow as ever lived, took my hand he burst into tears and said, goot py Jim, if I ever does come back, I will bring an army mit me, and take yours and your daddy's bones from dis tammed country, for it is worse as hell.' I should have laughed heartily at him, had not his tears pre-

vented me, for I knew, that they came from his heart. Mounting
their mules they now set off. Their only arms were old Spanish
muskets, which, when fired, I would almost as soon have stood before as behind. Under such circumstances, knowing, that they
would be obliged to pass through numbers of hostile tribes of Indians, I was very doubtful of their return.

On the 8th, Captain Bradshaw came to my prison, and asked me,
why I was in prison, and my companions at liberty? I told him the
whole story. When he had heard it, he expressed doubts in regard
to their returning. I replied to him, that I was not at all in doubt
of their return, if they lived. He then told me, that he intended to
go to the general, and demand his papers on the 11th, and if they
were not given up to him, he would cut cable, and run out in spite
of any one, adding his advice to me, which was, that I should write
to the consul at Wahu and inform him of my imprisonment. He
seemed to think, I might thus obtain my release. Mr. R. Perkins
would undertake, he said, to place it in the hands of the consul, as
he was acquainted with him. I answered, that I had neither ink nor
paper. He said I should have some in a few minutes, and took
leave of me. A soldier soon entered with writing materials, and I
wrote my letter to Mr. Jones, for that was the name of the consul,
stating every circumstance relative to our imprisonment, and the
death of my father, giving the names of all our party, and begging him, if it was not in his power to obtain our freedom, that
he would inform our government of our situation. I supposed it
was in his power to grant my first request, placed as he was, in
the midst of a foreign nation.

On the 11th, at the request of the general, I was conducted to
his office, to serve as interpreter for the captain and Mr. P. The papers were now demanded by them. The general refused to comply
with the demand, and told them, that both the vessel and cargo
were condemned, but that if they would discharge the cargo, and
deliver it to him, he would allow them to clear the vessel, to go
and seek redress, wherever they pleased. The captain's answer to this
was, that it was not in his power to do so, and that the laws of his
country would hang him, if he thus gave up his ship and cargo at
the request of an individual. The general now became enraged,

and repeating the words, at the request of an individual, added, the ship and cargo have both been lawfully condemned, and if they are not given up peaceably, I have soldiers enough to take the ship, and every thing belonging to it. In reply the captain remarked, that he came to trade on the coast, and not to fight, that if he was disposed to seize the vessel or cargo, he had nothing to say farther, than that he should not aid, or advance in any shape the unlading of the vessel himself, and taking up his hat walked away. I asked permission of the general to go to Miss. Peaks, to get a change of clothing, which was granted. He, however, told me to be in haste. My principal business there was to give my letter to Mr. P., for I knew that captain B., would set sail with the first breeze, of which he could avail himself. I found both the gentlemen in the house, when I entered. I was assured by Mr. P., that he would give the letter to the consul, and endeavor to interest him in my behalf. I thanked him, and was upon the point of taking leave, when captain B. asked me to take a note from him to the general, and to tell him that he would like to have an answer, and would wait an hour for it. I took the note and went to the general's office, gave him the note and told him what the captain had said. He bade me sit down, after he had read the note, for a few minutes. I obeyed, and he passed into the adjoining room, and ordered his porter to call the ensign Ramirez. The porter hastened to execute his commission, and in a few minutes the ensign entered. The general and ensign then began to converse, drawing near the door, behind which I was seated. I heard distinctly the former tell the latter, that captain B., and Mr. P., were both at Peak's awaiting an answer from him, and that he would send me to tell them that he was engaged at present, but at the expiration of an hour and a half they should have their answer through me. Meantime he, the ensign, was to provide a guard of soldiers, with which to take them prisoners, and then the vessel and cargo would be sure. All this, as I have said, I heard distinctly. He then came in, and told me to go and inform them, as he told the ensign, he should direct me. I hastened to captain B., and told him what I had heard from the general concerning him. I advised him to go to the vessel immediately, for that the ensign and guard would soon be upon the spot. Both he and Mr. P. went directly to the vessel, and I returned to the general, to inform him that I had delivered his message. He then ordered me to return to prison. It was now three o'clock.

In a few hours the ensign returned from the pursuit of captain B., and as he passed the prison on his way to the general's office he shook his sword at me with vengeance in his face, saying, 'Oh! you traitor'! I inferred from this, that he supposed I had informed the captain of the projected attempt to take him prisoner. My situation now seemed to me desperate. I thought more of my comrades than myself, for I could not expect to live. Concluding that I should soon be executed, I feared, that when they returned, they would be put to death also. In a few minutes I was summoned to the general's office. I expected to hear my sentence. When I entered the general bade me stand by the door, near a large table, at which several of his clerks were seated writing, and he then gravely asked me if I had overheard the conversation which took place between himself and the ensign, after he had read the note brought by me to him from captain B? I replied that I did not see the ensign at that time, and furthermore could not say positively, whether he had held any conversation, with the ensign, since my arrival on the coast or not. The general proceeded to question me, as to the fact of my having advised the captain to go on board his ship, and if I knew the motives, which induced him to do so, after saying that he would wait for an answer to his note.

He tried to extort an answer from me such as he wished, threatening me with death if I did not relate the truth. I regarded all this as no more than the threats of an old woman, and went on to state what was most likely to be favorable to my cause. I was now remanded to prison with the assurance, that if found guilty, death would be my doom.

A few days only elapsed before, the breeze serving, the Captain slipped anchor, and ran out of the port. He was compelled to perform this under a heavy shower of cannon balls poured forth from the fort, within two hundred yards of which he was obliged to pass. When he came opposite it, he hove to, and gave them a broadside in return, which frightened the poor engineers from their guns. His escape from the port was made without suffering any serious injury on his part. Their shots entered the hull of the vessel, and the sails were considerably cut by the grape. I was greatly rejoiced when I heard of their escape from these thieves. The General pretended great disgust at the cowardly conduct of the engineers, but, I believe, had he been there, he would have run too. I have no faith in the courage of these people, except where they have greatly the advantage, or can kill in the dark, without danger to themselves. This in my view is the amount of a Spaniard's bravery.

But to return to myself, I remained in prison, until a sufficient time had elapsed, as I thought, for the return of my companions. I still did not entirely despair of seeing them; but the Spaniards came daily and hourly to my prison with delighted countenances to tell me that my companions had deserted me, and that the General would soon have me executed. Some consoled me with the information, that at such an hour or day, I was to be taken out, and burnt alive; and others, that I was to be stationed at a certain distance, and shot at, like a target, or hung. These unfeeling wretches thus harrassed and tormented me, until the arrival of my companions on the 30th Sept. put an end to their taunts, with regard to their desertion of me. They brought no fur however, it having been all spoiled as I had expected, by an over flow of the river. Our traps which they did bring, were sold, and a part of the proceeds paid to the old priest for the hire of the mules.

I have failed to remark, that my comrades had returned with the loss of two of their number, one of whom we learned, had married in New Mexico. When the party reached the river, these two concluded that rather than return to prison, they would run the risk of being killed by the Indians, or of being starved to death; and set forth on their perilous journey through the wilderness to New Mexico on foot. The probability of their reaching the point of their destination was very slight, it being a great distance and through great dangers. Happily for us, their not returning, did not appear to strengthen the General, in his opinion of our being spies. I had the pleasure of conversing with my companions an hour, or more, after which they were again disarmed, and all of us returned to our separate places of confinement. I had now no prospect before me, but that of lingering out a miserable and useless life in my present situation; as I was convinced, that the only inducement, which operated in the General's mind, to allow a part of us to go in search of our property was the hope of taking a quantity of furs and other valuables from us. I was thankful that he obtained nothing but the traps, which, as he knew no more how to use, than a blind horse, could be of no utility to him. This feeling may seem a poor gratification, but it was certainly a natural one.

In this condition we remained for months, never seeing the outside of our prison, deprived of the pleasure we had received from the visits of the charitable young lady, formerly allowed entrance to us, and the advantage we had derived from the generous nourishment she so kindly furnished us, and compelled by hunger to eat the food set before us by our jailors; and cofined principally to dried beans, or corn boiled in water, and then fried in spoiled tallow.

At length the small pox began to rage on the upper part of the coast, carrying off the inhabitants by hundreds. Letters from the distressed people were continually arriving, praying the general to devise some means to put a stop to the disease, which seemed to threaten the country with destruction. The general was thus beset by petitions for several weeks, before he could offer a shadow of relief for them. He was much alarmed, fearing that the disorder might extend its ravages to that part of the coast where he resided.

One day the soldiers, through mere inquisitiveness, asked the Dutchman if he knew any remedy for the complaint? He answered that he did; but that he had none of the article that constituted the remedy. He added, however, that he thought that my father had brought some of it with him, as he recollected his having vaccinated the people at the copper mines. This conversation was communicated to the general immediately, who sent a sergeant to me to inquire if I had any of the remedy spoken of by the Dutchman, as brought by my father? I answered in the affirmative; I then showed him where I had been vaccinated on the right arm, and assured him that it had effectually protected me from the small pox. Upon his demand whether I knew the method of applying it, I again answered in the affirmative; but when he asked me to show him the remedy, and let him have it to apply to his own arm, as he was fearful of losing his life from the spread of this dreadful disease, I told him I would not. This sergeant, who wished the matter, was my friend, and brother of the charitable young lady who had procured my father's burial, and for whom I would have sacrificed my life. But thinking this my only chance for regaining liberty, I refused it to him, saying, that I would neither show it to any one, nor apply it, unless my liberty and that of my companions was rendered secure; and that in sustaining this resolution I would sacrifice my life. I also mentioned that I must be paid, over and above my liberty. My object in this, was to influence the fears of the general. If he acceded to my proposition, my friend and his sister would share the benefit in common with others. If I granted the request of the sergeant to inoculate him, I might lose my advantage; but my gratitude decided me against allowing himself and his sister to be exposed to an imminent danger, which I could avert. I told him that if he would pledge himself, solemnly, for his own part, and that of his sister, that he would not communicate the matter to another individual, I would secretly vaccinate them. He replied that I need not fear his betraying me, as he would much rather aid me in my design, which he thought excellent, and likely to accomplish my wishes. He then left me to communicate the result of our conversation to the general.

This incident, so important in its influence upon my fortunes, occurred December 20th. The sergeant had not been absent more than a half hour, when he returned and told me that the general said he would give me a passport for a year, if I would vaccinate all the people on the coast; and furthermore, if I conducted properly during that period, that he would at the expiration of it, pay me for my services, and give me my liberty. His countenance was bright with delight, as he related this to me, not dreaming that I could refuse what seemed to him so good an offer. When I repeated, in reply, my resolution not to vaccinate any one, except on the conditions I had stated, and added that I would not agree to any terms without an audience from the general, his pleasure vanished, giving place to gloom as he told me he did not think the general would accede to the proposal to set my companions and myself at liberty upon parole for one year, for any consideration; but that, if I persisted in my refusal, he feared I should incur some violent punishment, and perhaps death. My answer was, that in my present situation I did not dread death. I then requested him to tell the general I wished to talk with him personally upon the subject.

He went, and in a few minutes returned with orders to conduct me to the General's office. Upon my arrival there, the General questioned me with regard to the efficacy of the remedy of which he had been much informed in the same manner as I have related in the conversation between the sergeant and myself; and he then repeated the same terms for the matter and the application of it, that he had transmitted me through my friend, to which I replied as before. When I had finished, he asked me in a surly manner, what my own terms were? I told him, as I had done the sergeant, that I would vaccinate all the inhabitants on the coast, provided he would allow myself and companions to leave our prison on parole for one year, with liberty to travel up or down the coast, in order to find some occupation, by which we could obtain food and clothing. Upon hearing this his rage burst forth. He told me I was a devil; and that if I did not choose to take the offer he had made, he would compel me to perform its conditions, or put me to death. I replied, that he could take my life; but that it was beyond his power to compel me to execute his commands, adding, that life or liberty would be no object to me, if my companions were denied the enjoyment of them with me. They had had the alternative in their power of leaving me in prison to suffer alone, or returning to share my captivity, and had chosen the latter; I concluded by saying, that rather than accept of liberty while they remained in prison, I would undergo all the torments his *excellency* could devise. He said he might as well let loose so many wolves to ravage his country, as give myself and companions the liberty I required; adding, that he gave me twenty-four hours to reflect on the alternative of his wrath, or my liberty upon the conditions he had proposed. I was now remanded to prison. As I walked out, I remarked to the General, that my resolution was fixed beyond the possibility of change. He made no reply, and I proceeded to prison. The soldiers who accompanied me, tried to induce me to conform to the General's wishes, saying, that he was a terrible man when enraged. I made them no answer, and entered my prison, where I remained until 8 o'clock the next day; when I was again escorted to the office, and asked by the General, what security I would give for the good behaviour of myself and companions, if he let us out on parole for one year? I told him I would give none, for no one here knew me. He then ordered me back to prison, where he said I should lay and rot, calling me a *carracho picaro,* and similar names, which I did not regard. I walked to my prison as undauntedly as I could. I now felt somewhat encouraged; for I perceived he was not inflexible in his resolutions, and by adhering firmly to mine, I hoped finally to conquer him.

In the course of the night he received a letter containing information of the death of one of his priests, and that great numbers were ill of the small pox. Early in the morning of the 23d I received a summons to attend him at the usual place. When I arrived, he said he wanted to see my papers, that is, those I had mentioned as being my father's commission, and his discharge from the service of a ranger. I told him they were at Miss Peak's, which was the name of the young lady who had been so kind to me. He sent a soldier for them, who soon returned with them. I translated them to him. He said that was a sufficient proof of my being an American; and asked if my companions could produce proofs of their belonging to the same country? I replied that I did not know.

He sent orders for them to come to the office; and before their arrival, told me that all he now wanted, was proof that they were Americans, to let us go on a parole, as all Americans were tolerated in his country. My opinion with regard to his motive in the case was, that he was less unwilling to grant our liberty, as the payment for my services in spreading the vaccine disease, now that he knew we had no property for him to extort from us.

He talked, too, about rendering himself liable to suffer the rigor of the laws of his country, should he set us free, without our establishing the fact of our being Americans.

My companions entered: I was glad to see them. Their beards were long, and they were haggard and much reduced in flesh. I gave them to understand what was wanting, and they readily produced some old black papers, furnishing in themselves proof of any thing else, as much as of their owners being American citizens. I, however, so interpreted them, that they established the point with the General. I believe he had as firmly credited this fact from the first hour he saw us, as now. He concluded to let us out a week upon trial, before he gave us freedom on parole, although he compelled me to engage to vaccinate all the people in the fort. He then directed us to endeavor to find some employment around the fort, which would procure us food, and to return every night to the guard house to sleep. The guard bell now tolled eight o'clock, and according to the permission given, we walked in the direction of our inclinations.

I went directly to Miss Peak's, who was much astonished, and apparently delighted to see me at liberty. She had expected, she said, every day to see me on my way to be shot, or hung. The manifestation of kindness and benevolence to us having been forbidden by our jailors, she now indemnified her humanity and good feeling by telling me how much she had regretted not being allowed to send me proper food, asking me if I was not hungry? and proceeding, before I could answer, to spread a table with every thing good, of which I partook plentifully; after which we had a pleasant conversation together. My enjoyment of my fortunate change of situation was, however, mingled with uncertainty, as to the length of its duration. I felt that I was still in the lion's jaws, which might close upon me from the first impulse of petulance or anger.

I therefore, endeavoured to devise some way of availing myself of my momentary freedom, to place myself beyond the possibility of losing it again. That one which suggested itself to me, was to prevail upon the officer, who had our rifles in charge to allow us possession of them for a short time, to clean them. When we should once more have them in our hands, I hoped we would have resolution to retain them, until death rendered them useless to us. I went to my companions, and imparted my plan to them. They agreed with me upon all points. The only difficulty now was, to lay our hands upon our arms. I went directly to the apartment of the officer, in whose care they were, one of the best hearted Spaniards I have ever seen. I appealed to his goodness of heart in order to obtain my purpose, telling him, that we only wanted the rifles a few minutes, in order to rub off the rust, and dirt, which must have accumulated upon them. I told him after this was done, they should be returned to him. He did not answer for some minutes; and then said, that if he complied with my request, and was discovered by the General to have done so, he should be punished. I replied that there was no danger of an act of this kind, a mere kindness of this sort being known by any, but those immediately concerned; concluding by slipping ten dollars in silver, which had been given me by Capt. B. into his hand. He then handed me the rifles, and all belonging to them, through a back door, cautioning me not to let my having them in possession be known. I answered, that I would be upon my guard. I was now joined by my companions. We found an old and unoccupied house, into which we entered, and soon put our guns in order, and charged them well, resolving never to give them into the hands of a Spaniard again. We had been so treacherously dealt with by these people, that we did not consider it any great breach of honour to fail in our promise of returning our arms, particularly as the officer had taken my money.

We then concluded to coneal our rifles in a thicket near at hand, and to keep our pistols, which the officer had also given us as a part of our arms, concealed around our persons. At night we went to the guard house to sleep, as we had been commanded to do. The officer who gave me the rifles, came to me, and asked why I had not returned the arms according to promise? I told him that I had not finished cleaning them, and repeated, that the General should not know I had them. He charged me to fulfill my former promise of returning the arms on the succeeding morning. I satisfied him, thinking as before, that it made no great difference what is said to such persons, in a position like ours.

Early the next morning we met a countryman by the name of James Lang, who had come upon the coast to smuggle, and kill sea otters for their skins, which are very valuable. He was now here secretly, to enquire if sea otters were to be found in abundance higher up the coast; and to obtain information on some other points connected with his pursuits. He told us he had a boat distant eighty miles down the coast, with men in search of otters, and proposed that we should accompany him to it, offering to furnish every thing required for this species of hunting, and give us half of whatever we caught, adding, that when his brig returned from the Gallipagos islands, where it had gone in search of tortoise shell, he would give us a free passage to our own country.

We all considered this an offer advantageous to us, as it held out the prospect of our being enabled to obtain something in the way of gain, after which a way would be open for our return to our homes, and we agreed to meet him on a certain day at *Todos Santos,* in English All Saints. This took place on the 24th. Our new friend set off to rejoin his companions, and we fell to consultation upon the best method of conducting in our present circumstances. We did not wish to do any thing, that would render us amenable to the laws of the country, should we be detected in our attempt to escape. We were consequently precluded from relying on horses to aid us in hastening beyond the reach of pursuers. The night was chosen, as the time for our experiment; but in the course of an hour after this determination was made, all my companions excepting one, receded from it, pronouncing the plan of running off without any cover for our intentions, not a good one. They proposed instead of it, that we should ask permission of the General to go a hunting, assigning as our reason for this request, that we were barefoot, and wanted to kill some deer in order to obtain their skins to dress, to make us moccasins. I consented to this plan, and to try its efficacy immediately, I went to the General's office. It was late, but I related my errand. He asked me, where I could get arms, to kill deer with? I replied, that if he would not allow us to use our own arms, we could borrow some. He refused the permission, I had asked of him.

On Christmas night, the one among my companions, whom I have mentioned, as agreeing with me, in regard to the original plan for our escape, set off with me at 12 o'clock, while the people, who were all Catholics, were engaged in their devotions at church. We were obliged to leave our comrades, as they would not accompany us in our enterprise. We travelled entirely by night, and reached the before mentioned place of rendezvous on the 28th. We found Mr. Lang and his men in confinement, and his boat taken by the Spaniards. We gained this information in the night, without committing ourselves. We retreated to the woods, in which we remained concealed through the day. At night our necessities compelled us to enter a house, in order to obtain some food. It was occupied by a widow and her two daughters. They gave us bread, milk and cheese, treating us with great kindness. We spent a week passing the day in the woods, and going to this friendly house to get food in the night; in the hope of hearing of some vessel, by means of which we might escape from this hated coast. But no such good fortune awaited us.

We then concluded to return, and see our comrades, whom we supposed to be again in prison; although we were determined never again to be confined there ourselves alive, with our own consent. So we walked back to San Diego, killing some deer by the way, the skins of which we carried to the fort.—To our great admiration and surprize, we found our companions at liberty. They informed us, that the General was exceedingly anxious for my return, and that our arms had not been demanded, although the officer, through whose means we obtained them, had been placed under guard.

I felt grieved by the latter part of this information, as I had deceived the unfortunate man, when he intended to do me a kindness, of the utmost importance to my interests, as I viewed it. He would probably, be severely punished. But I nevertheless was firm in my purpose to retain my arms. It was late in the day; but the companion of my flight and myself proceeded to present ourselves before the General, leaving our rifles concealed in a safe place. Our pistols we carried in our bosoms, determined not to be taken to prison without offering resistance.

The General appeared much surprised to see us, and asked where we had been? I told him, that we had been out upon a hunting expedition; upon which he wished to know if we had killed any thing? We answered in the affirmative. He then looked serious, and demanded of me, if I was not aware that it was wrong to go off, without taking leave of him? My reply was, that I did; and that he refused it to me; and that then I concluded to go without permission, knowing it could not be a crime. His next question was, how I obtained my arms? I told him the truth with regard to this point. The succeeding demand was, why I did not return them, according to my promise? To which I replied, that I did not intend to return them from the first; and I now declared that they should never be taken from me for the time to come, while I drew my breath. He smiled, and said he did not want them; but that I must begin to vaccinate the people of the garrison; for that he wished me to go up the coast soon to practice vaccination there.

On the 18th of January, 1828, I began to vaccinate; and by the 16th of February had vaccinated all the people belonging to the fort, and the Indian inhabitants of the mission of San Diego, three miles north of the former place. It is situated in a valley between two mountains. A stream runs through the valley, from which ships obtain fresh water. An abundance of grain is raised at this mission. Fruit of all kinds, growing in a temperate climate, is also plentiful. The climate is delightfully equal. The husbandman here does not think of his fields being moistened by the falling rain. He digs ditches around them, in which water is conveyed from a stream, sufficient to cover the ground, whenever the moisture is required. Rains seldom fall in the summer or autumn. The rainy season commences in October; and continues until the last of December, and sometimes even through January; by which time the grass, clover and wild oats are knee high. When the rain does come, it falls in torrents. The gullies made in the sides of the mountains by the rains are of an enormous size.

But to return to my own affairs. Having completed my vaccinations in this quarter, and procured a sufficient quantity of the vaccine matter to answer my purpose, I declared myself in readiness to proceed further. I communicated the matter to one thousand Spaniards and Indians in San Diego.

February 28 the General gave us each a legal form, granting us liberty on parole for one year, at the expiration of which period it was in his power to remand us to prison, if he did not incline to grant us our freedom. He likewise gave me a letter to the priests along the coast, containing the information that I was to vaccinate all the inhabitants upon the coast, and an order providing for me all necessary supplies of food and horses for my journey. These were to be furnished me by the people, among whom I found myself cast. They were, also, directed to treat me with respect, and indemnify me for my services, as far as they thought proper. The latter charge did not strike me agreeably; for I foresaw, that upon such conditions my services would not be worth one cent to me. However, the prospect of one whole year's liberty was so delightful, that I concluded to trust in Providence, and the generosity of the stranger, and think no more of the matter. With these feelings I set forth to the next mission, at which I had already been. It was called San Luis.

I reached it in the evening. I found an old priest, who seemed glad to see me. I gave him the General's letter. After he had read it, he said, with regard to that part of it which spoke of payment, that I had better take certificates from the priests of each mission, as I advanced up the coast, stating that I had vaccinated their inhabitants; and that when I arrived at the upper mission, where one of the high dignitaries of the church resided, I should receive my recompense for the whole. Seeing nothing at all singular in this advice, I concluded to adopt it.

In the morning I entered on the performance of my duty. My subjects were Indians, the missions being entirely composed of them, with the exception of the priests, who are the rulers. The number of natives in this mission was three thousand, nine hundred and four. I took the old priest's certificate, as had been recommended by him, when I had completed my task. This is said to be the largest, most flourishing, and every way the most important mission on the coast. For its consumption fifty beeves are killed weekly. The hides and tallow are sold to ships for goods, and other articles for the use of the Indians, who are better dressed in general, than the Spaniards. All the income of the mission is placed in the hands of the priests, who give out clothing and food, according as it is required. They are also self constituted guardians of the female part of the mission, shutting up under lock and key, one hour after supper, all those, whose husbands are absent, and all young women and girls above nine years of age. During the day, they are entrusted to the care of the matrons. Notwithstanding this, all the precautions taken by the vigilant fathers of the church are found insufficient. I saw women in irons for misconduct, and men in the stocks. The former are expected to remain a widow six months after the death of a husband, after which period they may marry again. The priests appoint officers to superintend the natives, while they are at work, from among themselves. They are called *alcaides,* and are very rigid in exacting the performance of the allotted tasks, applying the rod to those who fall short of the portion of labor assigned them. They are taught in the different trades; some of them being blacksmiths, others carpenters and shoe-makers. Those, trained to the knowledge of music, both vocal and instrumental, are intended for the service of the church. The women and girls sew, knit, and spin wool upon a large wheel, which is woven into blankets by the men. The alcaides, after finishing the business of the day, give an account of it to the priest, and then kiss his hand, before they withdraw to their wigwams, to pass the night. This mission is composed of parts of five different tribes, who speak different languages.

The greater part of these Indians were brought from their native mountains against their own inclinations, and by compulsion; and then baptised; which act was as little voluntary on their part, as the former had been. After these preliminaries, they had been put to work, as converted Indians.

The next mission on my way was that, called St. John the Baptist. The mountains here approach so near the ocean, as to leave only room enough for the location of the mission. The waves dash upon the shore immediately in front of it. The priest, who presides over this mission, was in the habit of indulging his love of wine and stronger liquors to such a degree, as to be often intoxicated. The church had been shattered by an earthquake. Between twenty and thirty of the Indians, men, women and children, had been suddenly destroyed by the falling of the church bells upon them. After communicating the vaccine matter to 600 natives, I left this place, where mountains rose behind to shelter it; and the sea stretched out its boundless expanse before it.

Continuing my route I reached my next point of destination. This establishment was called the mission of St. Gabriel. Here I vaccinated 960 individuals. The course from the mission of St. John the Baptist to this place led me from the sea-shore, a distance of from eighteen to twenty miles. Those, who selected the position of this mission, followed the receding mountains. It extends from their foot, having in front a large tract of country showing small barren hills, and yet affording pasturage for herds of cattle so numerous, that their number is unknown even to the all surveying and systematic priests. In this species of riches St. Gabriel exceeds all the other establishments on the coast. The sides of the mountains here are covered with a growth of live oak and pine. The chain to which these mountains belong, extends along the whole length of the coast. The fort St. Peter stands on the sea coast, parallel to this mission.

My next advance was to a small town, inhabited by Spaniards, called the town of The Angels. The houses have flat roofs, covered with bituminous pitch, brought from a place within four miles of the town, where this article boils up from the earth. As the liquid rises, hollow bubbles like a shell of a large size, are formed. When they burst, the noise is heard distinctly in the town. The material is obtained by breaking off portions, that have become hard, with an axe, or something of the kind. The large pieces thus separated, are laid on the roof, previously covered with earth, through which the pitch cannot penetrate, when it is rendered liquid again by the heat of the sun. In this place I vaccinated 2500 persons.

From this place I went to the mission of St. Ferdinand, where I communicated the matter to 967 subjects. St. Ferdinand is thirty miles east of the coast, and a fine place in point of position.

The mission of St. Buenaventura succeeded. Not long previous to my arrival here, two priests had eloped from the establishment, taking with them what gold and silver they could lay their hands upon. They chose an American vessel, in which to make their escape. I practised my new calling upon 1000 persons in this mission.

The next point I reached was the fort of St. Barbara. I found several vessels lying here. I went on board of them, and spent some pleasant evenings in company with the commanders. I enjoyed the contrast of such society with that of the priests and Indians, among whom I had lately been. This place has a garrison of fifty or sixty soldiers. The mission lies a half a mile N. W. of the fort. It is situated on the summit of a hill, and affords a fine view of the great deep. Many are the hours I passed during this long and lonely journey, through a country every way strange and foreign to me, in looking on the ceaseless motion of its waves. The great Leviathan too played therein. I have often watched him, as he threw spouts of water into the air, and moved his huge body through the liquid surface. My subjects here amounted to 2600. They were principally Indians.

The next mission on my route was that called St. Enos. I vaccinated 900 of its inhabitants, and proceeded to St. Cruz, where I operated upon 650. My next advance was to St. Luis Obispes. Here I found 800 subjects. The mission of St. Michael followed in order. In it I vaccinated 1850 persons. My next theatre of operations was at St. John Bapistrano. 900 was the number that received vaccination here. Thence I went to La Solada, and vaccinated 1685, and then proceeded to St. Carlos, and communicated the matter to 800.

From the latter mission I passed on to the fort of Monte El Rey, where is a garrison of a hundred soldiers. I found here 500 persons to vaccinate. The name of this place in English signifies the King's mount or hill. Forests spread around Monte El Rey for miles in all directions, composed of thick clusters of pines and live oaks. Numberless grey bears find their home, and range in these deep woods. They are frequently known to attack men. The Spaniards take great numbers of them by stratagem, killing an old horse in the neighborhood of their places of resort. They erect a scaffold near the dead animal, upon which they place themselves during the night, armed with a gun or lance. When the bear approaches to eat, they either shoot it, or pierce it with the lance from their elevated position. Notwithstanding all their precautions, however, they are sometimes caught by the wounded animal; and after a man has once wrestled with a bear, he will not be likely to desire to make a second trial of the same gymnastic exercise. Such, at any rate, is the opinion I have heard those express, who have had the good fortune to come off alive from a contest of this kind. I do not speak for myself in this matter, as I never came so near as to take the *close hug* with one in my life; though to escape it, I once came near breaking my neck down a precipice.

From Monte El Rey I advanced to the mission of St. Anthony, which lies thirty miles E. from the coast. In it I found one thousand persons to inoculate. I had now reached the region of small pox, several cases of it having occurred in this mission. The ruling priest of this establishment informed me, that he did not consider it either necessary or advisable for me to proceed farther for the purpose of inoculating the inhabitants of the country, as the small pox had prevailed universally through its whole remaining extent. As I had heard, while in San Diego, great numbers had been carried off by it. I then told him that I wished to see the church officer who had been described to me by the first priest whom I had seen on my way up the coast. He furnished me a horse, and I set off for the port of San Francisco, vaccinating those whom I found on the way who had not had the small pox.

I reached the above mentioned place, on the twentieth of June, 1829. Finding the person of whom I was in search, I presented him all the certificates of the priests of the missions in which I had vaccinated, and the letter of the General. I had inoculated in all twenty two-thousand persons. After he had finished the perusal of these papers, he asked me, what I thought my services were worth? I replied, that I should leave that point entirely to his judgment and decision. He then remarked, that he must have some time to reflect upon the subject, and that I must spend a week or two with him. I consented willingly to this proposal, as I was desirous of crossing the bay of St. Francisco to the Russian settlement, called the Bodego.

I proceeded to carry my wish into execution on the 23d, accompanied by two Coriac Indians, whose occupation was the killing of sea otters for the Russians, who hire them into their service. Those who pursue this employment, have water crafts made of the sea lions' skins, in the shape of a canoe. Over this spreads a top, completely covered in such a manner as to preclude the possibility of the entrance of any water. An opening is left at the bow and stern, over which the person who has entered draws a covering made of the same material with that of the boat, which fastens firmly over the aperture in such a manner, as to make this part entirely water proof, as any other portion of the boat. Two persons generally occupy it. No position can be more secure than theirs, from all the dangers of the sea. The waves dash over them harmless. The occupants are stationed, one at the bow, and the other at the stern; the latter guides the boat, while the other is provided with a spear, which he darts into the otter whenever he comes within its reach. Great numbers are thus taken.

But to return to myself: We crossed the bay, which is about three miles in width. It is made by the entrance of a considerable river, called by the Spaniards Rio de San Francisco. After we reached the north shore, we travelled through a beautiful country, with a rich soil, well watered and timbered, and reached the Russian settlement in the night, having come a distance of thirty miles. As our journey had been made on foot, and we had eaten nothing, I was exceedingly fatigued and hungry. I accompanied my fellow travellers, who belonged here, to their wigwams, where I obtained some food, and a seal skin to sleep upon. Early in the morning I arose, and learning from one of my late companions where was the dwelling of the commander of the place, I proceeded towards it. I had become acquainted with this person while I was vaccinating the inhabitants of San Diego. He came there in a brig, and insisted upon my promising him that I would come and communicate the remedy to the people of his establishments, offering to recompense me for my services. I agreed to do what he wished, should it be in my power. Accordingly, finding that the Spaniard did not intend to keep a strict guard over my movements, I availed myself of this opportunity of fulfilling the expressed wish of Don Sereldo, for so was he called. I reached the place pointed out to me by the friendly Indian, and was received by the above mentioned gentleman with the warmest expressions of kindness and friendship. He said that so long a time had elapsed since he saw me, he was afraid I had forgotten our conversation together, and that circumstances had rendered my coming to him impossible. He had suffered greatly from the fear that the small pox would spread among his people, before he should be enabled to prevent danger from it, through the means of the kine pox.

After breakfast, he circulated an order among the people, for all who wished to be provided with a safe guard against the terrible malady that had approached them so near, to come to his door. In a few hours I began my operations; and continued to be constantly occupied for three days, vaccinating during this period fifteen hundred individuals. I reminded them all that they must return on the fourth day, provided no signs of the complaint appeared; and that they were not to rub, or roughly touch the spot, should the vaccine matter have proper effect.

This done, Don Sereldo offered to accompany me through the fort and around the settlement, in order to show me the position, and every thing which might be new and interesting to me. Its situation is one of the most beautiful that I ever beheld, or that the imagination can conceive. The fort stands on the brow of a handsome hill, about two hundred feet above the level of the sea. This hill is surrounded on all sides for two miles with a charming plain. A lofty mountain whose side presents the noblest depth of forest, raises a summit, glittering with perpetual ice and snow on one hand, and on the other the level surface is lost in the waves of the sea. Clear cold streams pour down the mountain, unceasingly from different points, and glide through the plain, imparting moisture and verdure. The same multitudes of domestic animals, that are every where seen in this country, graze around in the pastures. They find abundant pasturage in the wild oats, which grow spontaneously upon this coast. Very little attention is paid to cultivation, where so many advantages are united to favor it. The amount of produce of any kind raised is small, and the inhabitants depend for bread entirely upon the Spaniards.

I remained in this delightful place one week. At the expiration of this time Don Sereldo gave me one hundred dollars, as payment for my services, and then mounted me upon a horse and conducted me back to the bay himself, and remained on the shore, until he saw me safe upon the other side.

I soon saw myself again in the presence of the Spanish priest, from whom I was to receive my recompense for the services performed on my long tour. He was not aware where I had been, until I informed him. When I had told him, he asked me what Don Sereldo had paid me? I stated this matter as it was. He then demanded of me, how I liked the coast of California? I answered, that I very much admired the appearance of the country. His next question was, how I would like the idea of living in it? It would be agreeable to me, I returned, were it subject to any other form of government. He proceded to question me upon the ground of my objections to the present form of government? I was careful not to satisfy him on this point.

He then handed me a written piece of paper, the translation of which is as follows:

I certify, that James O. Pattie has vaccinated all the Indians and whites on this coast, and to recompense him for the same, I give the said James O. Pattie my obligation for one thousand head of cattle, and land to pasture them; that is, 500 cows and 500 mules. This he is to receive after he becomes a Catholic, and a subject of this government. Given in the mission of St. Francisco on the 8th of July, in the year 1829.

JOHN CABORTES

When I had read this, without making use of any figure of speech, I was truck dumb. My anger choked me. As I was well aware of the fact, that this man had it in his power to hang me if I insulted him, and that here there was no law to give me redress, and compel him to pay me justly for my services, I said nothing for some time, but stood looking him full in the face. I cannot judge whether he read my displeasure, and burning feelings in my countenance, as I thus eyed him, and would have sought to pacify me, or not; but before I made a movement of any kind, he spoke, saying, 'you look displeased, sir.' Prudential considerations were sufficient to withhold me no longer, and I answered in a short manner, that I felt at that moment as though I should rejoice to find myself once more in a country where I should be justly dealt by. He asked me, what I meant when I spoke of being justly dealt by? I told him what my meaning was, and wished to be in my own country, where there are laws to compel a man to pay another what he justly owes him, without his having the power to attach to the debt, as a condition upon which the payment is to depend, the submission to, and gratification of, any of his whimsical desires. Upon this the priest's tone became loud and angry as he said, 'then you regard my proposing that you should become a Catholic, as the expression of an unjust and whimsical desire!' I told him 'yes, that I did; and that I would not change my present opinions for all the money his mission was worth; and moreover, that before I would consent to be adopted into the society and companionship of such a band of murderers and robbers, as I deemed were to be found along this coast, for the pitiful amount of one thousand head of cattle, I would suffer death.'

When I had thus given honest and plain utterance to the feelings, which swelled within me, the priest ordered me to leave his house. I walked out quickly, and possessed myself of my rifle, as I did not know, but some of his attendants at hand might be set upon me; for if the comparison be allowable the priests of this country have the people as much and entirely under their control and command, as the people of our own country have a good bidable dog. For fear they should come barking at me, I hastened away, and proceeded to a *ranch,* where I procured a horse for three dollars, which I mounted, and took the route for Monte El Rey. I did not stop, nor stay on my journey to the place. I found upon my arrival there, an American vessel in port, just ready to sail, and on the point of departure.

Meeting the Captain on shore, I made the necessary arrangements with him for accompanying him, and we went on board together. The anchor was now weighed, and we set sail. In the course of an hour, I was thoroughly sick, and so continued for one week. I do not know any word, that explains my feelings in this case so well as that of heart sickness. I ate nothing, or little all this time; but after I recovered, my appetite returned in tenfold strength, and I never enjoyed better health in my life. We continued at sea for several months, sailing from one port to another, and finally returned to that of Monte El Rey, from which we had set sail.

It was now the 6th of January, 1830, and I felt anxious to hear something in relation to my companions, from whom I had so long been separated. I accordingly went on shore, where I met with a great number of acquaintances, both Americans and English. The latter informed me, that there was a revolution in the country, a part of the inhabitants having revolted against the constituted authorities. The revolted party seemed at present likely to gain the ascendency. They had promised the English and Americans the same privileges, and liberty in regard to the trade on the coast, that belonged to the native citizens, upon the condition, that these people aided them in their attempt to gain their freedom, by imparting advice and funds.

This information gladdened my very heart. I do not know, if the feeling be not wrong; but I instantly thought of the unspeakable pleasure I should enjoy at seeing the general, who had imprisoned me, and treated me so little like a man and a Christian, in fetters himself. Under the influence of these feelings, I readily and cheerfully appropriated a part of my little store to their use, I would fain have accompanied them in hopes to have one shot at the general with my rifle. But the persuasions of my countrymen to the contrary prevailed with me. They assigned, as reasons for their advice, that it was enough to give counsel and funds at first, and that the better plan would be, to see how they managed their own affairs, before we committed ourselves, by taking an active part in them, as they had been found to be a treacherous people to deal with.

On the 8th of the month, Gen. Joachim Solis placed himself at the head of one hundred and fifty soldiers well armed, and began his march from Monte El Rey to the fort of St. Francisco. He was accompanied by two cannon, which, he said, he should make thunder, if the fort was not quietly given up to him. Gen. Solis had been transferred from a command in the city of Mexico to take command of the insurgents, as soon as they should have formed themselves into something like an organized party, and have come to a head. He had left Monte El Rey with such a force as circumstances enabled him to collect, recruiting upon his route, and inducing all to join him, whom he could influence by fair words and promises. As has been said, he threatened the fort of St. Francisco with a bloody contest, in case they resisted his wishes. He carried with him written addresses to the inhabitants, in which those, who would range themselves under his standard, were offered every thing that renders life desirable. They all flocked round him, giving in their adhesion. When he reached the fort, he sent in his propositions, which were acceded to, as soon as read by the majority. The minority were principally officers. They were all imprisoned by General Solis, as soon as he obtained possession of the place. He then proceeded to make laws, by which the inhabitants were to be governed, and placed the fort in the hands of those, upon whom, he thought he could depend.—These arrangements being all made, he began his return to Monte El Rey, highly delighted with his success.

There now seemed little doubt of his obtaining possession of the whole coast in the course of a few months. He remained at Monte El Rey increasing his force, and drilling the new recruits, until the 28th of March, when he again marched at the head of two hundred soldiers. The present object of attack was Santa Barbara, where the commander under the old regime was stationed. The latter was Gen. Echedio, my old acquaintance of San Diego, for whom I bore such good will. He was not in the least aware of the visit intended him by Gen. Solis; the latter having prevented any tidings upon the subject reaching him, by posting sentinels thickly for some distance upon the road, that lay between them, to intercept and stop any one passing up or down. The insurgent General had as yet succeeded in his plans; and was so elated with the prospect of surprising Gen. Echedio, and completely dispossessing him of his power, and consequently having all in his own hands, that he did not consider it necessary any longer to conceal his real character. The professions of the kind purposes of the insurgent towards the English and Americans will be recollected; and also, that it was at a time when application was made by these Spaniards to them for aid. The tone was now changed. Threats were now made, with regard to the future treatment, which we, unfortunate foreigners, might expect, as soon as Gen. Solis became master of the coast.

We learned this through a Mexican Spaniard, whose daughter Captain Cooper had married. This old gentleman was told by the General, that he intended either to compel every American and Englishman to swear allegiance to the government, which should be established, or drive them from the country. This information was, however, not communicated to us, until the General had departed. We held a consultation upon the subject, to devise some means, which should render him incapable of carrying his good intentions towards us into effect. No other expedient suggested itself to us, but that of sending General Echedio information of the proposed attack, in time to enable him to be prepared for it. We agreed upon this, and a letter was written, stating what we deemed the points most necessary for him to know. The signatures of some of the principal men of the place were affixed to it; for those who think alike upon important points soon understand one another; and the character of Solis had not been unveiled to us alone. It was important, that General Echedio should attach consequence to our letter, and the information, it contained, would come upon him so entirely by surprize, that he might very naturally entertain doubts of its correctness. I added my name to those of the party to which I belonged. The object now was to have our document conveyed safely into the hands of Gen. Echedio. We sent a runner with two good horses and instructions, how to pass the army of Solis in the night undiscovered. All proceedings had been conducted with so much secrecy and caution, that the matter so far rested entirely with ourselves. We occasionally heard the citizens around us express dislike towards the insurgent General; but as they did not seem inclined to carry their opinions into action, we concluded these were only remarks made to draw out our thoughts, and took no notice of them. From after circumstances I believe, that the number of his enemies exceeded that of his friends; and that the remarks, of which I have spoken, were made in truth and sincerity. Mean while we impatiently awaited some opportunity of operating to the disadvantage of the General, and to hear what had taken place between him and Gen. Echedio. A messenger arrived on the 12th of April with the information, that the commander of the insurgents had ranged his men for three days in succession before the fort upon the plain. A continual firing had been kept up on both sides, during the three days, at the expiration of which Gen. Solis, having expended his ammunition, and consumed his provisions, was compelled to withdraw, having sustained no loss, except that of one horse from a sustained action of three days! The spirit with which the contest was conducted may be inferred from a fact, related to me. The cannon balls discharged from the fort upon the enemy were discharged with so little force, that persons arrested them in their course, without sustaining any injury by so doing, at the point, where in the common order of things, they must have inflicted death.

Upon the reception of this news, we joined in the prevalent ex-

pression of opinion around us. The name and fame of Gen. Solis
was exalted to the skies. All the florid comparisons, usual upon
such occasions, were put in requisition, and all the charges were
sung upon his various characteristics wit, honor and courage. The
point was carried so far as to bring him within some degrees of relationship to a supernatural being. Then the unbounded skill he
displayed in marshalling his force, and his extreme care to prevent
the useless waste of his men's lives were expatiated upon, and placed
in the strongest light. The climax of his excellence was his having
retreated without the loss of a man. This was the burden of our
theme to his friends, that is, the fifty soldiers, in whose charge he
had left the command of the fort. The Captain Cooper, of whom I
have spoken, looked rather deeper into things, than those around
him; and consequently knew the most effectual means of operating upon the inefficient machines, in the form of men, which it was
necessary for our present purpose, to remove out of the way for a
time. Accordingly he rolled out a barrel of good old rum, inviting
all the friends of the good and great Gen. Solis to come, and drink
his health. The summons was readily obeyed by them. Being somewhat elevated in spirit by the proceedings of their noble general,
previous to swallowing the genuine inspiration of joy, the feeling
afterwards swelled to an extent, that burst all bounds, and finally
left them prostrate and powerless. We, like good Christians, with
the help of some of the inhabitants, conveyed them into some
strong houses, which stood near, while they remained in their helpless condition, locking the doors safely, that no harm might come
to them. In our pity and care for them, we proposed, that they
should remain, until they felt that violent excitements are injurious, from the natural re-action of things. We now proceeded to cir-
culate another set of views, and opinions among the inhabitants in
the vicinity of the fort; and such was our success in the business
of indoctrination, that we soon counted all their votes on our side.

General Solis was now pitched down the depths, as heartily as
he had before been exalted to the heights. Huzza for Gen. Echedio
and the Americans! was the prevailing cry.

The next movement was to make out a list of our names, and
appoint officers. Our number including Scotch, Irish, English,

Dutch and Americans, amounted to thirty-nine. The number of Americans, however, being the greatest, our party received the designation of American. Captain Cooper was our commanding officer. We now marched up to the castle, which is situated on the brink of a precipice, overlooking the sea, and found four brass field pieces, mounted on carriages. These we concluded to carry with us to the fort. The remainder placed so as to command a sweep of the surface of water below, and the surrounding ground, we spiked fearing, if they fell into the hands of Solis, that he might break down our walls with them. This done, we went to the magazine, and broke it open, taking what powder and ball we wanted. We then posted sentinels for miles along the road, to which we knew Solis was hastening in order to prevent news of our proceedings from reaching him, before it was convenient for us, that he should know them. We were aware of his intention to return here to recruit again, and it was our wish to surprize him by an unexpected reception, and thus obtain an advantage, which should counterbalance his superiority of numbers. In so doing, we only availed ourselves of the precedent, he had given us, in his management with regard to Gen. Echedio. He had not derived benefit from his plan, in consequence of his too great confidence of success, which led him to discover his real feelings towards our people.

We hoped to avail ourselves of what was wise in his plan, and profit by his mistakes. We shut up all the people, both men and women, in the fort at night, that it might be out of their power to attempt to make their way, under the cover of darkness, through our line of sentinels, to give information, should the inclination be felt. Our precautions were not taken through fear of him, should he even come upon us, prepared to encounter us as enemies: but from the wish to take both himself and army prisoners. Should they learn what we had done, we feared, they would pass on to St. Francisco, to recruit, and thus escape us.

Our designs were successful; for in a few days General Solis and his men appeared in sight of the first of our sentinels, who quickly transmitted this information to us. Our preparations for receiving him were soon made, with a proper regard to politeness. A regale of music from air instruments, called cannons, was in readiness to incline him to the right view of the scene before him, should he seem not likely to conform to our wish, which was, simply, that he should surrender to us without making any difficulty.

Our fortification was in the form of a square, with only one entrance. From each side of this entrance a wall projected at right angles from it fifty yards. The Spaniards call them wings; and it seems to me a significant and fitting name for them. We intended to allow the approaching party to advance between these walls, before we began our part. Our cannons were charged with grape and balls, and placed in a position to produce an effect between the walls. Every man was now at his post, and General Solis approaching within sight of the fort, a small cannon which accompanied him was discharged by way of salute. No answer was returned to him. The piece was reloaded, and his fife and drum began a lively air, and the whole body moved in a quick step towards the fort, entering the space between the wings, of which I have spoken. This was no sooner done than our matches were in readiness for instant operation. Captain Cooper commanded them to surrender. He was immediately obeyed by the soldiers, who threw down their arms, aware that death would be the penalty of their refusal. The General and six of his mounted officers fled, directing their course to St. Francisco. Six of our party were soon on horseback with our rifles, and in pursuit of them. I had been appointed orderly sergeant, and was one of the six. We carried orders from the principal Spanish civil officer, who was in the fort, and had taken an active part in all our proceedings, to bring the General back with us, either dead or alive. The commands of our military commander, Captain Cooper, spoke the same language.

I confess that I wanted to have a shot at the fugitive, and took pleasure in the pursuit. We went at full speed, for our horses were good and fresh. Those belonging to the party we were so desirous to overtake, would of course be somewhat weary, and jaded by their long journey. We had not galloped many miles, before we perceived them in advance of us. As soon as we were within hearing distance of each other, I called upon them to surrender. They replied by wheeling their horses and firing at us, and then striking their spurs into their horses' sides, to urge them onward. We followed, producing more effect with our spurs than they had done, and calling upon them again to surrender, or we should fire, and give no quarter. They at length reined up, and six dismounted and laid down their arms. The seventh remained on horse back, and as we came up, fired, wounding one of our number slightly in the right arm. He then turned to resume his flight; but his horse had not made the second spring, before our guns brought the hero from his saddle. Four of our balls had passed through his body. The whole number being now assembled together, victors and vanquished, General Solis offered me his sword. I refused it, but told him, that himself and his officers must accompany me in my return to the fort. He consented to this with a countenance so expressive of dejection, that I pitied him, notwithstanding I knew him to be a bad man, and destitute of all principle.

The man who had lost his life through his obstinacy, was bound upon his horse, and the others having remounted theirs, we set out upon our return. Our captives were all disarmed except General Solis, who was allowed to retain his sword. We reached the fort three hours before sunset. The General and his men were dismounted, and irons put upon their legs, after which they were locked up with those who had forgotten themselves in their joy at the good fortune of their poor general.

These events occurred on the 18th of March. On the 20th the civil officer of whom I have before spoken, together with Captain Cooper, despatched a messenger to General Echedio, who was still in Santa Barbara with written intelligence of what we had accomplished. It was stated that the Americans were the originators of the whole matter, and that their flag was waving in the breeze over Monte El Rey, where it would remain, until his excellency came himself to take charge of the place; and he was requested to hasten his departure, as they who had obtained possession were anxious to be relieved from the care and responsibility they found imposed upon them.

We were very well aware that he would receive our information with unmingled pleasure, as he expected Solis would return in a short time to Santa Barbara, to give him another battle. It was said, that upon the reception of the letter he was as much rejoiced as though he had been requested to come and take charge of a kingdom. As soon as he could make the necessary arrangements he came to Monte El Rey, where he arrived on the 29th. We gave the command of the place up to him; but before he would suffer our flag to be taken down, he had thirty guns discharged in honor of it. He then requested a list of our names, saying, that if we would accept it, he would give each one of us the right of citizenship in his country. A splendid dinner was made by him for our party. On the night of the 29th a vessel arrived in the port. In the morning it was found to be a brig belonging to the American consul at Macho, John W. Jones, esq., who was on board of it. This was the same person to whom I wrote when in prison at San Diego by Mr. Perkins. I met with him, and had the melancholy pleasure of relating to him in person my sufferings and imprisonment, and every thing, in short, that had happened to me during my stay in this country. This took place in my first interview with him. He advised me to make out a correct statement of the value of the furs I had lost by the General's detention of me, and also of the length of time I had been imprisoned, and to take it with me to the city of Mexico, where the American minister resided, and place it in his hands. It was probable, the consul continued, that he would be able to compel the Mexican government to indemnify me for the loss of property I had sustained, and for the injustice of my imprisonment.

The probability of my success was not slight, provided I could establish the truth of my statement, by obtaining the testimony of those who were eye witnesses of the facts. I informed the consul that I had not means to enable me to reach the city of Mexico. A gentleman who was present during this conversation, after hearing my last remark, mentioned that he was then on his way to that place, and that if I would accompany him he would pay my expenses; and if circumstances should happen to induce me to think of returning thence to the United States, I should do so free of expense. I expressed my thanks for this offer, and said that if I succeeded in recovering only a portion of what I had lost I would repay the money thus kindly expended in my behalf; but the obligation of gratitude imposed by such an act, it would be impossible for me to repay.

In conformity to Mr. Jones' advice and instruction, I sat myself down to make out an account for the inspection of the American minister. When I had completed it, I obtained the signatures, of some of the first among the inhabitants of Monte El Rey, and that of the civil officer before mentioned, testifying as to the truth of what I said, so far as the circumstances narrated had come under their observation. The General having received the list of our names, which he had requested, he now desired, that we might all come to his office, and receive the right of citizenship from his hand, as a reward for what we had done. I put my paper in my pocket, and proceeded with my companions and Mr. Jones to the indicated place. The General had been much surprized to find my name in the list furnished him; but as I entered the room, he arose hastily from his seat and shook my hand in a friendly manner, after which I introduced him to the consul. He seemed surprised as he heard the name of this gentleman, but said nothing. After pointing us to seats, he walked out of the room, saying he should return in a few moments. I concluded, that he thought, I had brought the consul, or that he had accompanied me for the purpose of questioning him on the subject of my imprisonment and that of my companions. He returned, as soon as he had promised, having some papers in his hand. After he had seated himself, he began to interrogate, me with regard to what had happened to me, during the long time that had elapsed since he had last seen me, adding, that he did not expect ever to have met me again; but was happy to see me a citizen of his country. My answer in reply to the last part of his remarks was short. I told him, he had not yet enjoyed any thing from that source, and with my consent never should.

He looked very serious upon this manifestation of firmness, or whatever it may be called on my part, and requested to know my objections to being a citizen of the country?

I replied that it was simply having been reared in a country where I could pass from one town to another, without the protection of a passport, which instead of affording real protection, subjected me to the examination of every petty officer, near whom I passed, and that I should not willingly remain, where such was the order of things. Besides, I added, I was liable to be thrown into prison like a criminal, at the caprice of one clothed with a little authority, if I failed to show a passport, which I might either lose accidentally, or in some way, for which I might not have been in the least in fault.

The General, in reply, asked me if in my country a foreigner was permitted to travel to and fro, without first presenting to the properly constituted authorities of our government, proof from those among the officers of his own government appointed for that purpose, of his being a person of good character, who might safely be allowed to traverse the country? I told him I had once attempted to satisfy him on that head, and he very abruptly and decidedly contradicted my account; and that now I did not feel in the least compelled, or inclined to enter upon the matter a second time. All which I desired of him, and that I did not earnestly desire, was, that he would give me a passport to travel into my own country by the way of the city of Mexico. If I could once more place my foot upon its free soil, and enjoy the priceless blessings of its liberty, which my unfortunate father, of whom I could never cease to think, and who had died in his prison, assisted in maintaining, I should be satisfied.

While I thus spoke, he gazed steadily in my face. His swarthy complexion grew pale. He read in my countenance a strong expression of deep feeling, awakened by the nature of the remembrances associated with him. He felt that there was something fearful in the harvest of bitterness which the oppressor reaps in return for his injuries and cruelties. I thought, he feared, if he did not grant my request for a pass, that I might carry into execution the purposes of vengeance; to which I used to give utterance in my burning indignation at his conduct at the time of my father's death. Whenever I saw him pass my prison I seized the opportunity to tell him, that if my time for redress ever came, he would find me as unflinching in my vengeance as he had been in his injuries. I only expressed the truth with regard to my feelings at the time, and even now I owe it to candor and honesty to acknowledge, that I could have seen him at the moment of this conversation suffer any infliction without pity.

He did not hesitate to give the pass I desired; but asked me what business led me out of my way to the United States around by the city of Mexico? My direct course, he remarked, lay in a straight direction through New Mexico. For reply, I drew out of my pocket the paper I had written before coming to his office, and read it to him, telling him that was the business which led me to the city of Mexico. I then asked him if all the facts there stated were not true? His answer was in the affirmative; 'but,' added he, 'you will not be able to recover any thing, as I acted in conformity to the laws of my country. If you will remain in this country I will give you something handsome to begin with.' I assured him that I would not stay, but I wished him to show me the laws which allowed, or justified him in imprisoning myself and my companions for entering a country as we did, compelled by misfortunes such as ours. In return, he said he had no laws to show, but those which recommended him to take up and imprison those whom he deemed conspirators against his country. 'What marks of our being conspirators did you discover in us,' rejoined I, 'which warranted your imprisoning us? I am aware of none, unless it be the evidence furnished by our countenances and apparel, that we had undergone the extreme of misfortune and distress, which had come upon us without any agency on our part, and as inevitable evils to which every human being is liable. We were led by the hope of obtaining relief, to seek refuge in your protection. In confirmation of our own relation, did not our papers prove that we were Americans, and that we had received legal permission from the very government under which we then were, to trade in the country? The printed declaration to this effect, given us by the governor of Santa Fe, which we showed you, you tore in pieces before us, declaring it was neither a license nor a passport.' The General replied, that he did tear up a paper given him by us, but that in fact it was neither a passport nor a license.

"Now sir," said I, "I am happy that it is in my power to prove, in the presence of the American consul, the truth of what I have said with regard to the license." I then produced another copy of the paper torn up by him, which had been given my father by the governor of Santa Fe, at the same time with the former. He looked at it, and said nothing more, except that I might go on, and try what I could do in the way of recovering what I had lost.

The consul and myself now left him, and returned to Capt. Cooper's. The consul laughed at me about my quarrel with the General. In a few moments the latter appeared among us, and the remainder of the day passed away cheerfully in drinking toasts. When the General rose to take leave of us, he requested the consul to call upon him at his office; as he wanted to converse with him upon business. The consul went, according to request, and the General contracted with him for the transportation of Gen. Solis, and sixteen other prisoners to San Blas, on board his vessel, whence they were to be carried to the city of Mexico. The 7th of May was fixed for the departure of the brig, as the General required some time for making necessary arrangements, and preparing documents to accompany the transmission of the prisoners. When I heard that this delay was unavoidable, I went to the General and returned my passport, telling him I should want another, when the vessel was ready to sail, as I intended to proceed in it as far as San Blas. He consented to give me one, and then joked with me about the honor, I should enjoy, of accompanying Gen. Solis. I replied in the same strain, and left him.

Captain William H. Hinkley and myself went to the mission of San Carlos, where we spent three days. During the whole time we did little beside express our astonishment at what we saw. We had fallen upon the festival days of some saint, and the services performed in his honor all passed under our eyes. They were not a few, nor wanting in variety, as this was a noted festival. Our admiration, however, was principally excited by the contest between grizzly bears and bulls, which constitutes one of the exhibitions of these people.

Five large grey bears had been caught, and fastened in a pen built for the purpose of confining the bulls, during a bullbaiting. One of the latter animals, held by ropes, was brought to the spot by men on horseback, and thrown down. A bear was then drawn up to him, and they were fastened together by a rope about fifteen feet in length, in such a manner, that they could not separate from each other. One end of it is tied around one of the forefeet of the bull, and the other around one of the hind feet of the bear. The two were then left to spring upon their feet. As soon as this movement is made, the bull makes at the bear, very often deciding the fate of the ferocious animal in this first act. If the bull fails in goring the bear, the fierce animal seizes him and tears him to death. Fourteen of the latter lost their lives, before the five bears were destroyed. To Captain Hinkley this was a sight of novel and absorbing interest. It had less of novelty for me, as since I had been on the coast, I had often seen similar combats, and in fact worse, having been present when men entered the enclosure to encounter the powerful bull in his wild and untamed fierceness. These unfortunate persons are armed with a small sword, with which they sometimes succeed in saving their own lives at the expense of that of the animal.

I once saw the man fall in one of these horrible shows; they are conducted in the following manner: the man enters to the bull with the weapon, of which he avails himself, in the right hand, and in the left a small red flag, fastened to a staff about three feet in length. He whistles, or makes some other noise, to attract the attention of the animal, upon hearing which the bull comes towards him with the speed of fury. The man stands firm, with the flag dangling before him, to receive this terrible onset. When the bull makes the last spring towards him, he dexterously evades it, by throwing his body from behind the flag to one side, at the same time thrusting his sword into the animal's side. If this blow is properly directed, blood gushes from the mouth and nostrils of the bull, and he falls dead. A second blow in this case is seldom required.

Another mode of killing these animals is by men on horseback, with a spear, which they dart into his neck, immediately behind the horns. The horse is often killed by the bull. When the animal chances to prefer running from the fight to engaging in it, he is killed by the horseman, by being thrown heels over head. This is accomplished by catching hold of the tail of the bull in the full speed of pursuit, and giving a turn around the head of the saddle, in such a manner, that they are enabled to throw the animal into any posture they choose.

After we returned to the fort, it took us some time to relate what we had seen, to the consul. Feeling it necessary to do something towards supporting myself, during the remaining time of my stay in this part of the country, I took my rifle, and joined a Portuguese in the attempt to kill otters along the coast. We hunted up and down the coast, a distance of forty miles, killing sixteen otters in ten days. We sold their skins, some as high as seventy-five dollars, and none under twenty-five. Three hundred dollars fell to my share from the avails of our trip. Captain Cooper was exceedingly desirous to purchase my rifle, now that I should not be likely to make use of it, as I was soon to proceed on my journey to the city of Mexico. I presented it to him, for I could not think of bartering for money, what I regarded, as a tried friend, that had afforded me the means of subsistence and protection for so long a time. My conscience would have reproached me, as though I had been guilty of an act of ingratitude.

The period of my departure from this coast was now close at hand, and my thoughts naturally took a retrospect of the whole time, I had spent upon it. The misery and suffering of various kinds, that I had endured in some portions of it, had not been able to prevent me from feeling, and acknowledging, that this country is more calculated to charm the eye, than any one I have ever seen. Those, who traverse it, if they have any capability whatever of perceiving, and admiring the beautiful and sublime in scenery, must be constantly excited to wonder and praise. It is no less remarkable for uniting the advantages of healthfulness, a good soil, a temperate climate, and yet one of exceeding mildness, a happy mixture of level and elevated ground, and vicinity to the sea. Its inhabitants are equally calculated to excite dislike, and even the stronger feelings of disgust and hatred. The priests are omnipotent, and all things are subject to their power. Two thirds of the population are native Indians under the immediate charge of these spiritual rulers in the numerous missions. It is a well known fact, that nothing is more entirely opposite to the nature of a savage, than labor. In order to keep them at their daily tasks, the most rigid and unremitting supervision is exercised. No bondage can be more complete, than that under which they live. The compulsion laid upon them has, however, led them at times to rebel, and endeavor to escape from their yoke. They have seized upon arms, murdered the priests, and destroyed the buildings of the missions, by preconcerted stratagem, in several instances. When their work of destruction and retribution was accomplished, they fled to the mountains, and subsisted on the flesh of wild horses which are there found in innumerable droves. To prevent the recurrence of similar events, the priests have passed laws, prohibiting an Indian the use or possession of any weapon whatever, under the penalty of a severe punishment.

On the 25th I addressed the companions of my former journeyings and imprisonment in San Diego by letter. They had remained in the town of Angels, during the months which had elapsed since my separation from them, after our receiving liberty upon parole. I had kept up a constant correspondence with them in this interval. My objects at present were to inform them of my proposed departure for my native country, and request them, if they should be called upon so to do, to state everything relative to our imprisonment and loss of property, exactly as it took place. I closed, by telling them, they might expect a letter from me upon my arrival in the city of Mexico.

On the 8th of May I applied for my passport, which was readily given me, and taking leave of the General and my friends, I entered the vessel, in which I was to proceed to San Blas, at 8 o'clock in the morning. The sails of the brig, which was called the Volunteer, were soon set, and speeding us upon our way. The green water turned white, as it met the advance of our prow, and behind us we left a smooth belt of water, affording a singular contrast to the waves around. I watched the disappearance of this single smooth spot, as it was lost in the surrounding billows, when the influence of the movement of our vessel ceased, as a spectacle to be contemplated by a land's man with interest. But no feeling of gratification operated in the minds of the poor prisoners in the hold. They were ironed separately, and then all fastened to a long bar of iron. They were soon heard mingling prayers and groans, interrupted only by the violent vomiting produced by sea sickness. In addition to this misery, when fear found entrance into their thoughts, during the intervals of the cessation of extreme sickness, it seemed to them, as if every surge the vessel made must be its last. In this miserable condition they remained, until the 19th, when we arrived at San Blas. The prisoners here were delivered into the charge of the commanding officer of the place.

Captain Henkley, his mate, Henry Vinal, and myself disembarked at this place, in order to commence our journey over land to Mexico. The necessary arrangements for our undertaking occupied us three days. We found the season warm on our arrival here. Watermelons were abundant, and also green corn, and a great variety of ripe fruit. Two crops of corn and wheat are raised in the year. A precipice was shown me, over which, I was told, the Mexicans threw three old priests at the commencement of the revolt against the king of Spain.—This port is the centre of considerable business in the seasons of spring and fall. During the summer, the inhabitants are compelled to leave it, as the air becomes infected by the exhalations, arising from the surrounding swamps. Myriads of musquitos and other small insects fill the air at the same time, uniting with the former cause to render the place uninhabitable.

Great quantities of salt are made upon the flats in the vicinity of San Blas. I did not inform myself accurately, with regard to the manner, in which it is made; but as I was passing by one day, where the preparation of it was carried on, I observed what struck me as being both curious and novel. The earth was laid off in square beds. Around their edges dirt was heaped up, as though the bed, which I have mentioned, was intended to be covered with water.

We began our journey well armed, as we had been informed that we should, in all probability, find abundant occasion to use our arms, as we advanced. Our progress was slow, as we conformed to the directions given us, and kept a constant look out for robbers, of whom there are said to be thousands upon this route.

On the 25th we reached a small town called Tipi, where we remained one day to rest from our fatigue, and then set off again for Guadalaxara, distant eight days' journey. Our path led us through a beautiful country, a great portion of which was under cultivation. Occasionally we passed through small villages. Beggars were to be seen standing at the corners of all the streets, and along the highways. They take a station by the road side, having a dog or child by them, to lead them into the road when they see a traveller approaching. They stand until the person reaches the spot upon which they are, when they ask alms for the sake of a saint, whose image is worn suspended around their neck, or tied around the wrist. This circumstance of begging for the saint, and not for themselves, struck me as a new expedient in the art of begging. At first we gave a trifle to the poor saint. As we went on we found them so numerous that it became necessary for us to husband our alms, and we finally came to the conclusion that the large brotherhood of beggars could occasionally diversify their mode of life by a dexterous management of their fingers, and shut our purses to the demands of the saints. The country for some time before we drew near Guadalaxara, was rather barren, although its immediate vicinity is delightful.

We reached that city on the 2d of June, and spent three days in it. It is situated upon a fine plain, which is overspread by the same numbers of domestic animals that I had seen in New Mexico and California. The city is walled in, with gates at the different entrances. These gates are strongly guarded, and no one is allowed to enter them until they have been searched, in order to ascertain if they carry any smuggled goods about them. The same precaution is used when any one passes out of the city. A passport must be shown for the person, his horse, and arms, and a statement from the principal peace officer, of the number of trunks with which he set out upon his journey, and their contents. This caution is to prevent smuggling; but it does not effect the purpose, as there is more contraband trade here, than in any place I was ever in before. I was not able to ascertain the number of inhabitants of this city. The silver mines of Guanaxuato are near Guadalaxara. They are carried on at present by an English company. The evening before our departure we went to the theatre. The actresses appeared young and beautiful, and danced and sung charmingly.

The 5th day of June we resumed our journey to the city of Mexico. Again we travelled through a charming country, tolerably thickly settled. On our way we fell in company with an officer belonging to the service of the country. He had ten soldiers with him. Upon his demanding to see our passports we showed them to him, though he had no authority to make such a demand. After he had finished their perusal he returned them with such an indifferent air, that I could not resist an inclination to ask him some questions that might perhaps have seemed rude. I first asked him what post he filled in the army? He answered, with great civility, he was first lieutenant. I then requested to know, to what part of the country he was travelling? He said, still in a very civil manner, that he had had the command of some troops in Guanaxuato, but was now on his way to the city of Mexico, to take charge of the 6th regiment, which was ordered to the province of Texas, to find out among the Americans there, those who had refused obedience to the Mexican laws. He added, that when he succeeded in finding them, he would soon learn them to behave well. The last remark was made in rather a contemptuous tone of voice, and with something like an implied insult to me. This warmed my blood, and I replied in a tone not so gentle as prudence might have counselled a stranger in a foreign land to have adopted, that if himself and his men did not conduct themselves properly when they were among the Americans, the latter would soon despatch them to another country, which they had not yet seen; as the Americans were not Mexicans, to stand at the corner of a house, and hide their guns behind the side of it, while they looked another way, and pulled the trigger. At this he flew into a passion. I did not try to irritate him any further, and he rode on and left us. We pursued our way slowly, and stopped for the night at Aguabuena, a small town on the way. We put up at a house, a sort of posada, built for lodging travellers.—Twenty-five cents is the price for the use of a room for one night. It is seldom that any person is found about such an establishment to take charge of it but an old key bearer. Provisions must be sought elsewhere. It is not often necessary to go further than the street, where, at any hour in the day until ten o'clock at night, men and women are engaged in crying different kinds of eatables. We generally purchased our food of them. After we had finished our supper two English gentlemen entered, who were on their way to the city of Mexico. We concluded to travel together, as our point of destination was the same, and we should be more able to resist any adversaries we might encounter; this country being, as I have before mentioned, infested with robbers and thieves, although we had not yet fallen in with any.

These gentlemen informed us that the greatest catholic festival of the whole year was close at hand. If we could reach the city of Mexico before its celebration, we should see something that would repay us for hastening our journey. As we were desirous to lose the sight of nothing curious, we proceeded as fast as circumstances would permit, and reached the city on the 10th, late in the evening, and put up at an inn kept by an Englishman, although, as in the other towns in which we had been, we were obliged to seek food elsewhere, the only accommodation at the inn being beds to sleep in, and liquors to drink. We found supper in a coffee house.

We were awakened early in the morning by the ringing of bells. As we stepped into the street we met three biers carried by some men guarded by soldiers. Blood was dropping from each bier. The bearers begged money to pay the expenses of burying the bodies. I afterwards learned that these persons were murdered on the night of our arrival, upon the Alameda, a promenade north of the city, in one of the suburbs. We visited this place, and found it covered with thousands of people, some walking, and others sitting on the seats placed around this public pleasure ground. Small parties are sheltered from view by thickets of a growth, like that in our country, used for hedges. The open surface is surrounded by a hedge of the same shrub. These partially concealed parties are usually composed of men and women of the lowest orders, engaged in card playing. Such are to be seen at any hour of the day, occupied in a way which is most likely to terminate the meeting in an affray, and perhaps murder. Blood is frequently shed, and I judged from what I saw of the order of things, that the accounts of the numerous assassinations committed among this populace, were not exaggerated. One of the characteristics of this people is jealousy. Notwithstanding the danger really to be apprehended from visiting this place after certain hours, my two companions and myself spent several evenings in it without being molested in the slightest degree. But one evening as we were returning to our lodgings, we were compelled to kneel with our white pantaloons upon the dirty street, while the host was passing. We took care afterwards to step into a house in time to avoid the troublesome necessity.

We attended a bull baiting, and some other exhibitions for the amusement of the people. Being one evening at the theatre, I had the misfortune to lose my watch from my pocket, without being aware when it was taken. It would have been useless for me to have thought of looking around for it, as I stood in the midst of such a crowd that it was almost an impossibility to move.

The accounts of this city which I had met with in books led me to expect to find it placed in the midst of a lake, or surrounded by a sheet of water. To satisfy myself with regard to the truth of this representation, I mounted a horse, and made the circuit of the city, visiting some villages that lay within a league of it. I found no lake; but the land is low and flat. A canal is cut through it, for the purpose of carrying off the water that descends from the mountains upon the level surface, which has the appearance of having been formerly covered with water. A mountain which is visible from the city, presents a circular summit, one part of which is covered with snow throughout the year: upon the other is the crater of a volcano, which is continually sending up proof of the existence of an unceasing fire within.

Early upon the first day of my arrival in this city, I waited upon Mr. Butler, the American charge d'affairs. After I had made myself known to him he showed me a communication from President Jackson to the President of this country, the purport of which was, to request the latter to set at liberty some Americans, imprisoned upon the coast of California. I then handed him the statement I had made according to the advice of Mr. Jones. He asked me many questions relative to the losses I had sustained, which I answered, and then took my leave.

A number of coaches were to leave the city for Vera Cruz on the 18th of June. My companions and myself took places in one of them. On the 15th I again called upon Mr. Butler to obtain a passport to Vera Cruz, where I intended to embark for America. He took me to the palace of the President, in order that I might get my passport. This circumstance was agreeable to me, as I was desirous to see this person, of whom I had heard so much. Upon arriving at the palace I found it a splendid building, although much shattered by the balls discharged at it by the former President Guerero, who is now flying from one place to another with a few followers, spreading destruction to the extent of his power. A soldier led me into the presence of the President. He was walking to and fro when I entered the room, apparently in deep meditation. Several clerks were present, engaged in writing. He received me politely, bowing as I advanced, and bade me sit down. In answer to his inquiry what I wished of him? I told my errand. He then asked me from what direction I came? I replied, from California. California! said he, repeating the word with an air of interest. I answered again, that I left that part of the country when I began my present journey. You must have been there then, rejoined he, when the late revolution took place, of which I have but a short time since received information. I remarked, that I was upon the spot where it occurred, and that I took my departure from the coast in the same vessel that brought sixteen of the captives taken in the course of its progress, and that I disembarked at St. Blas at the same time that they were taken from the vessel. He resumed the conversation by saying, you were probably one of the Americans who, I am told, assisted in subduing the revolted party. I told him, he was correct in his opinion; and by so doing I had had the good fortune to gain my liberty. His countenance expressed surprize at the conclusion of my remark; and he proceeded to ask me, what meaning I had, in saying that I had thus regained my own liberty? I then related my story; upon which he said he had understood that General Echedio had acted contrary to the laws, in several instances, and that, in consequence, he had ordered him to Mexico to answer for his conduct. I was surprised at the condescension of the President in thus expressing to me any part of his intentions with regard to such a person. I accounted for it by supposing that he wished to have it generally understood, that he did not approve of the unjust and cruel treatment which the Americans had received. The president appeared to me to be a man of plain and gentlemanly manners, possessing great talent. In this I express no more than my individual opinion; to which I must add, that I do not consider myself competent to judge of such points, only for myself. He gave me a passport, and I returned to Mr. Butler's office, who informed me that he wished me to take a fine horse to Vera Cruz, for the American consul at that place. He said that I would find it pleasant to vary my mode of travelling, by occasionally riding the horse. I readily consented to his wish, requesting him to have the horse taken to the place from which the coach would set off, early in the morning, when I would take charge of it. I now took leave of Mr. Butler and proceeded to my lodgings.

I found both my companions busily engaged in packing, and arranging for departure. I immediately entered upon the same employment. I had two trunks; one I filled with such articles as I should require upon my journey; and in another I placed such as I should not be likely to use, and a great many curiosities which I had collected during my long wanderings. The latter trunk I did not calculate to open until I reached my native land.

At 8 o'clock on the morning of the 16th our coach left the city, in company with two others. We were eight in number, including the coachman. Three of the party were ladies. One was a Frenchwoman, a married lady travelling without her husband. Another was a Spanishwoman, who had married a wealthy Irishman, and was accompanied by her husband. The third was the wife of a Mexican officer, also one of the eight. This gentleman was an inveterate enemy of the displaced President General Guerero. We journeyed on very amicably together, without meeting with the slightest disturbance, until the second day, when, about three o'clock in the afternoon, we were met by a company of fifty men, all well mounted and armed. At first sight of them we had supposed them to be a party which had been sent from the city in search of some highwaymen who had commited murder and robbery upon the road on which we were travelling, a few days previous to our departure. A few minutes served to show us our mistake.—They surrounded the coaches, commanding the drivers to halt, and announcing themselves as followers of General Guerero. They demanded money, of which they stated that they were in great need. The tone of this demand was, however, humble, such as beggars would use. while they addressed us in this manner, they contrived to place themselves among and around the persons of our party in such a way as to obtain entire command of us. The instant they had completed this purpose, they presented their spears and muskets, and demanded our arms. We resigned them without offering an objection, as we saw clearly, that opposition would be unavailing. They now proceeded to take from us what they thought proper. I was allowed to retain my trunk of clothing for my journey. The Mexican officer was sitting by his wife in the coach. Some of the sol-

diers seized him, and dragged him from his almost distracted wife
out of the carriage. His fate was summarily decided, and he was
hung upon a tree. When this dreadful business was terminated, we
were ordered to drive on. We gladly hastened from such a scene
of horror. But the agony of the unfortunate wife was an impressive
memorial to remind us of the nature of the late occurrence, had we
needed any other than our own remembrances. We left this afflicted
lady at Xalapa, in the care of her relations. A great quantity of jalap,
which is so much used in medicine, is obtained from this place.
After leaving Xalapa, we advanced through a beautiful country. We
passed many small towns on this part of our route.

Our course had been a continued descent, after crossing the
mountain sixteen miles from the city of Mexico. The road is excellent, being paved for the most part. It is cut through points of
mountains in several places. This work must have been attended
with immense labor and expense.

We reached Vera Cruz on the 24th. On the 27th Captain Hinkley
and his mate embarked for New York. I remained with the consul
Mr. Stone, until the 18th of July. A vessel being in readiness to sail
for New Orleans at this time, I was desirous to avail myself of the
opportunity to return to the United States. Mr. Stone and some
others presented me money sufficient to pay my passage to the
point to which the vessel was bound. It was very painful to me to
incur this debt of gratitude, as I could not even venture to hope that
it would be in my power to repay it, either in money or benefits of
any kind. The prospect, which the future offered me, was dark.
It seemed as if misfortune had set her seal upon all that concerned
my destiny. I accepted this offering of kindness and benevolence
with thanks direct from my heart, and went on board the vessel.

It would be idle for me to attempt to describe the feelings that
swelled my heart, as the sails filled to bear me from the shores of a
country, where I had seen and suffered so much. My dreams of success in those points considered most important by my fellow
men, were vanished forever. After all my endurance of toil, hunger,
thirst and imprisonment, after encountering the fiercest wild beasts
in their deserts, and fiercer men, after tracing streams before un-
measured and unvisited by any of my own race to their source, over
rugged and pathless mountains, subject to every species of danger,

want and misery for seven years, it seemed hard to be indebted to charity, however kind and considerate it might be, for the means of returning to my native land.

As we sped on our way, I turned to look at the land I was leaving, and endeavored to withdraw my thoughts from the painful train into which they had fallen. Vera Cruz is the best fortified port I have ever seen. The town is walled in, and well guarded on every side with heavy cannon. The part of the wall extending along the water's edge, is surmounted by guns pointing so as completely to command the shipping in the harbour. A reef of rocks arises at the distance of half a mile from the shore opposite the city, and continues visible for several miles in a south direction, joining the main land seven or eight miles south-west of Vera Cruz. A fort stands upon that part of the reef which fronts the town. Ships in leaving or entering the harbour are obliged to pass between the fort and the town.

We reached New Orleans on the first of August, although the wind had not been entirely favorable. It blew a stiff breeze from a direction which compelled us to run within five points and a half of the wind. As I approached the spot where my foot would again press its native soil, my imagination transported me over the long course of river which yet lay between me, and all I had left in the world to love. I cannot express the delight which thrilled and softened my heart, as I fancied myself entering my home; for it was the home I had known and loved when my mother lived, and we were happy that rose to my view. Fancy could not present another to me. There were my brothers and sisters, as I had been used to see them. The pleasant shade of the trees lay upon the turf before the door of our dwelling. The paths around were the same, over which I had so often bounded with the elastic step of childhood, enjoying a happy existence. Years and change have no place in such meditations. We landed, and I stood upon the shore. I was aroused by the approach of an Englishman, one of my fellow passengers, to a sense of my real position. He asked me if I had taken a passage in a steamboat for Louisville? I immediately answered in the negative. He then said he had bespoken one in the Cora; and as I had not chosen any other, he would be glad if I would go on in the same one with him, and thus continue our companionship as long as possible.

So saying he took me by the arm to lead me in the direction of the boat of which he spoke, that we might choose our births. As we advanced together, it occurred to me to ask the price of a passage to Louisville? I was answered, forty dollars. Upon hearing this I stopped, and told my companion I could not take a birth just then, at the same time putting my hand in my pocket to ascertain if the state of my funds would permit me to do so at all. The Englishman seeing my embarrassment, and conjecturing rightly its origin, instantly remarked, that the passage money was not to be paid until the boat arrived at Louisville. I was ashamed to own my poverty, and invented an excuse to hide it, telling him, that I had an engagement at that time, but would walk with him in the evening to see about the passage. He left me in consequence. I then discovered, that so far from being able to take a cabin passage I had not money enough to pay for one on the deck.

I re-entered the vessel in which I had arrived. As I approached the captain I saw him point me out to a person conversing with him, and heard him say 'there is the young man I have been mentioning to you. He speaks Spanish, and will probably engage with you.' When I was near enough he introduced me to the stranger whom he called Captain Vion. The latter addressed a few remarks to me, and then requested me to accompany him into his vessel. I consented and followed him on board. He then told me, that he wished to engage a person to accompany him to Vera Cruz, and aid in disposing of his vessel and cargo; and asked if I was inclined to go with him for such a purpose? I said, in reply, that it would depend entirely upon the recompense he offered for the services to be performed. He remarked, that he would give a certain per cent upon the brig and cargo, in case it was sold. I partly agreed to his proposal, but told him that I could not decide finally upon it until I had considered the matter. He then requested me to come to him the next day at 12 o'clock, when I would find him at dinner.

I left him, after promising to do so, and wandered about looking at the city until evening, when I met the Englishman from whom I had parted in the morning. He said he would now accompany me to the steam boat, that we might choose our births according to our engagement. I had no longer any excuse to offer, and was compelled to acknowledge that the contents of my purse were not sufficient to justify me in contracting a debt of forty dollars. I added, that I had an idea of returning to Vera Cruz. He replied, that in regard to the passage money I need have no uneasiness, nor hesitate to go on board, as he would defray my expenses as far as I chose to go. In respect to my plan of returning to Vera Cruz, he said that it would be exceedingly unwise for me to carry it into execution; as the yellow fever would be raging by the time I reached the city, and that it was most likely I should fall a victim to it. I had, however, determined in my own mind that I would run the risk, rather than ask or receive aid from a person to whom I was comparatively unknown, and accordingly I refused his kindly proffered assistance, telling him at the same time, that I felt as grateful to him as though I had accepted his offered kindness, and that I would have availed myself of his benevolent intentions towards me, had he been a resident of my country; but as I knew him to be a traveller in a foreign land, who might need all his funds, he must excuse me. He then asked me if I had no acquaintance in New Orleans, of whom I could obtain the money as a loan? I replied, that I did not know an individual in the city; but if I carried my plan of returning to Vera Cruz into execution, I should probably be enabled to proceed to my friends without depending on any one. Upon this we separated, and each went to his lodging.

At ten the succeeding morning my English friend came to my boarding house, accompanied by Judge Johnston, who accosted me with a manner of paternal kindness, enquiring of me how long I had been absent from my country and relations? I naturally enquired in turn, if he was in any way acquainted with them? He replied, that he was; and advised me to ascend the river, and visit them. I expressed to him how pleasant it would be to me to visit them, but assured him that it was out of my power to enjoy that pleasure at present. He enquired why? I avoided a direct answer, and remarked, that I proposed returning to Vera Cruz. He not only urged strong objections to this, but offered to pay my passage up the river. It may be easily imagined how I felt in view of such an offer from this generous and respectable stranger. I thankfully accepted it, only assuring him that I should repay him as soon as it was in my power. He replied that it was a matter of no consequence. He advised me to go on board the steam boat and choose my birth, alleging, that he had business in the city which would not allow him to accompany me on board.

My English friend seemed highly gratified by this good fortune of mine, and went with me on board the steam boat, where I chose a birth. The name of this gentleman was Perry, and he was one of the two whom I have already mentioned, who had travelled in company with me from the city of Guadalaxara to Mexico. On the fourth, at nine in the morning, the starting bell rung on the steam boat, and Judge Johnston, Mr. Perry and myself went on board. This was the first steam boat on which I had ever been. Scarcely was the interior of the first ship I was ever on board at San Diego, a spectacle of more exciting interest. How much more delighted was I to see her stem the mighty current of the Mississippi.

As I remarked the plantations, bends and forests sinking in the distance behind me, I felt that I was rapidly nearing home; and at every advance my anxiety to see my relations once more, increased. To the many enquiries, made by Judge Johnston, touching the interior of the continent where I had been wandering, I am sure I must have given very unsatisfactory answers, much as I wished to oblige him. My thoughts dwelt with such constant and intense solicitude upon home, that I felt myself unable to frame answers to questions upon any other subjects. Home did I say? I have none. My father and mother sleep—widely separated from each other. They left nine orphans without resources to breast this stormy and mutable world. I, who ought to supply the place of a parent to them, shall carry to them nothing but poverty, and the withering remembrances of an unhappy wanderer, upon whom misfortune seems to have stamped her inexorable seal.

I parted with Judge Johnston at Cincinnati, who gave me a line of introduction to Mr. Flint, for which I felt under renewed obligations to him, hoping it would be of service to me. I left Cincinnati; and on the 30th of August arrived at the end of my journey. I have had too much of real incident and affliction to be a dealer in romance; and yet I should do injustice to my feelings, if I closed this journal without a record of my sensations on reaching home. I have still before me, unchanged by all, that I have seen, and suffered, the picture of the abode of my infant days and juvenile remembrances. But the present reality is all as much changed, as my heart. I meet my neighbors, and school fellows, as I approach the home of my grandfather.—They neither recognize me, nor I them. I look for the deep grove, so faithfully remaining in my memory, and the stream that murmured through it. The woods are levelled by the axe. The stream, no longer protected by the deep shade, has almost run dry. A storm has swept away the noble trees, that had been spared for shade. The fruit trees are decayed.

I was first met by my grandmother. She is tottering under the burden and decline of old age, and the sight of me only recalls the painful remembrance of my father, worn out by the torture of his oppressors, and buried in the distant land of strangers and enemies. I could hardly have remembered my grandfather, the once vigorous and undaunted hunter. With a feeble and tremulous voice, he repeats enquiry upon enquiry, touching the fate of my father? I look round for the dear band of brothers and sisters. But one of the numerous group remains, and he too young to know me; though I see enough to remind me, how much he has stood in need of an efficient protector.—I hastily enquire for the rest. One is here, and another is there, and my head is confused, in listening to the names of the places of their residence. I left one sister, a child. She is married to a person I never knew; one, who, from the laws of our nature, can only regard me with the eye of a stranger. We call each other brother, but the affectionate word will not act as a key, to unlock the fountains of fraternal feeling.

They, however, kindly invite me to their home. I am impelled alike by poverty and affection, to remain with them for a time, till I can forget what has been, and weave a new web of hopes, and form a new series of plans for some pursuit in life. Alas! disappointments, such as I have encountered, are not the motives to impart vigor and firmness for new projects. The freshness, the visions, the hopes of my youthful days are all vanished, and can never return. If any one of my years has felt, *that the fashion of this world passeth away,* and that all below the sun is vanity, it is I. If there is a lesson from my wanderings, it is one, that inculcates upon children, remaining at the paternal home in peace and privacy; one that counsels the young against wandering far away, to see the habitations, and endure the inhospitality of strangers.

**END OF THE NARRATIVE**

# APPENDICES

# NOTE

THE FOLLOWING ARTICLES are given, as containing fresh and important information with regard to the countries, through which the Author passed. Dr. Willard's 'Tour' was extensively quoted, by the periodicals of the day, at the time of its publication. Views taken, upon the spot, by an impartial observer, of this comparatively unknown country, so interesting in itself, and from its vicinity to our own country, and the increasing relations, which connect us with it cannot fail to interest the reader. By comparing the statements of individuals differing entirely in training, position, and circumstances, and the purpose for which a country is observed, such statements, in short as are comprised in this volume, the real advantages and disadvantages of a country, its healthfulness, fertility, climate, beauty and the character of its inhabitants, and institutions may be known.

These travellers note down what passed under their eyes, "nothing extenuating, nor setting down aught in malice." It probably did not occur to them, that the imagination might almost work at will, without fear of being caught in the fact, in the desert and unvisited regions of which they speak.

# INLAND TRADE WITH NEW MEXICO

INTO WHAT NOOK of our globe can we penetrate, and not find our citizens with their 'trade and traffic?' We not long since read in a paper, that a Yankee captain was running a steam boat in the Yellow sea. In farthest India—in the islands of the gentiles—along the new countries recently discovered in the Antarctic sea, the undisputed throne of winter, and the habitation of sea monsters—wherever winds can waft, human foot-step be imprinted, or the Argus ken of industry and enterprise discover the most distant prospect of a harvest, there we shall find Americans. We delight to consort, as a listener, among the crowds of American tars. Their peculiar dress and step, walking the firm earth as if 'she' reeled; their frank, reckless and manly port; their voice, formed to its tones and expression amidst the roar of the winds and the dash of the waves; their dialect, their outlandish phrase, all furnish food for imagination. We hear them speak of China, of Japan, of Borneo, the Cape of Good Hope, and Cape Horn, as familiarly as the transit from New York to Greenwhich. Their language seems to imply that distance and space are ideas unknown to them. Imagination follows them in their long and dangerous course through the trackless brine, and realizes how many storms they have encountered, how many hardships endured, and deaths dared, during these passages; of which they speak as familiarly as of their diurnal visits on shore.

Though the adventures and voyages of the mariner furnish most food for the imagination; though the immense distances and the mysterious depths, that he traverses, and the indifferent hardihood, with which he encounters his perils and toils, naturally inspire an undefined admiration; yet the real exposure, toils and dangers of the interior journeys of our adventurous landsmen are, probably, quite as numerous, though they elicit much less of that feeling of romance and homage to daring, which is so readily called forth in the case of the other. The sailor carries his home with him. The fathomless and swelling cerulean is to him as the scenery of his birth place. No verdure, no enclosures of his paternal home are more pleasant, desired or natural, than good sea room. The winds and waves are chartered alike to convey him from danger, and to furnish him with the spectacles, varieties and pleasures of new ports. Not so with the landsman, far from home in the land of the stranger. Every new object, every variety of soil, climate, vegetation, strange plants and trees, strange men, dresses, religions, modes of building, strange customs, and, more than all, strange speech, awaken every moment those feelings, which made the Romans denominate the strange host by a word, that implies an enemy. At every step nature puts on new forms of hostility, and warns him against uncalled espionage of her privacy, and familiarity with her secrets. His weary steps, his worn down horse or mule, furnish no facilities of escape from those combinations of danger that imagination so readily creates, where they do not really exist. A whole community, with all their innate and national likes and dislikes, are always ready to yield to the natural human repugnance to whatever is a departure from its own ways, and to make a war of extermination upon the defenceless and desolate strangers. The ancient bard admired the temerity of those, who first dared, with only a thin plank to interpose, between them and death, to commit themselves to the winds and waves. If we viewed the daring in all its aspects and bearings it would furnish equal ground for admiration, to contemplate one or a few solitary travellers setting forth on a journey of a thousand leagues, through strange countries, among people at war with each other, and in language, manners and religion furnished with a radical and unchangeable ground of jealousy, dislike and hostility. How happens it, under such circumstances, that men ever break the tender ties, the natural and strong charities of home, and go far away, to enter askance, embarrassed and afraid the habitation of the stranger, knowing nothing of his language and character, and only knowing that the stranger has a religion and customs, not only different, but hostile? The love of gain, curiosity, the disposition to meet adventures, and the wandering protuberance can only furnish adequate motives.—We believe, that Americans, and particularly the New Englanders have more ample endowments of these combinations, than any other people. If we have ever for a moment given place to the traveller's vanity, in thinking,

that in visiting some new and distant region, we had achieved an exploit,
—on reaching the desired point, that vanity has been instantly corrected
by finding compatriots there before us, who seemed quite at home, and
wholly unconscious, that the attainment of their new domicil had given
them any claims to celebrity.

We were recently indulged with the reading of a manuscript journal
of an overland tour from Jackson, in Tennesee, by way of Memphis, the
Arkansas, and one of its long and undescribed branches, over the wide
prairies to the mountains that separate between our territory and that
of New Mexico; to Santa Fe and the towns in that vicinity; and thence
back, over the arid plains between Santa Fe and the Council Bluffs, on
the Missouri. The caravan noted in their journal, as a common matter,
that their trip had extended between five and six thousand miles. It was
not a little amusing, or furnishing moderate excitement of interest
and play of the imagination, to become acquainted with the thoughts
of these hardy denizens of the forests of Tennessee, as they first emerged
from the dark woods upon the ocean prairies of the Arkansas. Their
reasonings upon the strange country over which they past, in one place
covered with countless buffaloes, in another with moving sands, and
still in another offering the temperature of winter in summer, in
parallels south of their nativity; upon the different soils, temperatures
and configurations of the country, have an intrinsic interest. They are
not the reasonings of cosmogonists, or geologists, or chemists, or bota-
nists, or philosophers; but of men, who reason from first impressions,—
who make short work of knotty and debateable points, and where they
cannot untie the Gordian knot, make no ceremony in cutting it with the
hunter's knife. Nothing could be more interesting, than to witness this
little caravan surrounded by hordes of the ruthless red Tartars of the
desert, brandishing their lances on horseback, and scenting the plunder
with panther keennes of instinct. Forewarned by the fate of caravans that
had preceded them, how little they had to hope, except from the fears of
these Ishmaelites, they poise themselves on their native intrepidity,
arrange their little phalanx, and remind the classical reader of the deportment of the ten thousand amidst the strange and innumerable hordes of
barbarians, through which, partly by battle, and partly by policy, they
made their way. The interest does not diminish, when we see them inter-
mix with the Spanish strangers, equally ignorant and bigoted; the one
calling in act cupidity and cunning, to countervail the cupidity and cunning of the other. What a spectacle must be furnished by the encounter of
such a band with countless thousands of buffaloes! What scenes are wit-

nessed in their encampments for a month, with no other itinerary, than the windings of an unknown river, the course of the planets, or the distant blue of mountains, whose peaks yet want a name! How different their incidents, thoughts, views, food and rest—their nightly encamping and morning departure along the grass plains, that vision cannot measure, from the pursuits and themes of us, who dwell in towns! Yet painful and laborious and hazardous as are these distant excursions, those who engage in them, soon acquire an invincible attachment to them, that renders all other pursuits in comparison stale and tedious!

After wandering six or eight weeks over these prairies, living on buffalo meat without bread or salt, and begrimmed with grease, smoke and the fine dust of the prairies to a brotherly resemblance with the red men, and not at all particular about making their toilet of a dress, which in the first instance smacked nothing of dandyism, nothing can be more amusing, than their ablutions, and beautifyings, and conversations, as, in a mountain-bounded vale, with a rivulet for mirror, they talk of the Spanish beauties, and lustrate and prepare for entering upon the scene of their profits and conquests.

In an article before us, we propose to take a brief survey of the journal of Dr. Willard, an amiable and very correct young man, now residing in our city, and calculating to become a permanent inhabitant, of a journey to the interior of New Mexico, and a residence for some years in the interior, and, more than all, a descent of the Rio del Norte from its head springs to Matamoras, at its mouth,—an immense extent of interesting country, as far as our reading extends, wholly unexplored. Our regret is equal to his own, that while passing down this long, interesting and undescribed river, he had not been more particular in noting the physical aspect of the country, the character of the soil and productions, animal and vegetable, on his route. But, not contemplating any thing beyond refreshing his own recollections, by noting down obvious and diurnal facts and incidents, the journal wants that fulness and variety, which he would probably give to it, were he privileged to travel over the same ground again. How much it is to be desired, that travellers should remember, while traversing new and unexplored regions, that what may seem trivial and common, while under the eye, will assume a different interest and importance, when surveyed anew by memory. No journal of travels in a new country can be uninteresting, so that the traveller is full and faithful in noting down, in the freshness of vision and actual occurrence, what is passing and spread under his eye.

Dr. Willard was a citizen of St. Charles, on the Missouri; and joined

a Missouri caravan to New Mexico, as it appears, with mixed induce-
ments. He had something of the common American propensity to seek
his fortune; and seems to have been disposed to make his *debut* and
perform his first quarantine among the Spaniards, choosing to make
his first experiment in spoiling the tents of the Philistine, rather than
the children of his own people.

Dr. Willard left St. Charles, May 6, 1825. The caravan consisted
of thirty three persons. He had not journeyed beyond the settlements of
the Missouri until the 16th, when he records in his tablets, that he slept
under a tent for the first time in his life. The greater part of the long
distance between St. Charles and the mountains at the sources of the
Arkansas, is a country of rolling prairies, until we reach the great plains
of the Arkansas, generally covered with grass, and of but moderate
fertility. A narrow belt of the last portion of the distance is not unlike
the deserts of Arabia,—a sterile plain of sand heaps, with but here and
there a few of the hardier weeds and plants, which seem to have settled
here, as outcasts from more fertile and genial regions. The route, laying
across the head sources of the larger rivers of the Missouri and Arkansas,
traverses but few rivers or creeks, that are not fordable. Although it
has the reputation of being an exceedingly arid region, one of the most
frequent occurrences noted in his journal, is being drenched with rains.
On the 22d, he remarks, that the earth, over which they travelled, was
completely saturated with rain; it having rained every day, save two,
since their departure. Another occurrence, which we have noted in all
similar journals, and one of the most unpleasant character, is the escape,
or what is called the breaking away of the horses. One mode of securing
them on these boundless grass plains is technically called 'hoppling'—
we imagine a corruption of the word 'hobbling.' The fore and hind legs
of the horse are fastened by a kind of fetter, generally of leather. Horses
accustomed to this kind of impediment can travel with ease far enough
to feed; but not with sufficient facility to evade the owner. But the more
general securiety is the feeling of companionship with each other, and
with their owners, which these generous animals soon acquire; and
which has so much influence, that affright, or the calls of wild horses,
or some extraneous circumstance, is necessary to overcome it. But these
circumstances frequently occur; and though the caravans have, or should
have a guard of one eighth of the company, of sleepless vigilance, to
guard against such disasters, it often happens, that the horses break
away; and we can imagine few employments, except dunning and bor-
rowing, more irksome and hopeless, than that of turning out upon the

great buffalo pasture a thousand leagues by five hundred in extent, in pursuit of horses, which after all make it a matter of choice, even if discovered, whether they will be taken or not. But it so happens, that these animals, with the municipal habits of settled life, and certain remembrances of country and home, start back on the track of their outward march, and with their heads towards the natal spot; and from this circumstance it seldom happens, that, when overtaken by their owners, they are not persuaded to be retaken.

On the 22d they see droves of elk, antelopes and deer; and of the latter kill two. Here is the view of prairies boundless to vision, of only moderate fertility, but covered with grass, and adorned with a great variety of flowering plants. A number of ravines, filled with water, are crossed with difficulty. It is mentioned as a difficulty of frequent occurrence, that they could not find sufficient wood for cooking. 24th, see two droves of elk—20 in each. Some deer among them; of which one is killed. At night they encamp on the banks of a creek, supposed to be a branch of the Verdigris of the Arkansas. Friday, 27th, depending on their guns, and game having failed, they start without breakfast. Between 10 and 11, a fine buck is killed; and they feast high again. This night encamped on the waters of the main Verdigris. Here they find a skirt of timber. Among the plants are noted wild onion, hog potatoe, wild tansy, prickly pears, and a great variety of flowering plants and shrubs. It is recorded on the 28th, that they went three miles out of their way, to arrive at wood and water. On the 29th they encamped by a little cotton wood tree, the only one in sight on the plain. They cut it down for fuel. Every one knows the difficulty of burning green cottonwood. The rains are frequent. On the 30th they see the first signs of buffaloes. Delighted with the fragrance of the flowering prairies overwhich they pass. On the 31st they passed mounds, composed of rocks resembling lumps of iron ore. They encamped on a small creek, skirted with a few lonely trees.

June 1st, they discover buffaloes. He thinks that they could not have been less than 100,000 before noon. Killed eight or ten. Dine upon buffalo soup and steaks; which although eaten without bread or salt, he considers delicious. Continual exercise on horseback, and associations with the sterility and desolation of the desert, would probably render any food such. This day they pased a very large town, or community of the animals called prairie dogs (*arctomys ludoviciana.*) Dr. Willard describes them, as larger than they have been commonly represented, and of the size of a domestic cat. They considerably resemble a dog in

appearance, except about the head, which bears a close analogy to that
of the squirril. Their community contains some hundred burrows; the
surface of their town being kept perfectly clean and smooth. On the
eminences made by the dirt carried out of their burrows, they sit, and
fiercely bark defiance at the approaching traveller. Their form seems
rather clumsy; and their hair is short, and of a light red color.

In crossing the creek before them they found two buffaloes mired in
the mud. They humanely endeavored to assist one of the unfortunate
animals out, and restore him to his free plains; but he was spent; and
drowned notwithstanding their efforts to disengage him. On the opposite
shore of the creek, the buffaloes covered the plains, as far as their eyes
could reach. Wolves and antelopes were bounding among them in all
directions. In the distance were red sand hills, which reflected the sun's
rays, and seemed like a burning wall, bounding this magnificent park of
nature. On the 7th they passed several dog towns; fed upon buffaloe
flesh; and found no other material for fuel, but the dried manure of
the animal. On the 8th they reached the main Arkansas; which they
found nearly half a mile wide, although it must have been, by its
meanders, 1,200 miles from its mouth. The velocity of the river at this
point was from three to three and a half miles an hour. The western
reader will not need to be informed, that this is the full width, and more
than the velocity of the river at its mouth. He found the waters potable;
which it is well known, they are not in its lower courses.

An unpleasant accident occurred here. In firing upon droves of buffaloes, they turned them out of their direction upon the course of the
caravan. Six pack horses broke from their ranks, probably in affright.
After pursuing them ten miles, three were recovered. The other three,
loaded with goods to the amount of three hundred dollars, and with
clothing and provisions, were never recovered. A Mr. Andrews, of the
company, who had gone out to hunt, was captured by the Indians; and
after being detained unharmed eight days, escaped from them, and
overtook his company.

On the 15th they crossed the Arkansas, to hunt, and lay in a stock
of provisions, on the opposite shore. On the 18th they left the Arkansas;
having thus far accomplished something more than twenty miles a day,
on an average. Hence they traveled, part of the way over sand hills,
forty-five miles; in which distance they found some water, though it is
commonly destitute. This brought them to the small river called the
Semirone. The 23d brought them to a fine spring, surrounded with
huge rocky knobs, on which were interesting, ancient, Indian fortifica-

tions. Small timber, wild plumbs, grapes and currants skirt the borders; affording a charming variety to the eye, after the long and dreary expanse of prairie, which they had traversed. They inhaled the fragrance of various aromatic flowers, and listened to the singing of birds. They here left the small creek, called the Semirone, upon which they had been travelling since they left the Arkansas, and took their direction for the mountains. On the 24th the summits of the Rocky mountains visible in the distance. On the 29th, mountains in view, white with snow, and supposed to be distant 100 miles. Passed a creek, which they judged to be a water of Red river.

The last day of June, they began to ascend the mountains. The latitude of their point of ascent is not laid down. But we should suppose their general course to have been west from the point, whence they started. This was an interesting point of their journey. From a vast expanse of naked plains they now began to ascend high mountains. Alpine scenery surrounds them. They inhale a highly oxygenated atmosphere. The sighing of the wind in mountain pines and evergreens is heard, and they rapidly pass from the dominions of scorching summer to the cool and brisk spring breeze. The atmosphere is that of March, and the strawberries, and vegetation of a similar character, are in blossom.

They here perform a lustration, preparatory to entering into the Spanish settlements. They wash away the dirt and greece coated on them, during their long march over the hot and dusty plains, and put themselves in trim to show themselves in presence of people of a certain degree of civilization. Here they met a party of ten or twelve Spaniards, who had come out from Taos to prevent them from smuggling their goods.

Their reception by the people would not furnish much interest in the description. We presume the chief effort between the parties was, to determine which should be most dextrous in circumventing the other. Dr. Willard boarded with a Spaniard of the name of Pablo Sucero, at twelve dollars a month. The country hilly, mainly destitute of timber, and by no means fertile. The church is a large mud building; and the people do not seem to him to be very attentive to the ceremonial and duties of their religion.

We think, the article would not be destitute of interest, if we were able to enter into ample details of Dr. Willard's residence among this people, where he remained two months, in the practice of physic. On the fourth of July, the American traders in that region, who then made a considerable of a showy concourse, turned out to celebrate the great festival of the natal day of their liberties. Dr. Willard prepared a flag with the American eagle. They went through their evolutions and firings much to the credit of their own patriotism; and no doubt, to the edification and delight of the good people, men, women and children, of Taos. The people received them in the different quarters of the town with shouts of *'Viva la Republica!'* Much of the journal is occupied with accounts of difficulties with the officers of the customs, in relation to the duties demanded by the Spaniards upon their goods.

Dr. Willard manifested a prudent regard to the observances of the Catholic ceremonial; and was soon in full practice of physic among the people. Among some hundreds of cases, which he records, there were all sorts of complaints, that flesh is heir to; and not a few bore evidence, that depravity had found its way, with its attendant penalties, to these remote recesses of the interior mountains, and among his simple and pastoral people, where such results ought not to have been expected. Among other patients, he prescribes for the acknowledged concubine of a priest; and in another case, a reverend personage, sworn of course to celibacy, hesitated not to admit the claims of his offspring. Some of his patients, as would be the case among us, disputed his charges. Others in gratitude repaid him far beyond his claims. He seems to us to have been a very discreet and sober faced young gentleman, prudently disposed to consult *Our Lady of good counsel;* in other words, to keep professional secrets; for the ladies trusted him. The old ladies, in particular, gave him the masonic and confidential grip, advised him to shrive and take a conversion, marry a young lady of the country and become one of them. These amiable *old Christians* thought, no doubt, that a man can take a conversion when he chooses; and that nothing more is necessary, as many of our enlightened friends here believe, than to feel, that it was a point of interest to become a good Catholic, really to become so. He very frequently attends *fandangoes,* which appear to be of a character similar to our country balls. His practice seems to have been constant and extensive. Among his patients, he numbers priests, the governor, the military; young and old, male and female; and not a few Indians, and among them some chiefs. He notes in his tablets very frequent attendance upon religious festivals; and they seemed to him poor and cheap shows, only capable of furnishing interest and curiosity for a people a little above the Indians in point of refinement. Though decent and respectful in his deportment, while among the people, and in view of the solemnities, he speaks of them with sufficient indifference, when away, and in communion with his own thoughts. He probably was not sufficiently aware of the influence of such a religion of forms and observances, in keeping in order a rude and ignorant people, who were incapable of a more spiritual service. However immoral they may have been with this superstition and these observances, we have no doubt, they would have been still more so without them.

While Dr. Willard shows an evident disposition to think kindly and respectfully of the people, among whom he sojourned, it is obvious from various incidental circumstances, noted in the journal, that the fandangoes and evening amusements were conducted in a style of the coarsest simplicity,—removed, it is true far above the intercourse of their red neighbors, but probably quite as far from that of our people in the same condition. Very few of the ladies were even tolerably pretty; and most of them were coarse, sufficiently forward, and not at all remarkable for attractions either of persons or manners. Some few were delicate, and some even beautiful.

From his recorded intercourse with the priests, it would seem, that he was almost uniformly treated with kindness and liberality. In fact, they evinced, so far as can be inferred from their deportment, a good degree of liberality. There can be little doubt, that the superstition of the people reacts upon them, and compels them to a seeming devotion to the formal and ceremonial part of their worship, from which they would gladly escape. With the progress of free inquiry, we confidently anticipate a consequent gradual triumph over the influence of bigotry.

One trait among them is worthy of all praise—a simple, unostentatious and noble hospitality. It is recorded in Dr. Willard's tablets, that one day he dined with the governor; and on another was invited to spend the evening with some *donna,* or family of respectability; that his patients and friends often called upon him, to invite him to ride with them to this point and to that; and that a horse or carriage was always provided on such occasions. Such hospitalities, it is true, are unexpensive in a country, where farmers have six or eight thousand horses or mules, forty thousand cattle, and twice as many sheep. But curlish and boorish people will always be inhospitable, cost the efforts to be otherwise little or much. This single trait in their character went far with us to conciliate kind feeling and good will towards them.

Writers on this country have generally represented its climate as variable and unequal. Dr. Willard found Taos, Sante Fe and Chihuahua to possess a very agreeable climate. It was never so warm there, as in some days of our summer. The temperature seemed to him equable, and seldom falling much below, or rising far above our temperate summer heat. The country suffers much from aridity, and the want of the shelter of our trees and noble forests. A few miserable, stinted shrubberies of a diminutive growth, like that which covers our shrub-oak plains, called musqueto wood, is only found at intervals. These countries are so elevated, that beyond 28° north latitude, the ground is sometimes whitened with snow and frost. Muriates of soda and lime, and nitrate of potash, and other saline substances, abound on the surface, and often so encrust the soil, as to bid defiance to cultivation. The mountains at the sources of the Arkansas are sublime elevations. There are sometimes cultivable table summits on their peaks. That the soil is underlaid with strata of calcareous rock, is manifest from a very astonishing recorded phenomenon. In 1752 the Rio del Norte became dry for an extent of 150 leagues. The water had sunk, and passed through subterranean channels, and so continued to flow for some weeks; when, no doubt, the chasm became choked, and the river resumed its former bed. Among the most important Indian tribes are the Commanche, Appache and Navijo. They live on horseback, and keep the inhabitants constantly on the alert and alarm. They are the Ishmaelites and Tartars of these deserts. It seldom rains; and when rains happen, the spring of that country may be said to have commenced. The naked, red and rolling surface of the wide prairies, only limited by rude and rugged mountains, become at once covered with a tender and deep verdure. This spring happens in September. The whole country becomes as an ocean of verdure. Few frosts occur. When the dry season returns, this grass may be said to be cured standing. The cattle feed and fatten upon it, when in its state of verdant tenderness. It afterwards sustains them as substantial hay. Hence, and from the mildness and alubrity of the climate, and its destitution of storms, its advantages for a grazing and a shepherd's country. Hence its infinite numbers of fine mules, horses, cattle and sheep; and hence, also, its innumerable droves of antelopes, deer and buffaloes.

All cultivation is caried on only by artificial irrigation; and it seems wonderful, how Providence has adapted a country, which could produce but few of the edible cerealia without it, for irrigation. Abundant rains fall on the mountains; and the flush waters are collected in the Rio del Norte, which rolls down these arid plains in such a channel, and by such a gentle slope, that each of the inhabitants along this water course can command just as much water as his necessities of cultivation require. Where the soil is fertile, it will naturally be imagined, how delightful and luxuriant those fields and gardens will be, when the owners can command just as frequent waterings as they choose. Art works a miniature sample; but it has a neatness and finish, which we look for in vain in the great scale of nature's rough operations. In Chihuahua, their trees, planted for ornament and shade, require to be irrigated; and a person is appointed by a municipality, whose business it is to take care of the trees, and see that they want not for water. Of course, native trees can only be expected on the misty and cool tops of the hills, and near the constant moisture of streams and ponds. It will not be difficult to imagine, that in a very windy climate—and this is such,—where, too, it rains moderately only a few days in the year, they will have ample opportunities to know what dust means. But it so happens, that there is little travel,—little cause to break the sward, or disturb the tranquil monotony of nature; and the people have become accustomed to look on the brown-yellow and sear surface, during a great portion of the year, with the same patient composure of endurance, with which we regard the mud, desolation and frost of winter.

These people live, as the honest Irishman said of his farm on Lake Erie, "a thousand miles from home, and five hundred from any place!" They are nearly a thousand miles from Matamoras, still farther from Mexico; and as far from the settled parts of our country. The mail goes and returns, so as that an answer can be had from Mexico in about two months. Our municipal arts are almost unknown to them. They make whiskey it is true; but all the saw they know, and all the water or steam power, for making building plank, is the human steam power of a broadaxe, or an awkward hatchet, applied to the cloven sections of a log. It seems incredible, that such can be the state of the mechanic arts among a policed people, living under a government; but such is the fact. Not a word need be said about the external improvement, the buildings, and finishings of dwellings, exterior and interior, when the plank are made with a broadaxe. Yet Dr. Willard mentions a splendid stone church at Chihuahua, which cost 300,000 dollars, was supported by Corinthian pillars, and glittered with gilding. The houses in the towns are generally built of unburnt bricks; in many instances in the form of a parallelogram, or hollow square, making the fronts at once mural defences, and the fronts of dwellings. The floors are, for the most part, brick or composition,—that is to say, clay, lime, &c. pulverized, and cemented with blood, or other glutinous and sizy liquids.

Dr. Willard's narrative incidentally brings to light, with a great degree of *naivete,* many of the interior lights and shades of their social intercourse and manners. Nothing can well be imagined, more unlike ours; and yet there are many points of resemblance, in which all civilized people must possess a similarity of manners. It is wonderful, how, with their extreme bigotry, they could so readily have admitted an unknown stranger to their intimacy and confidence. They evidently are a dancing generation; for fandangoes are matters of very frequent occurrence. Our young physician generally noted the presence of the minister at these places, which a reverend gentleman here has denominated 'squeezes,'—a word which, however, seems more vulgar and less respectable than fandango.

Upon surveying the state of society, and the progress of improvement, cultivation and refinement in these countries, we can hardly forbear something like a feeling of exultation, on comparing our condition with theirs. What an immense distance between the state of society in this place and Chihuahua, a place of nearly half the size, and thrice the age, and the same distance from the sea! What would a Cincinnatian think of building a house, if the planks were to be hewed from our oaks by a broadaxe? What a spectacle would be the state of things here to a citizen of that place! What surprise and astonishment would the *don creole* of that country experience, if transported to Lowell in Massachusetts, with its million wheels flying in dizzying, and at first view, inexplicable confusion! Yet they have mines innumerable, and ingots of silver; and one farmer owns ten thousand horses and mules,—and still sleeps under the puncture of fleas, on a wretched bed, supported upon an earth floor—without chairs, without hearths, and chimneys and fire places; in short, the lower classes dwell in habitations like the comfortless dens of Indians.

They want freedom. They want the collision of rival minds. They want liberty, that cannot be supplied either by constitutions, or laws, or enactments. So long as bigotry reigns, so long as the terrors of perdition are held up as determents from all freedom of thinking, and all mental elasticity, their condition cannot ameliorate. Let a miserable, ignorant priest lay down the law, and prescribe just how men may think and act—when they shall go to church, and when stay at home—when they must stand, kneel, or sit, and we should soon be here the same mischievous grown up infants, that they seem to be, with all the appetites and passions and stubbornness of men, and all the mental laziness and imbecility of children. Our free institutions are, no doubt, attended with their disadvantages; and their may be some peculiar pleasures belonging to such a state of society as exists at Chihuahua. But with all the licentiousness of our press, with all the bitterness of the hundred tongues of calumny, with all our rivalry and competition, and disposition to pull each other down, that we may fill the vacancy, give us our free institutions, with all their sources and all their curses; where men may be truly men; where the mind need not feel itself shut up between two adamantine walls; where no one need fear to think because a stupid doctor in divinity assures him he will be damned, if he dares to think. Give us freedom, with all its appendant drawbacks. Deliver us from the abominations of a dominant church establishment. Deliver us from a submission, and a cringing conformity, which is not enjoined by the voluntary movement of a free mind, but which is extorted by a creed maker, armed with a little brief and bad authority. It seems to us, as if even the sincere prayers of the people, who are compelled by law to pray, could not ascend acceptably to Him, whose only temple is the free heart. It is evident, that the hierarchy of New Spain has received an incurable shock from the revolution there. But it has been grafted on the ignorance and bigotry of centuries. It operates as cause and effect, acting and reacting for its own benefit; and it will be ages to come, before its bad predominance will pass away. We would not be understood to object to the Catholic church, as such. We believe it at present among the most tolerant and liberal churches; and they are wretchedly mistaken, who think, that bigotry belongs exclusively to that profession. It is a cheering consideration in our country, that the bigotry of one denomination neutralizes that of another; so that "all nature's discord makes all nature's peace." Heaven defend us from a dominant religion, or a worship enforced by law!

Various Spanish writers, Malte Brun, Humboldt, Gen. Pike, and others, have described this country superficially; Gen. Pike, perhaps, more satisfactorily, and more to the common apprehension, than any who preceded him. Baron Humboldt, only travelled it, and rapidly, in one direction. Pike was a kind of a state prisoner, while in it, and was necessarily, much restricted in his means for making observations. Perhaps no person has had more ample chances of this kind, than Dr. Willard. Unfortunately, he was there with the feeling and temperament, which are usually appended to the people from his section of the country, and whose principal object is to secure, what the New Englander calls the main chance. He now bitterly regrets, that he did not more highly appreciate, while he was in that interesting, and in a great measure undescribed and unexplored country, his opportunities to have made a book of travels of very high interest.

As it was, he remained in the country nearly three years, made his first essays at operating on the living fibre among the New-Mexicans, traversed the whole extent of country from Taos to Matamoras, a dis-

tance by the travelled line, of more than 2000 miles. He travelled leisurely,
and at intervals, through the country, practising physic at the more
important towns, making some stay at Santa Fe, Chihuahua, Monterey
Saltilleo, Maspimi, Matamoras, &c. We note in his journal, which details
the events and journeyines of each day, proofs of the hospitality of the
higher classes of the citizens, and of the readiness of the people to trust
themselves to an American stranger, who appears among them in the
character of a physician, although they consider him a heretic. This is
evidence conclusive of their deep respect for the supposed learning,
acuteness and talents of the people from our division of the continent.
He made money rapidly, as a physician among them. But it seems, he
looked from the 'leeks and fleshpots' of this distant and strange country,
with a filial remembrance, towards the common mother of us all, the
land of his birth; and preferred to return, and encounter the scramble
and competition of an over crowded profession, certainly with inferior
prospects of present pecuniary advantage. We admire that feeling, in
our countrymen, which prompts them, in remote and foreign lands, still
to turn their thoughts towards home, as the place of the charities, views
and motives, that render life desirable. A true hearted American, living
or dying, as long as pulsation lasts, *dulces reminiscitur Argos.* It will
gratify the reader to learn, that our enterprising, modest and amiable
traveller spoiled the Philistines, in an honorable and honest way, of a
sum of dollars, which to a young, sober and calculating New-Englander,
may be considered the embryo germ of a future fortune.

We left him last at Chihuahua. He left this place, August 5, 1827.
Unfrequent as rains are, he records being wet with a shower on the way
to San Pablo. On the 11th, another shower is recorded. From these casual
records, we should infer, that the aridity of the country has been over-
stated, as the records of rains occur in this journal almost as frequently,
as they would in our country at the same period. The loss of four mules
is mentioned on the night of the 12th. The loss of horses stolen is also
mentioned, as a frequent occurrence. Once or twice all his clothes, save
those he wore, were taken off, during his sleep, at his place of encampment. It is noted often, as a circumstance of hardship, that he encamps
at night without water; and, once or twice, that the beasts travel all day,
without finding either grass, or other feed. Frequent mention is made of
*haciendas, ranchos,* and small villages. Among them are noted Vera Cruz,
San Blas and San Bernardo. He arrives at Maspimi, September 7th. The
night before his arrival his best horse was stolen. He stays on the 14th at
San Lorenzo, where the grape is cultivated to a considerable extent;

wine, brandy, and dried fruit being important articles of their commerce. The large establishment here occupies from 150 to 200 hands. The whole of this magnificent and expensive establishment is owned by a young widow. He thinks the wine rich, and of a fine flavor, describing it, as having the sweetness of a Greek wine. On the 19th he arrives at Saltillio. This town he supposes to contain 10,000 souls; a great proportion of them Indians. The valley, in which it is situated, he describes, as one great beauty; deeply verdant, and productive of rich fruits. It is surrounded by rugged and lofty mountains. Great part of Baring's famous purchase lies between Paras and this place, a distance of 88 miles. He considers the intermediate country by no means a fertile one. In all these places he meets Americans, whom he names; and notes the places of their birth. On the 21st he records passing many fine farms, and in one instance a line of stone wall, laid perfectly regular and straight three miles in length, and enclosing a rich wheat field.

There is little in the subsequent notes of the journal, which would so much interest the general reader, as the mass of information, thrown together in the notes upon the country, which follow. We recommend them to the attentive perusal of the reader, as we give them substantially in the author's own words. The reader will not find in them the manner of Baron Humboldt, or Malte Brun. They have no resemblance, either, to the remarks of Gen. Pike. But they have the piquancy and freshness of being the views of a shrewd, and intelligent young man, who had his eyes open, and was accustomed to make observations, although to make money was his first vocation. It is, perhaps, from views like the following, that we form more definite and adequate conceptions of a country, than from the scientific and ambitious writings of practised scholars, and travellers, who commence their career with the professed purpose to make a book.

General aspect of the country embraced in a tour from Council Bluffs, Mo. to Santa Fe, New-Mexico, thence down the general course of the Rio del Norte to its mouth, comprising a distance of 2000 miles.

The physical appearance of that part of the country, lying between the limits of Missouri and the Rocky mountains, is generally well known to be, comparatively speaking, an illimitable expanse of prairie. That portion of country, situated between the Missouri and the head waters of the Osage rivers, is considerably undulating; the lower situations of which abound, more or less, with timber, grass and small streams; the higher portions are usually covered with grass only.

When arriving at the termination of this immense valley, we meet abruptly the Rocky mountains, or the southern extremity of that chain so celebrated for eternal snows and rocks. These mountains are mostly covered with pines, some spruce, hemlock and white birch. On the top of the mountain we found several vallies abounding with natural meadow, and having the appearance of receiving daily showers and heavy dews. Here the atmosphere was delightfully cool, while the plains on each side were so destitute of rain, as to render the air sultry, and to require irrigation for all the common products of agriculture.

The province of New Mexico is rather more mountainous, than that part formerly called New Biscay, now state of Chihuahua; but is interspersed with some rich vallies, particularly those bordering on the Rio del Norte. The city of Santa Fe is situated 25 miles from the river, at the barren foot of a mountain. It was established about the beginning of the 17th century, and seems to have been formerly a place of considerable importance, as a rendezvous for troops. It now contains perhaps not far from two thousand souls, the most of whom have the appearance of penury. The mines in the neighborhood of Santa Fe were formerly worked, but are now abandoned. The principal articles of commerce are sheep, blankets, buffalo hides, and sometimes their meat and tollow, peltry, salt, and the common productions of agriculture, as corn, wheat, beans, onions, &c.

At the Passo del Norte, an important village, the grape is cultivated to a very considerable extent, of which they prepare excellent wine and brandy, making use of hides for mashing vats. For these articles they find market at Santa Fe and Chihuahua. Dried grapes, apples, onions, &c. are taken down in great abundance. Chihuahua and its vicinity, with all the territory north of it, is supplied with salt from a lake in the neighborhood of the Passo. There is, also, about two day's ride west of this place, an exceedingly rich copper mine, which was worked for many years by Pablo Guerra, an European Spaniard, who realized some hundred *talegas* [a bag of 1000 dollars] from its proceeds. In consequence of the late law of expulsion, he was obliged to relinquish it. It is now worked by two Americans, Mr. Andrew Curcier, a merchant in Chihuahua, from Philadelphia, and Robt. McKnight, from St. Louis, Mo. A considerable amount of gold is found in this same mine; but, I believe, not incorporated with the copper.

That part of the republic called Sonora, bounded by the gulf of California, is celebrated for its rich mines of silver and gold. These metals, together with mules, horses, beeves, hides, and peltry, are exchanged for articles of merchandize, which are mostly supplied by the Americans from Missouri. They, however, procure some part by arrivals by sea in the port of Guimus, situated on the Gulf. It was in this part of the country that the Indians were most troublesome, during my residence there.

The tribe then hostile belonged to the *Yacqui* nation, united, I believe, to some of the Navajo tribe; both of which are exceedingly numerous and rapacious. Pitica, Arrispe, and Guimus are the principal towns or villages within that state. Upper California apparently has but little correspondence with that, or any other country; as brave Indian tribes inhabit the head of the Gulf, the Rio Colorado and adjacent country, so that the inhabitants are in a measure cut off from correspondence with the rest of the world.

Chihuahua is an incorporated city of about nine thousand souls, and the largest north of Durango. It is regularly laid out, but indifferently built; containing five or six churches, of which the Paroque is splendid, it being constructed of hewn stone, from base to spire. The temple of Guadaloupe, is also elegant but smaller. The numerous paintings, of course religious, which are suspended within, do honor to the nation in the art of painting; they being according to my taste, better executed, than the celebrated painting of Mr. West at Philadelphia. This town seems to have been established by the Jesuits, at an early day; and located to suit the convenience of the mining country. There is yet remaining abundant evidence of their superior skill and perseverence, in the arts of building, mining, &c. The place now contains about thirty smelting furnaces, the most of which are generally in blast, and which, in the course of the year separate a great quantity of the precious metals. The most part of the ore smelted at this place is brought from La Roche, some 150 miles, over an exceedingly mountainous country. Their only mode of transportation is on the back of mules, which are made to carry 300 lbs. each. These loads produce from 25 to 50 and $100 each, according to their quality. Price of smelting per load is $14; freight from 6 to $7. This mineral is bought and sold at the mines, as an article of merchandise, according to its purity. In regard to manufactures, there are few in Chihuahua; and, I believe, not many north of the city of Mexico; though in this place there is no lack of carpenters, shoemakers, hatters, tailors, blacksmiths, jewellers and painters. But they are of the most ordinary kind. The city is under municipal regulation. A board of twelve Alcaldes, constituting a junta, execute justice, according to common sense, and their notion of right and wrong, provided interest or partiality

do not happen to preside.—Law, I believe is seldom consulted in matters
of common place litigation. They, however, have higher tribunals to
which appeals can be taken, and by which criminal causes are tried; but
an appeal is almost an unheard of issue. The *carcel* or jail, abounds with
old and young, male and female, mostly committed under charges of
theft, assassination and murder. The court recently ventured to pass
sentence of death on a man between 25 and 30 years of age, after having
acknowledged that he had committed ten murders; yet a great deal of
commiseration was excited for his case by the priests and lower orders
of society. They have now a workhouse, where all the lower classes of
criminals are made to labor.

The lawyers are few, as likewise the physicians; the former are com-
missioned by the general government, and allowed a salary of $2000.
Their province seems to be to expound the law, or rather decide, as
judges of it. All bonds, notes, agreements, &c. have to be passed under
the official seal; and cost, according to the value, from 6 1-4 cents to
eleven dollars, and the proceeds go to support the revenue. Every village
or settlement has its priest and alcalde. The former presides over their
morals, and arrogates to himself the dictatorship of their consciences,
while the latter wields the sceptre of civil justice, and decrees, and exe-
cutes with all the dignity of a governor. If parties aggrieved enter a complaint, he despatches a foot page with his official cane, which is a
process of compulsion, or *forthwith;* and in case of non-compliance the
party is made liable to a discretionary fine.

Although these modes of judicature may seem to us despotic yet they
constitute, no doubt, the most salutary system for that people. In regard
to their national constitution, they have copied it from ours, or nearly so,
excepting religious intolerance. This they are aware, is anti-republican;
and yet their universal and bigoted attachment to this faith, and their
peculiar situation in a civil, religious, and military point of view, at the
close of the revolution, seem to have demanded it.

The constitution may be altered in the year 1830, by the concurrence
of two thirds of the members of congress; and at which time, it was expected by many, with whom I conversed, an attempt will be made to
tolerate all religious denominations. Their sources of revenue are the
following; on all merchandize they impose an enormous duty. I think
according to their last assessment, this duty is from 15 to 50 per cent.
according to the species of goods. Another very considerable revenue
accrues from the culture and manufacture of cigars. This business is
monopolized by the government, who furnish all parts of the republic

with this the greatest of their luxuries. To give an idea of the quantity consumed in Chihuahua, and the adjacent villages, I publish a note made at the time of my residence there, which states, that on the 16th October, 1826, one caravan of mules brought to the custom house, cigars valued at $95,000; and that a few days after, another arrived and brought $25,000 more; and at the same time it was remarked by good judges, that it was but about half the quantity consumed in the year. This may be well imagined, when we consider, that all smoke, both old and young, male and female. The duties arising from the precious metals smelted, which are 2 per cent., amount to something very considerable. All monies removed from one state to another are liable to 2 per cent; and if taken out of the government, another 3 1-2 per cent. Formerly each state claimed 2 or 3 per cent. on all merchandize, sold within its limits; but this tax was repealed more than a year ago; and was merged in the international duties. All produce of the farm, as beef, pork, grain, fruit, vegetables, &c. is subject to duty. And then comes the 'severest cut of all,' the *tithes*. Thus the poor farmer may at once make up his mind to devote himself a willing slave to the minions of superstition and credulity. But oppression does not stop here. It may be traced through the minute ramnifications of all social and religious intercourse. To explain these bearings, it would be necessary to pause in these remarks, and notice such characteristics, as compose, or help to compose, a body politic; and which comprise a variety of materials, which directly or indirectly influence the happiness or prove the bane of society. In illustrating this hint, it will be necessary to pass in review a subject, which, though variously understood, is nevertheless sacred to every christian believer. I shall, therefore, aim at *due deference* for *every* religious sect; and particularly that one, of which I am about to speak. Its claim I am assuredly not disposed to deny. But when I reflect on the situation of a people by nature free, and as a body, endowed with all the moral and physical advantages to make them great, wise, and happy, I can but enquire into the causes of the great and obvious distress, which pervades this fair portion of our continent.

During my residence with that people, no situation could be better calculated than mine, to facilitate the objects of this enquiry. My profession naturally led me into the sphere of intimacy and confidence, which brought into view, the most generous and noble traits of the human mind; while, at the same time, I was obliged to witness with disgust, the thousand meannesses incident to human nature, which found their way through all the avenues of avarice, prejudice, interest and power.

In the first place, we find them bound to observe all the enjoined feast days, amounting to more than one hundred, during which, they are not permitted to labor. Among these, Sundays are included. About fifty days in the year are devoted nominally to their patron saints. We will now suppose, that out of seven millions (the supposed amount of the population in Mexico,) three sevenths are laborers, at the moderate price of twenty-five cents per day, the loss would amount to seven hundred and fifty thousand dollars; and in the course of a year, to thirty-seven million five hundred thousand dollars! Added to this prodigality of time, no doubt some 12 1-2 cents at least would be spent by each, by way of drinking, recreation, or otherwise, which would amount to thirty thousand dollars per day, and for the year, one million five hundred thousand dollars; making an aggregate of thirty-nine millions of dollars of lost time in this way to the community. Added to this sum, would be the expense of rockets, illuminations, artificial bowers, church expenditures, civil and military uniforms, and a thousand other collateral expenses, that grow out of this established usage.

This of itself would seem to be sufficient to impoverish a nation. But we have yet to consider a few other items; such as pertain to births, deaths, marriages, &c. &c. In regard to baptisms, I have often witnessed them, but am unacquainted with the expense. The ceremonies of a common marriage are not considered decent, unless they cost one hundred dollars; burials about the same price, though regulated by the style, number of priests, musicians, part of the *campo sato,* in which the interment is made, and the number of masses subsequently said, &c. The funeral rites of infants usually cost from 20 dollars upwards. The high or low cross makes a great difference in the expense. All children who die before the age of accountability, are considered (and, I think, very properly) to have taken their departure for a better world. Hence the supposed propriety of festivity and rejoicing at such obsequies, and a grave solemnity at those of adults. The most exhilarating music is played at the house of the little innocent sojourner, and also on the way to the potter's field, together with discharge of rockets, accompanied by a rabble of boys, paupers, mendicants and priests.

It may not be uninteresting to notice some few of these civil and religious customs, inasmuch as they differ from our own; and border on what our people are apt to consider a puerile superstition.

The greatest personage of their adoration, is called *Nuestra Senora de Guadaloupe,* whom they esteem their patroness saint. She is said to have appeared near the city of Mexico, soon after the conquest of Cortez; calling herself by this name, and at the same time averring herself to be the true Mary, mother of Jesus. Her appearance was made to a poor Indian, who was civilized, and had some office in the church ceremonies.

He was by her ordered to go to the bishop of Mexico, and make known to him the wonderful apparition, and deliver him the following verbal message: 'That she had descended to the earth, the guardian protectress of that happy nation. That a temple must be built to her name in the vicinity of Mexico, where her benign influence would be shed to the healing of the nation.' This command seems to have much surprised the poor native, who declined being the messenger of this heavenly mission, alleging his lowness of birth, and the probability of his being considered an imposter by the bishop, when stating a circumstance so contrary to the common order of things. Whereupon she bade him not fear, but do as she should command him; and that she would suitably reward him. She then told him, that in order to convince the bishop, that the message was from heaven, he must go on to a neighboring mountain, where he should find in great abundance, a variety of blossoms, which at that time of the year, it being winter, could not naturally exist, and hence the evidence of a miracle. Many more mysterious circumstances are related in the history of this renowned personage, comprising a very considerable volume. But it is sufficient to say, that the message was received, the temple erected on the spot by her pointed out; and that she is now the object of devotion, and made the principal object of their mediatorial rites.

The anniversary of her appearance in the 12th of December, when a painting of her is taken from the temple, and carried to the *paroguia,* followed by a promiscuous procession. The next day she is returned to her temple; though there is always a duplicate representative kept at the church, which is carried out to visit the sick, and ward off disease. When any one falls sick, a greater or lesser catalogue of painted and wax images surround the patient's bed, which they almost incessantly implore.

Being naturally a credulous people, they place the most implicit confidence in all superiors; but more particularly in the priests and physicians. All such as are visited with sickness, usually meet with ample hospitality and commiseration. As it is a generally received opinion that the Spanish character is fraught with stealth, jealousy, perfidy, rapine and murder, I feel it an incumbent duty to contradict, or rather palliate it in a great measure. I grant, we find this a predominant feature in the lower ranks of society, and too much countenanced by the higher order. But where is the country that is not more or less afflicted in the same way? Even our own country is not without crimes from these sources. Though they are not perpetrated with impunity, they are suffered to rankle in the bosom of society. So, while we there find the suspicious rabble of the community addicted to these vices, we oftener find them here confined to those who assume the importance of gentlemen, who openly or covertly practice their crimes under the protection of the public countenance. The Spanish Don is generally a high minded, honorable and dignified character, who would not descend to meanness. Like all other nations, the people here watch their interest with tenacity. But so far as my experience goes, a respectable stranger meets with a hospitable reception, and is often loaded with favour. Among the wealthy we not unfrequently find the liberal heart and hand, to as great an extent as any other part of America can boast. Another beautiful trait in their character is a universal respect for seniority. Thus you find the elder brother respected and obeyed; while the parents command the most profound reverence to the end of their life. Common salutations are exceedingly cordial and polite. An embrace with the head uncovered, is the usual ceremony. If a servant is spoken to, he uncovers, before he makes his reply. Thus you find the most illiterate heathen looking characters among them, well versed in etiquette. The stranger is struck with the great discrepancy of dress between the high and low classes; as the former abounds more or less, with gold lace or rich embroidery, and the latter, polished with smoke and grease, is little more than a blanket.

As a people they seem to me to possess less versatility of genius, than perhaps, any other people. Such traditions as their forefathers sanctioned, are in no case questioned; but remain incorporated with their religion. All their manuel labor appears to be conducted in the ancient routine of almost savage simplicity; even their women, to this day, are made the efficient instruments in reducing all their maize to meal, of which their bread is mostly constituted. Every other process of labour is conducted with equal embarrassment and disadvantage.

Having thus far hinted at their customs, I shall have to consider the country lying between Chihuahua and the mouth of the Rio del Norte, both in a geographical and agricultural point of view. The reader will understand, that there is a great sameness in most of the Mexican Republic; as the general aspect is that of alternate low plains, high mountains of barren heaths, interspersed with arid plains, that would be productive, but for the want of seasonable rains, so necessary to fertility.—Those mountains lying S. W. between Chihuahua and the Pacific, are said to be much higher and more productive of timber, having great supplies of rain.

But in travelling from Chihuahua to the Atlantic coast, we seldom meet with water, more than once a day; and that furnished by trifling streams, or springs; and frequently from deep wells, where live a few shepherds, to water the flocks and sell water to passengers.

On almost all the streams, we find more or less inhabitants, according to the advantages of water and soil. On the rivers St. Pedro, Conchez, Guajaquilla, Parral, Napas, Parras, Pattas, Santa Catarina, &c. which are very small streams, we find more or less agriculture, conducted by irrigation, and for the most part, sufficient for the consumption of the inhabitants of the immediate vicinity. But the mining towns are mostly dependent on their supplies from abroad. Santa Cruz and St. Pablo, sixty miles from Chihuahua, on the river St. Pedro, afford many good farms. Parral, containing perhaps eight thousand, is altogether a mining town. St. Bartolomeo and Guajaquilla, 180 miles south of Chihuahua, containing two thousand souls, are mining villages, having some wealthy European Spaniards, who were the proprietors of the mines, but who were about to leave the country under the late law of expulsion.

In going from Mapimi to Parras, distance 120 miles, we cross Nassas, a small river which soon loses itself in a little lake. After crossing this river we enter extensive plains, as barren as the deserts of Arabia. It was in these I travelled three successive days, without being able to procure my horses and mules a single feed, as the country was literally dried up. At Parras I was delighted with the sudden change of scene. I should suppose this place and St. Lorenzo, which are contiguous, might contain six or eight thousand inhabitants, who cultivate the grape in great abundance, supplying all the adjacent country as far as Chihuahua and Durango with the articles of wine, brandy, and all kinds of dried fruit. I here noticed one vineyard, of, I should judge, 250 acres, owned by a young widow, which, together with the other farming departments, occupied 200 laborers the year round. From this place to Saltillio, distance 140 miles, we passed over a broken and mostly sterile country. This is the tract purchased by the house of Baring, London; said to contain 140, by not far from 200 miles square, for which, I was informed by his principal overseer, living at Pattas, he was to pay a little short of one million dollars, but had paid 100,000, and refused further payment from some dispute about the title. The haciendas are all worked under his direction. Saltillio is situated at the head of a large valley, affording a beautiful landscape, it being surrounded by a chain of picturesque mountains, which enclose the city, and an expanded series of cultivated farms. This place, I think something larger than Chihuahua, and better built, constitutes the Parogue, which is supposed to be the best of its size within the republic.

A great portion of the population of Saltillio, are civilized Indians. They occupy a large suburb of the city, and merit no small applause for their industry and ingenuity. I was delighted while passing their neat and even elegant cottages. Their little enclosures appeared teeming with verdure and fruit trees, which bespoke the frugal husbandman. I was pleased to observe the remarkable difference between the dress of these natives, and those of Chihuahua.

Here were similar fashions, but under an entirely different aspect; the Indian women were all clad in blue petticoats, a cotton *camisas*, with bosom and sleeves ruffled; then thrown gracefully over a blue and white striped *revoza* or scarf, all of their own manufacture. These revozas they likewise manufacture of the common sewing silk, which they so variegate, as to throw their work, when finished, into beautiful uniform, fancy figures. These are worth from thirty to fifty dollars each. —Blankets are also made in a similar manner and with equal elegance. Their apparatus for each consists of a little more than a few rods and strings, with one end of their piece fastened to a permanent stake, set in the ground; while the other is fastened by a strap, that goes round their waist, that they constitute at least half of the loom. Their position is that of a tailor, in which they sit, and fill in the various and beautiful colors, according to the sample before them.

I here met with several French and American merchants, though none permanently settled. They were about leaving for Durango and Chihuahua. I was also visited by an Italian, by the name of Don Jose Rose, who had resided here for many years. It being Friday, the market was destitute of meet, but said he, if there is any fish to be had, I shall expect you to dine with me; and I will let you know accordingly. It was not long before word came, that I should be expected precisely at 12 o'clock, and to bring my comrade with me. Accordingly, I waited on him at the time appointed, and sat down to a dinner served up in excellent style; and it concluded with a desert and wines of excellent quality. This gentleman (some forty-five years of age) had never seen proper to change a state of celibacy for that of a matrimonial life; but chose to govern alone his peaceful domicil in single blessedness.

From Saltillio to Montelrey, 60 or 70 miles distance, we pass Rinconada and Santa Catarina, which are small villages. The country is quite broken, rocky and sterile. At Montelrey, I remained eight or ten days. This place is about the same importance as Saltillio; but not quite so populous. They are both mostly built of stone; at this place the mountains diminish; and extensive v-alleys commence. Here was a great abundance of oranges and lemons in their prime. In its vicinity the cane is cultivated largely, which supplies all the country to Santa Fe with the article of sugar. It was worth at this place from five to six cents per lb. according to quality. I also found several French and American merchants residing here, who spoke of it as only a tolerable place for business. I also became acquainted with Col. Guttierez, former Governor of Tamulipas, who now resides here in command over the troops. He spoke of himself, as having been the principal agent in the proscription of the Emperor Iturbide, which proceedings he gave me in detail; his appearance and manner clearly indicate military enthusiasm and promptitude of decision. His volatile and unsophisticated look and manner, reminded me of the celebrated *Ringtail Panther of Missouri*. He certainly managed with great energy at that eventful crisis, when the fate of the nation depended on the decision of a moment.

From Montelrey to the coast the country lies exceedingly level, abounding more or less with musquito bushes, black ebony, and many other shrubs. In most part of the route the palm tree abounds, but they are much larger from Saltillio east.—This tree seems to be of a character, partaking of the shrub and plant in point of consistence, and general appearance, growing from six to thirty feet high. The Maguey, is a plant, that grows in many parts spontaneously, and from which they derive a liquor, called *pulk,* which is much used in large cities. They obtain this juice, by cutting off the plant, which is from six inches to eighteen in diameter; and at the same time they so excavate the stump, as that it will retain the juice, as it exudes upwards. This is afterwards laded out, and suffered to ferment for use. It is of this juice they make a kind of whiskey, called *vino meschal.*

Between Montelrey and the Rio del Norte, we passed a few small villages, of which Cadarota was the most considerable, it being a great sugar region. At Quemargo, we struck the del Norte, which I last saw at El Passo, more than a thousand miles above. A great part of the river between these two points traverses a savage country. Quemargo is something more than one hundred miles from the sea, and from which place to Matamoras it is thinly settled.

The village of Matamoras, formerly called Refugio, is forty miles from the harbour of Brassos Santiago; and stands immediately on the bank of the river, and is said to contain ten thousand inhabitants; but, I should think, not more than eight thousand. There are some two hundred Americans and French in this place, most of whom are merchants and mechanics. They have erected several very good brick buildings, and the place begins to wear the aspect of enterprise. There is a company or two of Mexican troops stationed here, which make great ado about nothing. A portion of them are kept at the Brassos, to protect the Custom-House, and prevent smuggling. But Americans have seen too much territory, to be deterred from saving 3 1-2 per cent. either by stratagem or by bribery; both of which are easily practised with the unconscionable Spaniard. In fact the American party is so strong in that place, that they do as they please. The consul (Daniel W. Smith) has great influence among them; as, whatever he says is law and gospel.

In regard to the harbour, it is both ample and safe, when once entered; but of dangerous entrance, owing to the channel being shallow, say six or eight feet water. It nevertheless commands considerable commerce during the year. There has been little exported from this port, except during the last two or three years. Since that, it has consisted mostly of passengers and their money: many of the European Spaniards embarked from this port, carrying with them large fortunes of silver and gold, on which the ship masters impose a tax of one per cent. They likewise export some hides, horns, mules, ebony, and some colouring woods. But these exports bear but a small proportion to the amount of specie taken out.

# DOWNFALL OF THE FREDONIAN REPUBLIC

WE WERE REMOVED scarcely a hundred miles from the scene, where was witnessed, during the past winter, the downfall of the Fredonian republic. The crash, however appalling in our ears, at that distance, was hardly heard at Washington, and if some better historian than ourselves, do not take the matter in hand, we fear that this catastrophe will perish from history. Although we do not expect the fame, and do not gird ourselves for the task of the historian of the 'the decline and fall of the Roman Empire,' yet it was no unimportant business of the original fifteen, who upreared the pillars of this short lived empire.

The fine country of Texas beyond our western frontier, from its peculiar configuration, its vast prairies, its long range of sea coast, and its numerous rivers on the south, and its range of unexplored mountains on the north, and from its peculiar position between the settled countries of the United States on the one hand, and those of the Mexican Republic, beyond the Rio del Norte, on the other, will always be a resort for outlaws, and desperate speculators from our country. Those who wish to get away from their conscience, and those who have visions of a *paradise in the wild,* in short, the 'moving generation' of the country will press to that region to find range. Until the Rio del Norte be our boundary, or a Chinese wall rise between the two states, or a continued line of military posts, interdicting transit, be kept up, it will be the refuge of negro-stealers, and the Elysium of rogues. During the past winter, it witnessed the rise and fall of a republic, which numbered fifteen citizens, and endured fifty days. They must allow us in this country, to have a wonderful faculty to over-stocking all kinds of markets, with the articles which we furnish. Every profession has three

260

aspirants for one that is needed. We furnish more orations, than all the other people on the globe, and we over-do, and parody every thing, that is great and noble.

We acknowledge, that the materials for this, our history, were no more than the common parlance of the people, the passing conversations of village news-mongers. We give as we have received. As we have understood it, a Mr. Edwards was the Romulus of this new republic. He had somehow obtained, or imagined that he had obtained at Mexico the conditional grant of some millions of acres, between the Sabine, and the grant of Col. Austin. We saw multitudes of emigrants repairing to this land of promise. Among others, there was a Mr. Chaplin, who we believe, was a respectable man. He married a sister of Edwards, a beautiful woman, over the events of whose life is spread no small coloring of romance. Mr. Chaplin was appointed by Mr. Edwards, the proprietor, and was elected by the people, chiefly Americans, *Alcaide,* and commandant of Nacogdoches, the only place, that had any resemblance to a town in the country. It seems that the Mexicans wanted to have a hand in the management of this business, and they appointed another *Alcaide,* and commandant. Hence arose a feud, and a collision of authorities between the old and the new *'residenters.'* The warm blood of the emigrants was roused. Fifteen men among them Col. Ligon, a man whom we had known elsewhere, in a respectable office and standing, took counsel from their free born minds, their stout hearts, and probably from the added influence of the cheering essence of the *'native.'* They repaired, on a set time, not without due pomp, and as they say, under desperate apprehensions of enormous bodily harm, to a stone house, the only one, we believe, of any consequence in the village. Here they promulgated a declaration of independence, adopted national banners and insignia, swore the customary oaths, pledged their 'lives, their fortunes, and their sacred honor,' earnestly invoked the aid of their fellow citizens in the United States, formed their constitution, and appointed their officers; and the offices were so numerous, that, we believe, every citizen of the republic held at least one. The aid of another republic, a band of renegade Cherokees, was invoked with as much form, as Æneas used in soliciting the alliance of Evander. The chief of these Indians was introduced under the most imposing formalities. Among the names of the Cherokee plenipotentiaries we observe the name of the thrice-famous *John Dunn Hunter.*

The Fredonians had expected aid from Col. Austin's settlement, about two hundred miles south west of them, on the Brassos and

Colorado. Not a few of the people of this colony were disposed to give in their adhesion to the new republic. But the shrewd Col. Austin was aware, on which side of the bread the butter lay, and he remained staunch in his loyalty to his adopted country. He issued a thundering proclamation, not unlike Gen. Hull's on the invasion of Canada, inviting his people to range themselves under the standard of the Mexican government. The Cherokee chain parted its links, like *a rope of sand.* The *'fifteen'* had inadvertently caused the death of one man, and otherwise shed some blood by dint of fist. Some of their more provident men said with the famous Dutch refugee,

> *'Timens lædi,*
> *His posteriora dedi.'*

In other words, made the best of their way east of the Sabine. The Mexicans embodied a small creole force, regained the *'stone house,'* and over-took some of the Fredonians, wisely treating them with a lenity, which rather savoured of contempt.

Some of the first magistrates of the fallen republic, on regaining the eastern shore of the Sabine, betook themselves to schoolkeeping, like Dyonisius, exchanging the sceptre for a rod. The Spanish vacher cracks his thong, as sonorously, and as carelessly, as before, and the surface of the vast prairies is at rest, like that of a lake, a few minutes after a projected stone has ruffled its sleepingwaters. *'Sic transit gloria mundi.'*

# MEXICO

## Some Account of Its Inhabitants, Towns, Productions, and Natural Curiosities

[EXTRACTED FROM THE UNIVERSAL GEOGRAPHY]

*Moral qualities of the* INDIANS.—In his present condition, the Mexican Indian is grave, melancholy, and taciturn, as long as he is not under the influence of intoxicating liquors. This gravity is particularly remarkable in the children of Indians, who, at the early age of four or five years, display infinitely greater intelligence and development of mind than the children of whites. They delight in throwing an air of mystery over their most trifling remarks. Not a passion manifests itself in their features. At all times sombre, there is something terrific in the change, when he passes all at once from a state of absolute repose to violent and ungovernable agitation. The energy of his character, to which every shade of softness is unknown, habitually degenerates into ferocity. This is especially the case with the inhabitants of Tlascala. In the midst of their degradation, the decendants of these republicans are still distinguished by a certain haughtiness with which they are inspired by the remembrance of their former greatness. The indigenous natives of Mexico, like all other nations who have long groaned under civil and religious despotism, are attached, with an extreme degree of obstinacy, to their habits, their manners, and their opinions.

*Assimilation of their Religious Belief.*—The introduction of Christianity among them has scarcely produced any other effect than merely substituting new ceremonies, the symbols of a mild and humane religion, —for the ceremonies of a sanguinary worship. From the earliest periods, semibarbarous nations have received new laws, and new divinities from the hands of their conquerors. The indigenous and vanquished gods give place to foreign deities. Indeed, in a mythology so complicated as that of the Mexicans, it was easy to discover an affinity between the divinities of Atzlan and those of the east. The Holy Spirit, for instance,

263

was identified with the sacred eagle of the Aztecs. The missionaries not only tolerated, they even favored this mixture of ideas, by which the Christian worship became more speedily established. The English collector, Mr. Bullock, readily obtained leave from the clergy and authorities, in 1823, to disinter and take casts from the image of the sanguinary goddess *Teoyamiqui.* During the time it was exposed, he adds, "the court of the University was crowded with people, most of whom expressed the most decided anger and contempt. Not so, however, all the Indians. I attentively marked their countenances; not a smile escaped them, or even a word—all was silence and attention. In reply to a joke of one of the students, an old Indian remarked, 'It is true we have three very good Spanish gods, but we might still have been allowed to keep a few of those of our ancestors.' I was informed that chaplets of flowers had been placed on the figure by natives, who had stolen thither unseen, in the evening, for that purpose; a proof that notwithstanding the extreme diligence of the Spanish clergy for 300 years, there still remains some taint of heathen superstition among the descendants of the original inhabitants." Yet it was, probably, a nobler impulse than superstition that wove the chaplet for the statue of Teoyamiqui; rather that mystery of nature, by which she links the present o the past with veneration, and to the future with anxiety,—that awful reverence with which the rudest nations look back to their origin and ancestors, and which even now, among the most enlightened, still consecrates the relics of Montmorillon and Stonehenge.

*Their talent for Painting and Sculpture.*—The Mexicans have preserved a particular taste for painting and for the art of carving on stone and wood. It is truly astonishing to see what they are capable of executing with a bad knife, upon the hardest wood and stone. They exercise themselves in painting the images, and carving the statues of saints; but from a religious principle, they have continued too servilely intimate for 300 years, the models which the Europeans brought with them at the period of the original conquest. In Mexico as well as in Hindoostan, the faithful are not allowed to make the smallest change in their idols; every thing connected with the rites of the Aztecs was subjugated to immutable laws. It is on this very account that the Christian images have preserved in some degree, that stiffness and hardness of feature which characterised the hyeroglyphical pictures of the age of Montezuma. They display a great deal of aptitude for the exercise of the arts of imitation, and still greater for those of a purely mechanical nature.

*Want of Imagination.*—When an Indian has attained a certain degree

of cultivation, he shows great facility of acquiring information, a spirit
of accuracy and precision, and a particular tendency to subtilize, or to
seize on the minutest differences in objects that are to be compared with
each other. He reasons coldly and with method; but he does not evince
that activity of imagination, that lively freshness of sentiment, that art
of creating and of producing, which characterises the people of Europe,
and many tribes of African negroes. The music and dancing of the indigenous natives partake of that want of cheerfulness which is so
peculiar to them. Their singing is of a melancholy description. More
vivacity, however, is observed in their women than in their men; but
they share the evils of that state of subjection to which the sex is condemned among most of those nations where civilization is still imperfect.
In the dance women take no part; they are merely present for the sake
of offering to the dancers the fermented drinks which they themselves
had prepared.

   *Their taste for Flowers.*—The Mexican Indians have likewise preserved the same taste for flowers that Cortez noticed in his time. We
are astonished to discover this taste, which, doubtless, indicates a taste
for the beautiful, among a people in whom a sanguinary worship, and
the frequency of human sacrifices, appear to have extinguished every
feeling connected with sensibility of mind and the softer affections. In
the great market of Mexico, the native does not even sell fish, or ananas,
or vegetables, or fermented liquor, without his shop being decked out
with flowers, which are renewed every succeeding day. The Indian shop-
keeper appears seated behind a perfect entrenchment of verdure, and
every thing around him wears an air of the most refined elegance.

   *Wild Indians.*—The Indian hunters, such as the *Mecos,* the *Apaches,*
and the *Lipans,* whom the Spaniards comprehend under the denomination
of *Indios bravos,* and whose hordes, in their incursions, which are often
made during night, infest the frontiers of New Biscay, Sonora, and
New Mexico, evince more activity of mind, and more strength of character, than the agricultural Indians. Some tribes have even language, the
mechanism of which appears to prove the existence of ancient civilization.
They have great difficulty in learning our European idioms, while, at
the same time, they express themselves in their own with an extreme
degree of facility. These same Indian chiefs, whose gloomy taciturnity
astonishes the observer, will hold a discourse of several hours, whenever
any strong interest rouses them to break their habitual silence.

   *Prerogatives of the* WHITES.—The greater or less quantity of European blood, and the skin being more or less clear, are at once decisive of

the consideration which a man enjoys in society and of the opinion which he entertains of himself. A white who rides barefooted, fancies that he belongs to the nobility of the country. Colour even establishes a certain equality between those who, as every where happens where civilization is either a little advanced, or in a state of retrograde movement, take pleasure in refining on the prerogatives of race and origin.—When an individual of the lower orders enters into a dispute with one of the titled lords of the country, it is no unusual thing to hear him exclaim to the nobleman, "It is possible that you really thought yourself whiter than I am?" Among the Metis and Mulattoes, there are many individuals who, by their colour their physiognomy, and theire intelligence, might be confounded with the Spaniards; but the laws keep them down in a state of degradation and contempt. Possessing an energetic and ardent character, these men of colour live in a state of constant irritation against the whites; and resentment too often hurries them into vengeance. It frequently occurs, too, that families who are suspected of being of mixed blood, claim, at the high court of justice, a declaration that they appertain to the whites. In this way, very dark colored Mulattoes have had the address to get themselves *whitened,* according to the popular expression. When the judgment of the senses is too palpably in opposition to the solicitations of the applicant, he is forced to content himself with somewhat problematical terms; for, in that case, the sentence simply states, that "such and such individuals may *consider themselves as white."*

NEW-MEXICO.—Many French writers, and, among others, the Abbe Raynal, have spoken in pompous terms of what they term the *Empire of New-Mexico;* and they boast of its extent and riches. Under this denomination they appear to comprehend all the countries between California and Louisiana. But the true signification of this term is confined to a narrow province which, it is true, is 175 leagues in length, but not more than thirty or forty in breadth.

*Towns.*—This stripe of country, which borders the Rio del Norte, is thinly peopled; the town of *Santa Fe* containing 4000 inhabitants; *Albuquerque,* 6000; and *Taos,* 9000, comprise almost one-half of the population. The other half consists of poor colonists, whose scattered hamlets are frequently ravaged by the powerful tribes of Indians who surround them, and overrun the province. It is true that the soil is amongst the finest and most fertile of Spanish America.

*Productions.*—Wheat, maize, and delicious fruits, especially grapes, grow most abundantly. The environs of Passo-del-Norte, produce the most generous wines. The mountains are covered with pine trees, maples, and oaks. Beasts of prey are met with in great numbers. There are also wild sheep, and particularly elks, or at least large deer, fully the size of a mule, with extremely long horns. According to the Dictionary of *Alcedo,* mines of tin have been discovered. There are several hot springs. Rivers with a saline taste, indicate the existence of rich beds of rock-salt.

*Mountains.*—The chain of mountains that border the eastern parts of New Mexico, seem to be of a moderate degree of elevation. There is a pass through them, called the *Puerto de don Fernando,* by which the Paducas have penetrated into New Mexico. Beyond this chain extend immense natural meadows, on which buffaloes and wild horses pasture in innumerable herds. The Americans of the United States hunt these animals, and sometimes pursue them to the very gates of Santa Fe. The principal mountains coast Rio del Norte, following its western banks. Some peaks, or *cerros,* are to be distinguished. Further to the north, in the country of *Nabaho,* the map of Don Alzate has traced mountains with flat summits, denominated in Spanish *mesas,* that is, *tables.*

*The Apache Indians.*—The *Apache* Indians originally inhabited the greater part of New Mexico, and are still a warlike and industrious nation. These implacable enemies of the Spaniards infest the whole eastern boundary of this country, from the black mountains to the confines of Cohahuila, keeping the inhabitants of several provinces in an incessant state of alarm.—There has never been any thing but short skirmishes with them, and although their number has been considerably diminished by wars and frequent famine, the Spaniards are obliged constantly to keep up an establishment of 2000 dragoons, for the purpose of escorting their caravans, protecting their villages, and repelling these attacks, which are perpetually renewed. At first the Spaniards endeavoured to reduce to slavery those who, by the fate of war, fell into their hands; but seeing them indefatigably surmount every obstacle that opposed their return to their dear native mountains, their conquerors adopted the expedient of sending their prisoners to the island of Cuba, where, from the change of climate, they speedily perished. No sooner were the Apaches informed of this circumstance than they refused any longer either to give or receive quarter. From that moment none have ever been taken prisoners, except those who are surprised asleep, or disabled during the combat.

*Manner of making war.*—The arrows of the Apaches are three feet long, and are made of reed or cane, into which they sink a piece of hardwood, with a point made of iron, bone, or stone. They shoot this weapon with such force, that at the distance of 300 paces they can pierce a man.

When the arrow is attempted to be drawn out of the wound, the wood detaches itself, and the point remains in the body. Their second offensive weapon is a lance, fifteen feet long. When they charge the enemy they hold this lance with both hands above their heads, and, at the same time, guide their horse by pressing him with their knees. Many of them are armed with firelocks, which, as well as the ammunition, have been taken in battle from the Spaniards, who never sell them any. The archers and fusileers combat on foot but the lancers are always on horseback, They make use of a buckler for defense. Nothing can equal the impetuosity and address of their horsemen. They are thunderbolts, whose stroke it is impossible to parry or escape.

We must cease to feel astonished at the invincible resistance which the Apaches oppose to the Spaniards, when we reflect on the fate to which they have subjected those other Indians who have allowed themselves to be converted.

*The Intendency of Mexico.*—The intendency of *Mexico,* the principal province of the Empire of Montezuma, formerly extended from one sea to the other; but the district of *Panuco,* having been separated from it, it no longer reaches the gulf of Mexico. The eastern part, situated on the plateau, contains several valleys of a round figure; in the centre of which there are lakes at present dried up, but waters appear formerly to have filled these basins. Dry and deprived of its wood, this plateau is at once subject to an habitual aridity, and to sudden inundations, occasioned by heavy rains and the melting of the snow. Generally speaking, the temperature is not so hot as it is in Spain; in fact, it enjoys a perpetual spring. The mountains with which it is surrounded still abound in cedars and other lofty trees, in gums, drugs, salts, metallic productions, marble and precious stones. The flat country is covered the whole year through with delicate and exquisite fruits, lint, hemp, cotton, tobacco, aniseed, sugar, and cochineal, with which they support an extensive commerce.

*Natural Curiosities.*—Besides the numerous volcanoes of which we have already spoken, some natural curiosities are met with. One of the most remarkable is the *Ponte-Dios,* or the bridge of God, a rock, under which the water has hollowed itself a canal, situated about one hundred miles to the southeast of Mexico, near the village of Molcaxac, on the deep river Aquetoyac. Along this natural bridge, the traveller may continue his journey as if he were on a high road. Several cataracts present a romantic appearance. The great cavern of Dante, traversed by a river; the porphyritic organ-pipes of Actopan; and many other singular objects excite the astonishment of the traveller in this mountainous region, where he is obliged to cross foaming rivers upon bridges formed of the fruit of the *Crescentia pinnata,* tied with ropes of Agava.

*City of Mexico.*—On the very ridge of the great Mexican plateau, a chain of porphyritic mountains encloses an oval valley, the general level of which is elevated 6700 feet above the surface of the ocean. Five lakes fill the middle of this valley. To the north of the united lakes of Xochimilco, and Chalco, on the eastern side of the lake Tezcuco, once stood the ancient city of *Mexico,* to which the traveller arrived by causeways constructed on the shallow bottom of the lake. The new city, although placed on the same spot, is situated on firm ground, and at a considerable distance from the lakes, the waters of which have retired, and the town is still intersected by numerous canals, and the public edifices are erected on piles. The draining of the lakes is further continued, by means of a canal which has been opened for that purpose, through the mountains of Sincoq, in order to protect the town from inundations. In many places however, the ground is still soft, and some buildings, amongst others the cathedral, have sunk six feet. The streets are wide and straight, but badly paved. The houses present a magnificent appearance, being built of porphyry and amygdaloid. Several palaces and private mansions have a majestic effect, and its churches glitter with metallic riches. The cathedral surpasses, in this respect, all the churches in the world; the ballustrade which surrounds the great altar being composed of massive silver. A lamp of the same metal, is of so vast a size that three men go into it when it has to be cleaned; and it is enriched with lions' heads, and other ornaments, of pure gold. The statues of the Virgin and the saints are either made of solid silver, or richly gilded, and ornamented with precious stones. Palaces, mansions of great families, beautiful fountains, and expensive squares, adorn the interior of this city. To the north, near the suburbs, is the principal public promenade, or *Alameda.* Round this walk flows a rivulet, forming a fine square, in the middle of which there is a basin with a fountain. Eight alleys of trees terminate here, in the figure of a star. But in consequence of an unfortunate proximity, immediately in front of alameda, the eye discovers the *Quemadero,* a place where Jews and other victims of the terrible Inquisition, were burned alive.

**FINIS**

# KEYSTONE BOOKS

## *Keystone Western Americana*

THE LEWIS AND CLARK EXPEDITION by Meriwether Lewis (3 vols.) (KB-34, -35, -36)

ASTORIA by Washington Irving (2 vols.) (KB-37, -38)

COMMERCE OF THE PRAIRIES by Josiah Gregg (2 vols.) (KB-52, -53)

MOUNTAINS AND MOLEHILLS by Frank Marryat (KB-49)

THE PERSONAL NARRATIVE OF JAMES O. PATTIE (KB-50)

THREE YEARS AMONG THE INDIANS AND MEXICANS by Thomas James (KB-51)

## *Keystone Short Stories*

COLOR OF DARKNESS by James Purdy (KB-25)

THE GAMES OF NIGHT by Stig Dagerman (KB-26)

THE DIGNITY OF NIGHT by Klaus Roehler (KB-27)

WHITE APPLES by Arno Karlen (KB-29)

THE SWING by Vera Cacciatore (KB-30)

THE GO-AWAY BIRD by Muriel Spark (KB-31)

TELL ME A RIDDLE by Tillie Olsen (KB-32)

THE END OF PITY by Robie Macauley (KB-39)

THE LAST HUSBAND by William Humphrey (KB-40)

HAPPY FAMILIES ARE ALL ALIKE by Peter Taylor (KB-41)


NEW WORLD WRITING 16 (KB-17)

NEW WORLD WRITING 17 (KB-20)

NEW WORLD WRITING 18 (KB-24)

NEW WORLD WRITING 19 (KB-33)

NEW WORLD WRITING 20 (KB-42)

THE ART OF MAKING SENSE by Lionel Ruby (KB-15)
MORE IN ANGER by Marya Mannes (KB-16)
THE ART SPIRIT by Robert Henri (KB-18)
GUY DOMVILLE by Henry James (with biographical chapters by Leon Edel) (KB-19)
RELIGION AND THE MODERN MIND by W. T. Stace (KB-21)
THE PICARESQUE SAINT by R. W. B. Lewis (KB-28)
POETRY AND MATHEMATICS by Scott Buchanan (KB-43)
THE PILGRIMAGE OF WESTERN MAN by Stringfellow Barr (KB-45)

## Keystone Discographies

THE COLLECTOR'S BACH by Nathan Broder (KB-3)
THE COLLECTOR'S JAZZ: *Traditional and Swing* by John S. Wilson (KB-4)
THE COLLECTOR'S HAYDN by C. G. Burke (KB-7)
THE COLLECTOR'S CHOPIN AND SCHUMANN by Harold C. Schonberg (KB-8)
THE COLLECTOR'S TCHAIKOVSKY AND THE FIVE by John Briggs (KB-9)
THE COLLECTOR'S JAZZ: *Modern* by John S. Wilson (KB-10)
THE COLLECTOR'S TWENTIETH-CENTURY MUSIC IN THE WESTERN HEMISPHERE by Arthur Cohn (KB-23)
THE COLLECTOR'S VERDI AND PUCCINI by Max de Schauensee (KB-46)
THE COLLECTOR'S BEETHOVEN by John Briggs (KB-47)

## Keystone Books in Medicine

EPILEPSY: *What It Is and What to Do About It* by Tracy J. Putnam, M.D. (KB-1)
LIVING WITH YOUR ALLERGY by Samuel M. Feinberg, M.D. (KB-2)
HELP FOR TEN MILLION: *Arthritis, Rheumatism and Gout* by Darrell C. Crain, M.D. (KB-5)
CATHARTICS AND COMMON SENSE by William Farrar, M.D. (KB-6)
HEARING LOSS by Greydon G. Boyd, M.D. (KB-11)
HIGH BLOOD PRESSURE by Eugene B. Mozes, M.D. (KB-12)
PARKINSON'S DISEASE by Lewis J. Doshay, M.D. (KB-13)
WILL MY HEART FAIL? by William A. Jeffers, M.D. (KB-14)
YOU AND YOURS: *How to Help Older People* by Julietta K. Arthur (KB-22)

41916

ook may be kept

**FOURTEEN DAYS**

A fine of ~~TWO CENTS~~ will be charged for each day
the book is kept over time.

| FEB 2 '68 | | | |
|---|---|---|---|
| MAR 9 '69 | | | |
| | | | |
| | | | |
| | | | |
| | | | |
| | | | |
| | | | |
| | | | |
| | | | |
| | | | |
| | | | |
| | | | |
| | | | |
| | | | |
| | | | |
| | | | |